Praise for Dr. Kalish's Book, The Lost Love Chronicles

*About **The Lost Love Chronicles**… FANTASTIC… I just LOVE it! It has such a wonderful balance of stories from every point of view.*

Sweet poems… sad stories… angry stories… supernatural occurrences… fairy tale reunions… funny situations… this book has it all. The best collection of love stories I have EVER read!!

*My lost love reunion ended very badly. It took me several years to recover (physically, financially, and emotionally) from the sadness, anger, and humiliation—and the complete loss of my long-time dream to be together again forever. So I didn't know if I would like reading stories about rekindled romances. But the stories in **The Lost Love Chronicles** are so compelling that they drew me in, and I couldn't put down the book. I feel like I met a lot of new friends in the book, people like me who understand the highs and lows of these reunions. I surprisingly loved this book and I recommend it most highly!*

Couldn't put it down! Forgot to eat, forgot to sleep—just sat reading, mesmerized by the terrific narratives in this book. Dr. Kalish said it took her several years to collect and edit these stories. Well, her time was well spent! Thanks, Dr. K!!

*Marvelous! I finished reading **The Chronicles** this weekend. Couldn't touch anything else until I finished it all. I continued to find almost all the entries to be very compelling, and was amazed at the depth of some of the feelings that came across in the writing. I like the way you arranged entries into the chapters. It really added some form to all the memories. Loved your selection for the last entry about the girl with the silver laugh.*

*This (the ebook) wasn't something I was going to buy. I am a hardcover diehard. I don't even like paperback books, let alone computer books. But I bought it at a friend's suggestion and printed it, and I'm really glad I did! That old saying that you can't judge a book by its cover (although **The Lost Love Chronicles** has a great cover) is so true. A book has to be judged by its contents. So set aside your prejudices about ebooks and treat yourself to some great stories.*

I finally printed the ebook this week and have begun reading it. I can hardly put it down! Each one is like a short story. Your editing is excellent, and I really like your chapter introductions. Some of the stories are so moving, they bring tears to my eyes. Makes me wonder what it would be like if I ever met my first love again!

The Lost Love
Chronicles

REUNIONS & MEMORIES OF FIRST LOVE

NANCY KALISH, Ph.D.

AUTHOR OF

LOST & FOUND LOVERS

The Lost Love Chronicles

REUNIONS & MEMORIES OF FIRST LOVE

NANCY KALISH, PH.D.

The Lost Love Chronicles

REUNIONS & MEMORIES OF FIRST LOVE

For more information, contact:

nancykalish@lostlovers.com

www.lostlovers.com

To protect the privacy of the individuals whose accounts appear in this book,
their names and biographical information have been changed.

Book Design by Kathleen R. Weisel, weiselcreative.com
Cover Photograph by M. Dewitt, 1906, Cupid Interested.
Cover Design by inksplatterdesign.com

ISBN 978-0-9991701-0-6

ISBN-10: 0999170104

To My Daughter, Robin

With Love Always

Contents

Preface

My favorite event of the book tour for *Lost & Found Lovers* was not my five "big city" bookstore signings, but the gathering at Barnes & Noble in my small hometown on the Jersey Shore. My grade school friends now live all over the country, but their parents came to buy signed books for these old buddies of mine. My parents and their friends attended and beamed at me from the audience as I talked about my research.

With the media coverage of my book's publication, mail arrived from my former students, from the supervisor of my first summer job, and from undergraduate classmates from my years at Douglass College. Lost friends arrived unannounced at my front door. What fun it was to reconnect with these people from my past, and how appropriate that they would find me through a book about lost and found love! Old friends and lost loves are keepers of memories; even when I am in California, when I talk with my friends from New Jersey, I am home.

As I investigated adolescent friendships and first loves over the last thirteen years—and with my personal experiences with these reunions as corroboration—it became very clear to me how important these early relationships really are. Readers of *Lost & Found Lovers* agree; many of these men and women sent their lost love narratives to me and urged me to write a second book, a book of first love stories. Their delightful, poignant, and remarkable love stories deserve to be shared; I am pleased to offer them to you in *The Lost Love Chronicles*.

Acknowledgements

First and foremost, I am indebted to all of the men and women who contributed their love stories to this book. Rekindlers with happy reunions are excited to tell you their stories. For other contributors, it took courage to trust that I would protect their identities; they agreed to share their painful experiences with the hope of helping others who may be experiencing similar difficulties.

I am grateful to the many talented journalists, webmasters, television and radio producers, hosts and anchors who publicized my research and book. Without them, I would never have found so many survey participants and narrative contributors.

My agent, Robert Wilson of Wilson Media, demonstrated tremendous patience and hard work throughout the process of bringing this love story book to its readers. His loyalty and belief in my writing (along with his humor and good nature) sustained me through the highs and lows of the publishing process.

Julie Olfe, my editor for *Lost & Found Lovers*, substantially improved this book during the early stages of manuscript preparation; I would not think of publishing anything without her expert guidance. I alone am responsible for any errors in the text.

Tom Galland has taken care of my web site design and modifications for many years. An artistic tech guy, he is always there when I need him.

The Lost Love Chronicles was designed by Kathleen Weisel (weiselcreative. com). She took several hundred ordinary text pages and quickly changed them into a beautiful book.

Special thanks to my family, my friends, and the members of Lostlovers.com for their kindness and unwavering support.

Introduction

Why are people from our past, especially from childhood and adolescence, so special, no matter how much time has elapsed between visits?

These compelling connections are the result of shared roots during the formative years. Our childhood friends and teenage sweethearts experienced with us all the wonderful, horrible, boring, and embarrassing moments that helped to make us who we are today, creating a bond like no other.

Yet when we were young, our parents may have regarded these ties as inconsequential. If our families moved to new neighborhoods and we had to leave close friends behind, so what? We would make new friends, our parents assured us. But *is* a friend as interchangeable as a new toy for an old one? Or is there more to friendship, even for childhood buddies? Why are we so elated to rediscover long lost friends in our adult years if, as many people believe, they were inconsequential to us as children?

Even more belittled by many adults is a teenager's love for a boyfriend or girlfriend. Parents often question the ability of children or teenagers to know what love is, yet they never question their teenager's love for *them;* parents accept their teenager's statement of "I love you" with full appreciation and at face value. If adults accept that teenagers can love parents, then shouldn't they also accept that teen love is real love?

Parents of adolescents often do not understand the magnitude of the loss of the first love. Perhaps it's amnesia: these adults seem to forget what a crushing blow it was when they lost their own first loves. They might try to comfort their teenagers with lighthearted lessons, assuring their teens that the pain will soon pass and be forgotten, or encourage them to date someone new. Quite a few adults and adolescents complained to me that their parents used an old joke about lost love to console them: "Don't worry. Boyfriends/girlfriends are like buses. A new one comes along every ten minutes." The parents meant well, but this attempt at humor was very upsetting to the grieving teenagers.

My extensive research on rekindled romances indicates that the pain of the breakup certainly does subside, but the love can stay buried and dormant for decades… until, perhaps, the first love returns. Of the 1001 participants in my original reunion survey for *Lost & Found Lovers,* and more than 2000 men and women who contacted me after my book was published, 85% of these adults tried reunions with their early sweethearts from junior high, high school, or their early twenties—the years that psychologists refer to as *adolescence*.

Not everyone thinks fondly about his or her first love. I recently surveyed 1300 adults who never tried lost love reunions and found that 70% of them separated from their early romantic partners and never looked back. There are many men and women who have only bitter memories of their first love experiences; yet even these adults reported that their first romances influenced their lifelong attitudes about love.

The stories presented in *The Lost Love Chronicles* describe the young love experiences of men and women who have tried reunions with their adolescent sweethearts, or who have thought about their former sweethearts longingly over the years. Perhaps they could have happily married their first loves when they were younger, if circumstances outside of their control (including being too young) had not torn them apart. They will never know. These are loves that were interrupted.

The romance stories in this book are arranged in topical chapters. Many of them, however, encompass more than one topic and could have been placed elsewhere. For example, many narratives of individuals who were married at the time they reunited may be found throughout the book, not exclusively in Married… With Ticking Time Bomb. There is a fluidity across the stories that belies the topical divisions.

A short introduction precedes each chapter. In some cases, there is brief reference to my survey research; however, *The Lost Love Chronicles* is meant to be a collection of stories. For information on the psychology of lost love reunions, I refer you to my web site, *Lostlovers.com*, and to my first book, *Lost & Found Lovers*. When people refer to "the book" in their stories, they are referring to *Lost & Found Lovers*.

These narratives are not composites. Each story is an actual lost love experience, presented in the words of the person who lived it. Identifying information has been changed to protect the confidentiality of the participants.

Most of these romances began in the teen years, when romantic feelings and sexual stirrings were new and when the slightest touch by the sweetheart sent shivers down the spine. First love, young love, is indeed real love. This intense love does not come along every ten minutes. For some people, it may come only once in a lifetime.

CHAPTER 1

Puppy Loves

A common reason why preteen and teen couples separate is that one of the sweethearts (usually the girl) just decides one day that the romance is over. And that's it. The decision may seem so arbitrary that, years later, a reunited couple may wonder why they broke apart. Often the reason is simply that they were too young for the romance to proceed to a full commitment. Although they were madly in love, they had no idea at that age what characteristics they wanted in their lifelong partners, and they thought they had a lifetime of unlimited, and successively better, loves ahead of them.

First love reunions confirm the lifelong significance of the first date, the first kiss, the first sexual stirrings. New research by neuroscientists suggests that the brain stores long-term memories of love and attachment: one area of the brain inhibits general contact-seeking and focuses on one person; another area stores sensory memories, associating them with pleasurable experiences; and another part of the brain stores memories of positive, emotionally significant events.

Remember the expression, "raging teenage hormones?" Neuroscientists are researching the hormones oxytocin and vasopressin, which may be involved in the formation of early love and sexual relationships by encoding these attachments into memory. First loves often yearn for each other; perhaps these hormones left a permanent emotional imprint of their love. Men and women tell me that their first loves became "the standard for all the rest." During their many years of separation, they felt that something was missing from their lives. The emotionally loaded memories of attachment were still there, but the person was not. When they reunited, the sight, smell, touch, and sound of the long-lost love activated these stored emotional memories. Like the key to a lock, the first love matched the memories, and everything felt right.

My family was British, but we lived in Lima, Peru, while my father was working for a textile company there. The English-speaking community was very close. We didn't have extended family nearby, so our friends meant a great deal to us. To this day, my friends are those I cherish from childhood.

Like most fourteen year old kids, I was terribly shy and lacking self-confidence. My older sister was not! She decided the best way for us to meet people was to join an amateur theatrical group that was staging *Brigadoon*. I was partnered for the dancing with an equally shy boy two years older than me. He and his pals had joined because one thought it was a good way to meet girls.

I didn't think he noticed me. I was short and athletic, and my short brown hair was not fashionably long and blond. I was British, not American, and in my eyes that was the uncoolest thing around. But maybe my being different was what made Jeffrey notice me. By the time we were in dress rehearsals, he'd definitely noticed, though unbeknownst to me.

As we watched the two leads rehearsing, from the highest seats in the huge auditorium, Jeffrey quietly told me that he loved me. I was stunned, and speechless. How could that totally cool guy (a surfer, even!) like me? Wow! The choreographer called us down for rehearsal, and Jeffrey took my hand. This was going to be wonderful.

We dated for six months, until I was fifteen. To this day I can't understand fully why I broke up with him. Maybe I thought he needed someone better? An American girl with long hair and long legs? I even suggested he go out with Marcia. It broke his heart. He wrote me a very sad poem, which I put in my scrapbook along with all of my other "Jeffrey keepsakes."

I suddenly realized what I had done. Too late. I guess he thought I gave him good advice, because after a few months I saw him walking with Marcia. Just to show I wasn't drowning in sorrow, I too started going out with someone new. My heart wasn't in it, though. I'd look through my scrapbook at everything connected to Jeffrey and mentally flog myself for my stupidity.

After graduation, I went back to England to study nursing. I kept in touch with three of my friends from Lima. One day I received a letter from Wendy telling me that Jeffrey had joined the Navy. What? News of Jeffrey? His parents and hers had become very good friends. A few years later, she sent me the news that he had married. I got on with my life.

I came to the States and loved it. For the first time, I felt I belonged somewhere. I started a new scrapbook and put the old one at the bottom of my trunk. Occasionally I'd bring it out and read the sad poem written by a very bright young man, and I'd wonder if he was happy. My own marriage ended in divorce, but my former husband is still one of my closest friends.

I had just turned forty, and I was working as a bank teller. One morning was particularly busy; one girl was out sick, and my line at the teller window was out the door, while the phone was ringing. "Can you hold, please?" I remember asking. But I never did put him on hold. He did reply, "Yes," but that one word changed my life forever. What a voice! Pure velvet! "May I ask who's calling?" I stammered. "Jeffrey." My knees gave way, my heart was doing the Macarena, and an angel settled on my shoulder. I got his number and called him back during my lunch hour.

Soon all kinds of wonderful things were happening. The phone company was making a lot more money for one thing, as we called each other daily from Washington state to Washington, DC. For an instant, I was glad he was so far away, because I had gained weight. I became determined to eat healthy foods. Gone were the nightly hot fudge sundaes, and fast food French fries became a thing of the past. Steamed veggies on a bed of rice with broiled chicken honestly became heavenly as I looked slimmer and felt great.

Jeffrey decided phone calls were not enough. He arrived at the airport for a two-day visit. I arrived late, had to park miles away, went running through the terminal in ridiculous sandals. I spotted him. Overnight bag flung over his shoulder. It had been twenty-eight years. I shouted his name and kept running, with a hop thrown in every now and then. Out of the corner of his eye, he saw a short red head hopping.

He was gorgeous! The seventeen year old kid had become a man, tall and slim. His slow smile was having that effect on my knees again.

The visit went so well, he flew back two weeks later. He was divorced with a teenage son. He sent me job clippings from Washington. I loved my job, had been there ten years, but there were lots of banks in Washington. My guardian angel worked overtime, and I got a job and apartment in Washington.

I can honestly say—hopefully without sounding too melodramatic—that my life truly did begin at forty. We married a year later. Many people thought that my move was rash and impulsive. After all, it was less than six months from his first phone call. But I know in my heart it was right, and I haven't a single regret.

The other day, I showed him his poem, and all the other treasures in my one scrapbook dedicated to him—even a napkin with the doodle he drew on it, that a fourteen year old girl had saved.

From when we were twelve, she was a part of me. Through high school we were friends, but I didn't know how to tell her what was in my heart. I went away to the service, and she went to college, and by the time I got back to the States four years later, she was committed to the man she married. I lost myself.

I married a woman who wanted me, even on the rebound. Neither of us wanted to be alone, and we had so much love to give. For nearly thirty years I kept the thoughts and memories of my truest love hidden.

One day I sent a letter to a friend whom I hadn't talked to for all those 30 years, and I mentioned the name of that "someone" we both knew. My friend told me the woman of my dreams was alone, having been left recently by her husband of thirty years. I was stunned. I hesitated briefly, then sent an email letter to this heart of my heart. I simply asked if she remembered me. I couldn't breathe. Days went by. I checked with my friend to see if I got the address wrong. I was told that my love hardly ever responded to email, and never quickly. So I sent another email message to ask if the first one was received. This time I got a reply that said she did remember me.

Here I was, over fifty, married with children. And here was the truest love I had ever known, and she wanted to talk. So we talked in email. I learned of her hardship and pain, her triumphs, her loves. And as she learned more about me, I told her what I could never tell her before.

She was shocked. And I had the weight of forever taken off my shoulders, because I had sworn I would find her and tell her I loved her more than my life, before I died. This was my deepest, most vulnerable self. There was much exchange after that.

She gave me her phone number. I tried to dial it several times, but I couldn't dial the last number. Hearing from her by email had sent me to heaven and hell in one moment. To hear her voice was a terror to me. One day she sent a letter that simply said, "The last number is three." I found a time to be alone and I dialed until I got to the last number. I took a deep breath, hit the 3, and closed my eyes. Her image from thirty years before filled my mind. She answered the phone, and as she spoke I knew she had grown old like me. But I also knew there was never anyone but her.

We talked. Mostly I listened because I just wanted to listen to her voice for the next thirty years. In spite of the passing of all the years and the fact that I was in a marriage, I knew I would give it all up to be able to listen to this voice for the rest of my life. Even today, over a year later, I am filled with the same feeling without measure.

We've met three times, talked on the phone hundreds of times, and written thousands of email letters. She wants me as a friend, and I will try to be the truest friend I can be. She knows I am miserable apart from her. We both know, too, that many obstacles are in the way. Still, when I ask her, she says she may someday be able to respond to me. I do not believe we will be together in this life, and that breaks my heart. I am in tears when alone. I know the time between now and the end of my life will be filled with thoughts of her, as the time until now has been.

Still, no matter how the rest of my life goes, I found her and told her I loved her—deeply, sincerely, completely, without reservation or regret. And if she would have me, I would shout it at the top of my lungs. But, as has been said, we live lives of quiet desperation.

I am a romantic in a world without romance. I love passionately in a world without passion. I am an old man waiting for the pain to end. Until then, if I am lucky, she will talk to me. If not, I have her as she is today in my heart.

Some would say this is a midlife crisis, or unhealthy obsession, or unresolved fantasy. I've thought a lot about it and analyzed it to death. It feels very complicated; I have taken more psychology courses than the average person. And having also been an observer of life as a writer of poems, I have taken every emotion apart and put it back together. Still, this I know if nothing else: when she is near me, the rest of the world is background noise. And when I think about never seeing her again, somehow the future ceases to exist.

Now, if this Kalish's Lost Love Project is just a scam, enjoy yourselves. But if the question is, "Does true love exist?"… it does. And it never goes away. It doesn't overcome everything. But, sometimes knowing she knows is enough.

The recent death of my mother has had a profound effect on the decision I made to reconnect with my first love. Perhaps I realized how precious people are to me, and that they are not easily replaced.

I remember when I first met Tony. I was 15, and my parents had a rule about not dating until 16. I met Tony at church. He was a year older than I and was in a class with my sister. I remember thinking that he was exciting and handsome. He had eyes the color of the ocean and was sun-colored and freckled with a physique sturdy enough to wrestle alligators. He was charming, entertaining and intriguing.

Tony was my first love and we were inseparable shortly after the dating ritual began. It is difficult to think of a time in my adolescence that we were not somehow together. And it is only through my accumulation of adult experiences that I can appreciate the power we had on each other.

When I was 18, it was my understanding that we would always be together. We were compatible in every way. We knew each other inside, outside, upside down. He was etched into my heart, as well as onto every notebook I carried to high school.

From early on, Tony was often a presence in my home, and later he stayed with us on weekend breaks from the university. He had become good friends with my sister, had gone away for summer jobs with my brother, and had gone hunting with my father. My aunts and grandmother loved him, too. He had become "family."

Now I realize my parents' wisdom in advising me that all eggs should not be gathered into one basket. They cautioned that I should experience a variety of relationships before I decided to settle down with someone. It seems now that this lesson came too late; by the time Tony and I separated, we had become imprinted on each other. I began a period of my life that I term "After Tony." I associate this with a feeling of great loss.

Tony and I drifted apart for reasons that seem unclear. We have talked about it together lately, and have concluded that he was uncomfortable when I talked about marriage, because he wanted to finish college. I interpreted his non-answers to mean that he could never make a commitment. So we separated and pursued educational interests apart from each other.

In spite of university life being one long party, I graduated with honors, with a do-gooder degree and a desire to change the world. I had participated in my share of sit-ins, candlelight vigils, and demonstrations in the name of women's rights, and now I sought the comfort and security of a home and family of my own.

I am now a mother and a professional in my field. My teenage son would describe me as old—I am 40. My marriage lasted only 8 years. I had tried for years to find my friend Tony, but after my mother passed away the desire became more intense. I needed to find some resolution or closure to what happened with us so long ago. I imagined him with a wife and children. I needed to see him and convince myself that we had done the right thing.

I was able to track down his brother from Directory Assistance, and he gave me a 2 minute synopsis of the last 22 years—including that Tony was single—and his telephone number. From there it took me a total of 10 minutes to leave a message on his answering machine and to crank out a brief letter with, "Hi! Remember me? We used to be pals. Call me if you want; I'm happy and not asking for anything."

It took forever (a week) to get a phone call back. Sitting in my living room and listening to this voice from the past was strange: a mixture of familiarity with spaces missing. We agreed to write to each other to flesh out the past 2 decades. He said he traveled frequently and would come to visit me some time within the next 6 months.

We continued to exchange letters and phone calls, with each becoming more personal—shifting from recalling facts and memories to sharing thoughts and ideas. Before long, curiosity made the promise of 6 months become unrealistic. We decided to see each other as soon as possible, even if for only a few hours at an airport. With promise blossoming into reality, I found myself wondering how those hours would be spent. Through a series of phone calls, we both communicated an urgency to complete something that neither of us dared to name.

At last we were able to arrange for a meeting. Tony had a pending business trip nearby and could spend several hours with me. We danced around a discussion of what the parameters of our meeting might be, both being careful not to offend or frighten the other away. He let me know his hotel and suggested I meet him there, in the lobby if that were most comfortable.

I called Tony at his hotel the evening before our arranged visit. He agreed to let me come to his suite. He answered the door before my knocking was completed; I reached to hug him and his response mirrored mine. There was so much to talk about. I felt a mixture of anxiety and amazement; I had searched a very long while for this precious friend and was not sure what to do with him now that he was found. We visited only briefly; I did not want to leave but knew I had to.

I slept very little that night, willing the night to be over. I had agreed to meet Tony at noon. I was fashionably late (12:07). The next 10 minutes is a blur. I recall hugging and kissing, at first carefully and then with a degree of frenzy. I remember saying something like, "Before we decide how to spend this day, there is something I have wanted to do for the past 20 years" and Tony gently guiding me to the bedroom.

That afternoon I experienced the wonder and excitement of my youth through the maturity of a woman. I honestly felt that if I had died that day, I would have died satisfied. As I left that night I knew that we had transcended the last 20 years as reunited soul mates with a new appreciation of what we had lost. I loved his touch, his feel, to nestle into his beard; everything about him was so much a part of my memory. It was as though we had never left each other.

I wrote to Tony the next day. I told him that I have never in my life felt as valued, loved, cherished, and honored as I did on that day. He appreciated my arms, my freckles, every part of me was significant. Though I believed that my appearance was of no consequence, Tony assured me that I was beautiful, absolutely perfect. I was, he said, the measure by which he had compared all women—The Standard.

The village where we grew up, in Canada, had a population of about 900 at the time. There was no community centre, except for a bowling alley, ball park and skating rink. Thankfully, one of the ministers in the village started a youth group where teenagers could get together every Friday night, make supper, dance, play games, and organize activities for the community.

I met Sylvain while ice skating with friends. We were 14 at the time. It was hard not to notice him. At the time, he stood 6'4" tall (he's now 6'5"). I was also quite tall at 5'9". Although Sylvain was francophone and I anglophone, we both spoke each other's language, which helped us connect. Before long, we were skating together. This was great, because I was a lousy skater, and so I had a great excuse to hold on to him. I then invited him to attend our youth group and things started flying from there. At Christmas, he gave me a gold ring as a symbol of his everlasting love for me. I was thrilled, as I wasn't accustomed to receiving something so fancy. After all, I was only 14. The following summer, while washing my hands, the ring slipped off my finger. I can remember that day as if it were yesterday. I immediately started screaming and my mother quickly ran to see what happened. Somehow my mother and I managed to retrieve the ring, which was caught in the curve of the pipe. Talk about a miracle!

Because Sylvain and I went to separate schools, we could only see each other on Friday nights at the youth group, and on weekends for skating or bowling. In the summer, Sylvain and I used to go biking, but only within the confines of the village. My parents were very strict about that. It also didn't help that my father was Chief of Police and, consequently, his children's behavior had to be exemplary. But I do remember once sneaking into Sylvain's house and playing pool with him in his basement. Of course, whenever he and I could get in a kiss without anyone seeing, we did. And wow, I got my first French kiss!

One thing that will always stand out in my mind is that Sylvain lived on the other side of the village from me, and virtually every nice summer day, my brothers and sister would tease me as Sylvain skateboarded by our house (back and forth several times), performing stunts. Instead of serenading me by the window with song, my sweetheart serenaded me with his upside down handstands on his skateboard. We were in love! Thankfully, my parents had a good opinion of Sylvain and saw our relationship as puppy love. It also helped that Sylvain wanted to become a police officer when he grew up.

We were girlfriend and boyfriend for a year, until a boy I previously had a crush on decided to look my way. I couldn't pass up the opportunity, and I dumped my current boyfriend. What can I tell you; kids do crazy things.

We ended up marrying each other six years later. What I didn't consciously know at the time was that my main reason for marrying him was to get away from home. I never stopped having a soft spot for Sylvain. It hurt me to have to hurt him.

It also didn't take me long to realize that my husband and I were two very different people, and that we were meant to be friends, not love partners. After moving to Montreal and having two beautiful daughters, I was sad to see that the spark between the two of us was just not there and hadn't been for years. My belief system said that we should work on the marriage, but my heart was empty. We divorced after 10 years of marriage.

I thought I would never marry again, but I encountered a man like no other, or so I thought. Almost everyone thought we made a perfect couple. We decided to get married in what was considered by many to be a fairy tale wedding. Unfortunately, behind the scenes, it was no fairy tale. I struggled, as I did not want a second divorce. What would people think? Well, my decision was made for me. After returning from a family vacation in 2002, he suddenly informed me that he was leaving and that he would let me know when, or if, he would be back. He had unknowingly opened the door for me to finally make my decision. I asked for a divorce.

During these years, my childhood sweetheart, his heart broken (so he tells me), left the village we grew up in at the age of 17 and joined the armed forces. His training as a military police officer eventually took him to British Columbia, where he married and had two children. Unfortunately, his relationship was not a happy one for the most part. Wanting so much to hold to the vow, "till death do us part," he did everything to try and make his marriage work, but it was not meant to be. Finally, after experiencing a very painful incident, he knew it was time for him to leave. He had been married for 18 years.

Twenty-six years passed. In late summer, 2002, I received a phone call. I chanced to look down at the call display and saw a name that made me say to myself, "I only know one person by this name, but it can't be." But it was. To be honest with you, I felt somewhat titillated hearing his voice. His tone was very warm and friendly. He voice sounded as wonderful now as it did twenty-seven years ago. He called to inform me that he was organizing a reunion for the village where we both grew up. We soon updated each other on our personal circumstances and, to my delight, I discovered that he was now residing only two hours away from me and not across the country.

After a couple more phone conversations, he surprised me with a visit. There was a knock at my apartment door and, when I opened it, I almost fainted. There he was, standing and holding a little plant for my daughter who was celebrating her 12th birthday. He asked me out to supper. Even though the restaurant was overly crowded, we felt like we were alone.

A couple days later, I received a call from Sylvain, asking me to go outside following our phone conversation. I was to go up to a gentleman (supposedly his colleague) who would be standing under a street lamp and ask him, "Excuse me, Sergeant, may I help you?" This Sergeant was supposed to deliver a gift to me from him. What Sylvain didn't know was that I knew that it was going to be him. He had forgotten that I had caller ID on my phone, and I could see that the number he was calling from was local and not from Ottawa, where he resided. I didn't let on, as I didn't want to spoil his surprise. His gift to me was a beautiful angel.

About a week later, we arranged to spend the day together. He picked me up in his pickup truck and took me up to the mountain. We parked at the bottom and walked up the trail to the top. It was almost dusk. At the lookout, he asked me if I cared to dance. I was in heaven. This couldn't be happening. He took out a CD player from his pocket and we each took an earphone and together we danced to one of my brother's songs.

I was smitten, but was worried about making another mistake. Five days later, Sylvain invited me to his mother's birthday party. The evening was beyond description. We laughed. We teased. We kissed. It was as if we had never been apart. I'm happy to say that we've been a couple since then, a little more than one year, and are now living together since last summer.

He is one of the most kindest, sweetest, most generous man I have ever met. As my daughters say, he's like a big puppy. Consequently, his pet name (pardon the pun) is Pitou (French slang for puppy).

I had kept the gold ring (circle of hearts) he had given me when I was 14, and I am wearing it today. Isn't life wonderful!!

When do kids first develop a sense of pairing equals? You know… the Captain of the football team goes with the prettiest cheerleader, and the most popular King of the class goes with the Queen? Dana always seemed beyond my reach.

I can't remember at what age I first thought girls were pretty. It must have been about the start of grade school. In second grade, I can recall in my mind's eye the school, the classroom, and Dana sitting behind me to my right.

Dana was incredibly sweet, quiet yet openly kind to everyone. There was a distance about her that I confused with unapproachable. She was the one about whom I daydreamed. I could only muster the courage to give her a candy heart at Valentine's Day. I debated about which heart to give her, and finally made the agonizing decision to give her the heart that said I LOVE YOU. It was exactly forty-five years later, bolstered by my confidence from a good business career, that I would say those words to Dana.

Since Dana accepted the heart, this seemed sufficient to consider her my girlfriend in second grade. When she moved across town at the end of the school year, I was heartbroken. To add to my misery, my family drove past her house on the way to visit my grandparents. But since it was out of my "play zone," the best I could hope for was a glimpse of her as we passed by in the car. The combination of small town, grade school boundaries and shyness frustrated my true love. I once saw Dana at a citywide grade school dance, but we were not paired as partners.

In seventh grade we were reunited at the same junior high school, and by the end of eighth grade, I found the courage to ask her to dance. Since Dana accepted the dance, once again I was sure she was my girlfriend. When she moved out of town that summer, I was once again heartbroken and resigned to never see her again.

Throughout the remainder of school, I had a series of girlfriends who mostly picked me. Midway through college, I got engaged. My fiancée and I were at a state park when we saw some friends. As we approached, the one friend said, "Bill, I'll bet you will never guess who this is?" When she said "Dana," I was speechless. Dana was taller, thinner and more beautiful that I ever could have imagined. Leaving the beach that day, I felt physically sick.

A few years ago, after many years and two marriages, my wife unexpectedly announced she wanted a divorce. Two weeks later, during my weekly phone call with my dad, he said he met Dana's brother and said that Dana's husband had died several years ago. I asked him if he knew where she lived. He said no, but would find out from her brother. It turns out, Dana was living in my hometown. We talked on the phone and agreed to meet for dinner over Labor Day weekend. I traveled from Chicago to Pennsylvania for the greatest reunion of my life.

We talked everyday by phone and dated long distance for nine months. We got engaged on the steps of the grade school - right where we had a second grade picture taken of us. I am now married to "MY ONE TRUE LOVE!"

My name is Brandi and I am writing to you with my fiancé, Paulo. We are residing in Santiago, Chile, at the moment. I am 28 years old and from Dallas, Texas, and he is 28 and from Iquique, Chile. We met when we were 13 in Chile in 1989, when I traveled with friends of my family who were Chilean. It was love at first sight for us both. Paulo was the first boy I kissed and my first love, and I was his first love, too. I stayed in Iquique for three wonderful months and then I had to return to the States. In the time we spent together, we promised our love forever.

On the day when I had to return to Texas, he gave me a red rose; I still keep it pressed in an album with all his letters. After I left Chile, we stayed in touch through letters for six years; he still has all the letters I wrote to him as well as the pictures I sent over the years, and I have all of his.

In 1994, when I was a freshman in college, I fell in love—or so I thought— and I sent Paulo a letter to tell him. In this final letter, I asked him to remain in touch with me, but he didn't. Years passed and I never forgot about him; for years I searched for him but with no luck. I didn't know that he had written to me, 2 1/2 years after that last letter of mine; I did not receive any of them… he wrote three. He even hired a search service through the Internet to find me, but he had no luck. Why? Because I had been living in Germany for 4 years.

The boy in college didn't work out; I seemed to be searching for something that I felt was missing. I met another guy and we married. I have a daughter and a son from the marriage. During all this time I still searched for Paulo, without luck. Even in the year 2000, when my brother died, I saw the family I visited Chile with and asked them to have their relatives search for him. Again no luck. But I never gave up and always went back to his letters that were filled with love. I moved back to Texas with my husband (now my ex) and children in August of 2002. Still searching for Paulo.

Finally, in June of 2003, I did an Internet search just on his last name and came across one number where the name looked familiar—I thought it might be his brother's—so I gave it a try. I called and left a message with a woman who answered the phone. My Spanish was really rusty, but with the help of Babble-fish Translator, I was able to get enough Spanish out to leave my number and name and ask if this person was the brother of Paulo. I didn't understand what the lady said in return, but she took down my number. Three weeks later, there was a message on my machine—it was him!!!! I called, he answered, and within 2 hours we both confessed our love for each other. It was only the second time in 14 years that I had heard his voice.

One week later I asked for a divorce; the marriage was never a good marriage to begin with. Paulo was also in a relationship when we found each other, for 6 years, with the promise of marriage; he made his decision as quickly as I made mine to end his relationship and try to have a future with me.

Five weeks later, almost 14 years to the day that I left him at the bus terminal in Iquique, I got on a plane and went to Santiago. The connection was instant, as we knew it would be, and we shared a wonderful three weeks. With much heart-ache I returned to Texas, to my children. My divorce was final in September and I got on a plane with a different heartache this time, because I was leaving my babies behind for a while.

I was destined for this magical kind of love and I am so lucky to have found him. He too felt this destiny, because before we met in 1989, he had always had a dream of a girl who physically looked like me. He said every year, "This is the year I am going to meet her," and finally that summer he did.

And a month before I found him again, he was dreaming every night about a man speaking only in English; the odd part of this is that his English was never very good. He was also thinking of me a lot during this time. So when I found him and we began corresponding, I was amazed at how his English had improved. He will tell you that he never spoke or wrote in English in the 9 years we were not in contact.

So 3 months after we found each other, here we are living together in Chile. I am teaching English, and he is finishing his law degree. We plan on marrying next December; my children will join us this July. He is the only person who has ever made me feel so complete. I knew he was the one, even at 13.

Kathy and I were born just 4 days apart, to mothers who were best friends. We grew up in South Lake Tahoe sharing birthday parties and warm afternoons on the beach. As Kathy says now, "I look at the pictures that we have and I can see that I'm adoring him, even when I'm one and two years old!"

But when we were 12, Kathy's family moved away, and we did not see each other again until we were 18. Our parents surprised us. They took us to the beach and didn't tell either of us that we were meeting each other. The chemistry between us was still there, but we were both involved with other people and were about to leave for different colleges.

Despite the distance, I always had Kathy in the back of my mind, even when I was dating someone; I always thought about her. In December of 1994, when Kathy was living in Southern California and had come to Nevada to visit her family for Christmas, she called me, in Stockton, to wish me a Merry Christmas. I HAD to see her! There was a terrible blizzard on Interstate 80 and my mom said, "You're not actually going to visit her, are you? There's a blizzard out there!" And of course I told her, "No, no. Of course I won't do that, Mom. Too risky." But my friend had a 4-wheel drive, and I told him, "Let's go!"

Seeing her again was so perfect. We spent the rest of that night confessing our lifelong feelings of love. I've always been attracted to Kathy, physically and to her personality. I've always loved her so much.

Kathy moved back to Northern California to be closer to me. On July 4, 1996, Kathy's 28th birthday, I took her to see the fireworks on the beach of Lake Tahoe. But Kathy didn't know that I had recorded something for her at the local radio station. We were sitting on a blanket, and the radio came on and she said, "Oh, that's so nice, you got a birthday wish for me on the radio." And I said, "Right. Keep listening." Sure enough, then it came on: "Kathy, will you marry me?" And I handed her a ring. The ring just about landed in the lake, because she was so excited that she swung her arms up!

I am now married to my one true love. We have a painting of a special photo of us, that was taken at Lake Tahoe when we were two years old, hanging in the living room. Under it is the caption, "I loved you then, I love you now."

Marina and I met in 1964 when I was 18, a product of an English Public (private) school and Marina was 16, born and bred in Las Palmas, Canary Islands. I was living in Las Palmas because my father had inherited property here and we had moved from Kenya where we had been living.

I was pretty single-minded in my pursuit of girls, particularly after having spent my youth in boarding schools in England. Marina still says to this day that when she first saw me she knew that we would be a couple some day. Well, she is beautiful and also she was correct—shortly thereafter we met and fell in love. We saw each other almost every day and went for romantic but frustrating evening walks, with her parents a few paces behind to make sure there was no hanky-panky on the part of "el Inglés!" Her school even threatened to expel her for dating a non-Catholic.

Apart from that, we did all the usual things that two teenagers madly in love do. I've always been an avid motorcyclist so we rode my Montesa a lot—in those days here "young ladies" didn't wear pants, so she always had to ride sidesaddle! Being in love seldom achieves a perfect state of being, but we came very close to it.

At the end of 1965, we broke up. While Marina was in bed with flu, the philandering part of me decided to take another girl to the local Debutante's Ball. Inexcusable, unforgivable, and it caused a very sad parting of the ways until 1992. I moved to England, Mallorca and then to North America in 1969.

In the meantime, we never forgot each other, although we did marry other partners. Marina married in 1970 for two years, and then had the marriage annulled (no mean feat for a Catholic in those days). She has one son who is now 33. I got married three times, twice in British Columbia and once in California, and have four children.

I always knew more or less how Marina's life was going, through a friend living in Las Palmas. On one of my visits, I flew from Vancouver to see my parents and looked Marina up. She was as gorgeous as I remembered her and I desperately wanted to hold and kiss her as all the old feelings came flooding back. She, however, would have none of that as she knew that I was married—even though I told her I had always loved her, a statement she probably received with some caution!

Driving down 101 South of San Francisco one day after my most recent divorce, I made up my mind to return to Las Palmas to see if Marina would have me.

Joy of joys, my first LOVE and ONLY soul mate said "Si," and in 1994 we were finally married, just a couple of miles from where we had always met 30 years earlier.

Our 10th anniversary comes up on April 29. Now we ride a Harley and Marina wears jeans! Isn't Life Great! Ride Free 'n Far !

My best friend introduced me to his fiancée, when she was 17 and he and I were both 22. Upon meeting her, I was a "goner," but he was my friend, so I backed off. But she was always in my thoughts. At one point I weakened, and arrived at her home, with bags packed, attempting to spirit her away (years later, she told me that if it hadn't been so close to their wedding, it might have happened.)

I was so upset when they married that I joined the Army, but whenever I was on leave, I would gravitate to their home. After one of these visits, as my friend walked me to my car, before driving off I turned and was about to say, "How lucky you are! That beautiful wife and lovely baby, and another on the way!" Before I could relate this, my friend exclaimed, "How lucky you are! Single, and driving a Cadillac!" So the grass is always greener on the other side!

All during my Army service, I kept looking for a girl, just like my lost love… to no avail. Every time I visited them, while on leave, it just tore my heart up, so when my discharge time was approaching, I decided not to see them again. I didn't know that my friend had died of cancer, and that she was now a 22 year old widow, with three babies.

Once I found out that she was again single, I made a beeline to her mother's home, where she and the children were living. Somewhere, I got it into my head that you wait a year to court a widow. That was the longest year of my life! I would visit her often, telling her that soon the year would be up (not realizing that here was a 22 year old female, dying to go out).

Near Christmastime, I knocked on her door; her father answered and said that she was out of town, visiting her deceased husband's parents, and that she was dating a contractor—with a big house, pool, and speedboat. My heart sank.

From then on, whenever I went on a date, I would take a "shortcut" past her house. And no matter the time, that darned contractor's truck was always parked in front of her house, with ladders and buckets hanging from it. If I drove by at 11:00 pm, he was there... 2:00 am, 3:00 am... he was always there!

Finally the year was up, it was a Saturday morning, and contractor or not, if he was there I was going in! Sure enough, I arrived and parked right behind this guy's truck. I was ready for fisticuffs! She let me in and as we talked, while she ironed clothes and folded diapers, it suddenly dawned on me... we're alone! I tried to sound casual, and I asked, "Who's truck is out front?" She replied, "Oh, that's the neighbor's." For six months, I had been dying!

We have now been married 43 years and have a total of 7 children, 13 grandchildren, and 2 great-grandchildren. I think God purposely kept me single, for all that time, in order that we would be together.

We talk of children and grandchildren
and marriages that were —
The innocent glow of high school youth
gives new luster
to our tarnished, dented lives
like a thick coat of silver.
The chance to hope, believe again
gives rise to fears.
So much has happened in so many years.
You come from the other coast,
from fabled California
where all the women are young blonde goddesses
with firm bodies proudly displayed
in string bikinis
to a nice old grandma who's soft
and comfortable as a pillow,
warm and sweet as hot cocoa,
fragrant as bread fresh from the oven.
As you come off the plane
I feel the airport smoldering.

In May, 1996, I was riding on a bus from the lowland rain forest of Ecuador across the Andes to Quito. The ride took eight hours, and I thought about many things to make time pass. I thought about being in new places, and how it felt when I arrived in Philadelphia to attend graduate school. There, a friend of a friend from college gave me a place to stay while I looked for an apartment.

I had noticed him often at school; he was boisterous and always made himself the center of attention. He studied art and always had interesting projects in student art shows. I was a shy country mouse, and didn't have the nerve to speak to him at first. I thought he would surely find me dull. But he was incredibly attractive, a bit mysterious, and he seemed dangerous to me. In Philadelphia we had a brief affair; it was important to me, my first love, but he soon told me goodbye.

My feelings about being in Ecuador seemed like my memories of Philadelphia. I felt lonely and felt sorry for myself for awhile. I wanted a partner in life. I had lived alone for ten years, had a few boyfriends, but still felt the empty space in my heart where love could have been. I wanted someone to sit beside me on that bus and be amazed with me at the forests, the waterfalls, the mountains!

I arrived in Quito late that afternoon. I found a bundle of letters in my mailbox and decided to check my computer for email. There was a message from my Lost Love! It began, "I was just reading again your letter written May 23, 1983... " At first I thought he must have made a typographical error, but *two* numbers? I realized he was talking about a letter I wrote so many years ago.

I had written it to an old address, not even knowing if it would ever reach him; in fact, his grandmother lived there and forwarded my letter to him. I had had fantasies of meeting him again, but he seemed to slip away, so I went on with my life. I later learned that he was meeting his wife at the time he received that letter. I wondered if he was married still.

We exchanged email, and I found that he was separated from his wife. I let him know I was also alone. Within three weeks (the time I had to stay in Quito where computers, email, and telephones are at least intermittently available), we had fallen in love. I suggested he read *Love in the Time of Cholera*. Since then, he signs his letters to me, "Florentino." We feel we've found missing halves of each other.

I returned to the rain forest; I had a Fulbright fellowship to study a specie of palm trees. I spent the next few weeks deciding if I could really make a commitment to a man with three small children (I had decided to have no children myself), who lived in the north (I had chosen to study tropical ecology and leave snow, sleet, and interminable winters behind), and whom I had not seen for twenty-two years.

I decided I could. I decided I would. I decided to allow myself the happiness, closeness, and shared experience that I had missed for so long.

Jack and I were high school sweethearts, and remained so, on and off, through three years of college. Several states between us during those years created a strain that our young love could not withstand. Finally, it was "off again" forever, and we each married someone else.

After a few years had passed, fate landed us both back "home" in the community of our youth. After a chance meeting on the beach—spouses and children in tow—our deep friendship and mutual admiration were rekindled, expanded to include our families. Our children attended grammar school and high school together, enjoyed each other's birthday parties, and shared various family excursions through the years. Eventually, they went in vastly separate directions, pursuing educations, careers, new friendships, etc.

Jack and I and our spouses remained dear friends, continuing to socialize, always sharing news of their offspring, but never dreaming the children would ever see each other again. An encounter was especially unlikely between Jack's daughter, Amy, happily living and working in New York City, and my son Eric, who was still quite comfortable living in the small town environs of his youth. However, they were reunited a few years ago at the wedding of a mutual friend, and we were all there to joyously witness the first buds of romance.

It was truly kismet, as Amy had declined her invitation with regrets. She was scheduled to fly south to help her sister with a family emergency; at the last minute, her flight was canceled, and she was welcomed to attend the wedding. A seat was available next to my son Eric. They chatted, laughed, danced, and fell in love.

After a wonderful courtship, they had a beautiful wedding right in our little hometown of Monmouth Beach, New Jersey, and are now living happily ever after.

So, Jack and I, along with his wife Bobbi and my husband Nick, are on cloud nine… spending holidays and other family events together, and looking forward to sharing grandchildren.

Here's Amy's perspective. It really touched my heart, especially the last few paragraphs:

I've known my husband, Eric, my entire life, thanks to my dad and his mom being high school sweethearts! But, more importantly, they all later became, and remain, close friends.

As I understand it, my father and my mother-in-law dated throughout high school and part of college. They broke up, married their respective spouses, and years later returned with their families to the neighboring, small beach town where they grew up together in New Jersey. That is when I first met my husband, I couldn't have been more than one year old and he about three years old.

With our parents' close friendships and our mothers quickly becoming inseparable, Eric and I literally grew up together, attending the same small school and taking family trips together. Throughout our childhoods, we knew that our parents had dated, but it was "way back in the '60's," so that was like a million years ago!

After Eric graduated from high school a few years before me, I didn't see him again for about 15 years. I moved to Manhattan and lived there for 10 years while he remained near his family in New Jersey. One day, I received an invitation to a friend's wedding, with whom we both grew up, and was terribly disappointed when I couldn't go, due to a surgery that my niece had to endure in North Carolina.

Well, that evening when I went to the airport, everything imaginable went wrong! I hit Yankee Stadium traffic on the way to the airport, then my cab broke down in Harlem, I got to the airport late, and my flight was canceled on a beautiful fall day; for some reason, there were no other flights, buses or trains that could get me there in time. Finally, my sister said, "Go home. There are too many signs saying that you are not supposed to come here this weekend."

On my way home from the airport, I called my mother to say that if there was still room at the wedding, I would love to make it! She called my now mother-in-law and they seated me right next to Eric.

When Eric and I danced for the first time, it struck me that he was my past, my present and about to be my future. There was an overwhelming feeling that came over me that had already shadowed every relationship I had ever had. Now I knew what I had been waiting for.

After our first date, there wasn't a doubt in my mind that he was going to be my husband. I couldn't believe, with all of my twenties spent wondering what my husband would look like or wondering about my future in-laws, that I would end up being so lucky—to already know and love my mother-in-law and sister-in-law, and that I had known my soul mate my entire life.

My dad, Jack, and Eric's mom, Janice, did not choose to make a family together. But through their love and subsequently the marriage of my husband and me, we made them family in the end.

If our parents hadn't been high school sweethearts, they never could have paved the way for Eric and me to have found each other. It was their initial love that was so innocent and pure that allowed for our families to be as close as they were later. As 19 year olds, I'm sure their breakup was hard, but in hindsight, it seems as if it was almost a sacrifice that they made for us. For, they wouldn't share children together, but they would share grandchildren—and the joy in the forever love that their children would have in their marriage together.

We met many years ago at a teachers' college, a long time ago. I wanted to teach kindergarten through second grade; Paul was training to teach junior high and high school. He was ahead of me by grade, and he was my orientation guide on my first day on campus. We were inseparable after that, until he graduated at the end of that year, and moved away. He was my first true love.

We wrote many letters to each other after that (and I still have all those letters), but that really wasn't enough to keep us together; back in those days, very few people had telephones or cars.

We did become teachers, in two different states, and we both dated other people while we were teaching. I met a man from Oregon, and after awhile our long friendship led to marriage. It was a happy marriage, and I have three wonderful grown children. My husband was a school superintendent.

I saw Paul once, just in passing, when I was 10 years into my marriage, and had two children. Paul was married too. After that, except for an occasional Christmas card, we had no contact until our renewed romance many years later.

I was widowed eleven years ago. Three years ago, Paul's wife passed away. He got lonely maybe and decided to try to find me. It wasn't very hard; one of his relatives knew my sister, so he attained my sister's telephone number that way. When he called my sister to ask her how to reach me, she was very protective. She tried to discourage him from seeing me, but she did give him my address.

From there, Paul wrote me a letter, asking to see me. It took him three days to write that letter—it had to be just right. He kept revising it until it was very general and casual. He didn't know my circumstances, so it was appropriate for him to sound friendly but no more than that. The letter said that coincidentally his four children were living not too far from me, and he asked if he could visit me.

I read the letter, and I was excited to know he was still alive! Three days later, we re-met. I expected to shake his hand at the door, but he opened his arms and we clasped. He proposed four days later.

We had a lot of news to catch up on. During our separation, Paul served in World War II as a radio operator. He was about to be drafted, so he decided to do it his way; he joined the Navy. Japanese torpedoes hit his ship, and sank it, and he floated around, hanging onto a rope, until he was rescued. He had been preparing for a raid in the Philippines.

We were married six weeks after that. It would have been sooner, but he had to have garage sales to sell the things we couldn't use, and to move to Oregon. We are newlyweds—we had a church wedding last Saturday in front of 200 guests.

Paul is 95 years old; I am 94. We had been apart for 75 years.

CHAPTER 2

Back to School

School reunions magically transform competent adults back to insecure, awkward adolescents as soon as they pass through the doors. Men and women are overwhelmed with hopeful (and anxious) feelings as they scan the room for their lost loves. Love-at-first-sight reactions set in when they spot their high school sweethearts, followed by confusion over the next few days as they wonder about what might have been and "What do we do now?" Even if one of the former sweethearts does not attend, the anticipation of a school reunion often serves as a catalyst for one to contact the other.

Many lost loves go to their school reunions innocently, bringing their spouses, but they are thrown into a terrible tailspin when they rediscover the dormant love that they thought they lost years ago—a love that can no longer be denied.

School reunions are like time machines, catapulting the lovers back to the innocence and angst of adolescence.

I ran into my lost love at a 30 year high school reunion. I knew he would be there—I was on the organizing committee and saw his name on the guest list—so I was filled with anticipation. But after scanning the room and noticing the other male class members, I decided I was probably setting myself up for disappointment: they were bald, plump, wrinkled, and in some cases completely unrecognizable.

Then I saw him, looking just as handsome as ever. We were both unattached; he came with his sister, and I came with my brother. Only one problem: I was suddenly too shy and intimidated to approach him! Evening over. I felt sooo stupid.

So the next day I wrote to him. I told him that I had seen him and felt silly for not talking with him. The letter was light, friendly, and warm, and I asked him to drop me a short note to tell me what he has been doing in all those years we have been apart. There! I did it.

Within a week, he wrote back and I was so surprised that I cried. He was warm, open, articulate and honest. He said his heart "skipped a couple of very large beats" when he saw me. He attended the reunion only to see me. But then—just like me—he did not have the nerve to approach and talk.

Since then we have been writing long, passionate letters and we are planning a visit. During all the years apart, we never forgot how much our young love had meant. And although we lost track of each other, we never really lost the love we now share again.

Read an article about you in the Los Angeles Times a few weeks back and am just now getting around to writing to you with my thoughts.

I discovered a common theme while at my last (35th) high school reunion. Most of the guys I spoke to had come back specifically to see a certain girl they'd lusted after during high school but hadn't had the nerve or social position to approach back then. Years went by, but despite their domestic circumstances they never got over that one unrequited love.

I fall into this category myself. I remained single, however, and never pursued any serious relationship. But I still dream about this one girl at least six or seven times a year, even though I'm old enough to know better. I was surprised to find out that other guys have this same hang-up.

A class reunion is one of those rituals that we, as a culture, have developed to satisfy our urge for nostalgia and belonging. Yes, there are other reasons for class reunions too. The word "reunite" is declarative, meaning to bring together again. But what else lurks in the process? What can we get from attending a reunion? What personal needs are served? What do we need to beware of? The answer is simply this: you've got to go, because you never know what will happen.

I think of myself as a fairly average guy. I really loved being a teenager; it was in high school that I began learning about life and fell in love for the first time. In the thirty years since I graduated from high school, I have led an average life. I have grown to prefer contentment and safety to thrills and danger. I trudge along, never quite finding fulfillment.

One night when I was bored, I sat down at the computer. I had not checked my email for a week, dreading those get rich quick ads, the warm fuzzy feeling chain letters, the notes from "Tina" promising to make my nights long and hard. In there among the junk was my invitation to the high school reunion.

I thought, Has it really been thirty years? How did they find me? And how long do I have until the event? I had left town when I was seventeen years of age, and I had not been around to observe any changes. For all I knew, everyone else was just the way I left them. I resolved to make no assumptions, but my mind reeled at the possibilities.

I arrived at the hotel and made my way to the meeting room about twenty minutes after registration began. I had planned the arrival time to be "fashionable," and in fact, everyone else thought this, too. Jeff was there just ahead of me. While we waited in line, Jeff turned and asked, "Who are you?" Then he said, "Don't remember ya" when I told him my name. I had to confess that I didn't remember Jeff either. He was an affable man and not being remembered didn't seem to bother him. I relaxed a bit. Then he asked, "What do you do?" "I'm a ferryboat captain," I told him. He looked at me in mild amusement.

Larry was working the registration table and he watched as I signed in. I didn't remember Larry either, but I liked him right away. He organized this reunion because he has kept up with many of our classmates over the years. He smiled. "Hey, someone asked if you were here." "Who's that?" I wondered. "Dunno, but they're inside." Though this sounded innocent enough, I soon found out that Larry was setting the stage for quite a surprise.

It was time to eat. The reunion crowd swelled in the room. I found myself in the food line behind Jeff again. We were chatting and I was scanning the crowd when the hairs on my neck rose. Larry was pointing my way with a mischievous smile.

Far ago and long away, about a week after my senior year started, I noticed this girl in class. It was hard not to notice her. She had that warmth that draws you to her, an innocent happiness and a modest nature. She was Italian, dark skinned, athletic and classically beautiful. In short, I had no right to even look in her direction, but I did. Being a clumsy teenager, all I ever managed to be able to say to her in class was a sheepish "hi." Thereafter, I would just sit near her, mesmerized.

About a week later, I happened to see her glumly standing alone in the parking lot after school. Her ride had left without her. I managed to offer to drive her home and she accepted. During the short trip, I couldn't speak. She would calmly offer directions and I would mumble "uh-huh." This trip was going too fast for my liking but 20 mph was as slow as I could go and not get run over. Hammers were banging away inside my head—"Speak, Think, DO SOMETHING." As we pulled into her driveway I choked out these words: "Er—uh uh uh Movie uh maybe?"

Later, as I drove home, I was marveling. I couldn't help but think that she may not be very smart. After all, she had just agreed to go out in public on a Friday night and be seen with me.

On our first date I brought best behavior to a new level. This girl turned out to be a very smart person. She was motivated, caring and tender. This was my first romantic love, an experience I knew nothing about, but she was patient, and I was smitten.

We spent all of the time we could together. At the beach, on picnics, having adventures, we just enjoyed each other. On the night of our Senior Prom I was so proud to be seen with her. She was elegant, stunning and every bit a lovely lady. We strolled along the decks of the cruise ship in our formal wear, having the time of our young lives. Later, we bundled ourselves into blankets, sat on the lounge chairs and held each other while we watched the sea and waited on the weather deck to see the sun rise.

Her father had been transferred and on the day after our graduation, she moved away with her family to a new city. I was determined to follow but before I could, I got that phone call, saying, "Maybe you shouldn't come to see me anymore." She had seen the writing on the wall for some time, while I had not. She was sorry, but she was right.

I have never cared for anyone so deeply before or since.

Larry smiled even more, puzzling me, so I turned and saw her just as she saw me. Then there was no one else in the room. She smiled and gave me that look of affection that I had remembered for years. I covered the ground between us instantly and took her hand. She glowed, and said, "You still hold my hand the same way," then pushed my hand aside and hugged me hard and kissed me tenderly. I had to bite my tongue until I tasted blood so that I wouldn't weep. She was every bit as beautiful as I had remembered, and more. She was lighter, stronger and had developed the character and presence of a woman without losing her girlish charm.

We sat, talked, and held hands while I learned about her life and told her of mine. The world came back into view and we realized that other people were there. Time and again we each went out to mingle, but we always found ourselves drawn back to one another. This went on all weekend.

I had offered to drive her to the airport and while on that drive we visited the old school and the houses where we grew up. When we arrived at the home of her youth, I noticed that she was misty. I adored her.

"Stay another day," I pleaded, but she could not. After all, she had a life, a business of her own and thirty years of history to return to. Now I could see the writing on the wall. I knew she cared for me. I wanted desperately for us to be together but this was not to be. I was about to lose the love of my life for a second time! At the airport I told her of my love and that I wanted us together again. We kissed, kissed again and she was gone.

I'm hooked on reunions; I'm going to them all. Meanwhile, I'm exercising, learning to dance, saving up and making plans. After thirty years, I had her in my arms again, even if only for a couple of days. This life isn't over yet, and I could still win the chance to make her happy for all time. Until then, I'm a ferry captain. And every morning I watch the sea and wait for the sunrise.

Almost fifty years ago, Ron and I met at a high school in Louisiana where we were both cheerleaders. We exchanged class rings with the understanding that we would get married after graduation. Our parents were very happy for us; on his birthday his folks invited me for pot roast and chocolate cake, and on my birthday mine invited him for fried oysters and chocolate pie.

But Ron was drafted out of high school in 1954 and sent to Germany. When I didn't hear from him, I assumed that he was no longer interested in me. The next year I married someone else, a politician, and we moved to Washington, D.C. The marriage worked for a while, but in 1970 my husband fell in love with his nineteen year old intern, and we began divorce proceedings. I moved back to Louisiana.

One morning shortly thereafter the telephone rang… at 3 am. It was Ron, who said he just had a feeling I was troubled. I told him that he was right. He, too, was in the middle of a divorce. We made tentative plans to see each other, but just like years before, I didn't hear from him again and thought, "same song, second verse."

(Later, much later, I learned that the reason I didn't hear from him was that he had been in a nearly fatal car wreck and had been given only a 5% chance to live. He had been in a coma.)

A couple of years later, I remarried and stayed married for twenty years. When our 40th class reunion was being planned in 1994, I didn't want to attend; I was still upset over my second divorce, and over being forced to retire from a satisfying career in banking because of a merger deal.

A girlfriend on the planning committee called me to say that Ron had signed up to attend. Indications were good that he was not married. At the last minute

I decided to go to the reunion. Ron didn't go at all on the first night, and on the final night he showed up late. I had retired early, and missed seeing him. But he called my hotel room to ask if I wanted to go dancing with another couple; I thought my girlfriend had set this up, that he wasn't sincere, so I said yes but I stood him up.

A week later I received a letter from Ron. He told me that when I didn't show up for dancing that evening, he decided to catch me for breakfast; I had already checked out. He added that he didn't know what was going on in my life, but that he sincerely hoped I would find happiness. I answered his letter with some reluctance, worried that he would disappear again. He called and this time we dated for a year.

All in that one year, Ron fell and tore his shoulder rotator cuff, almost burned to death in an apartment fire, and almost lost an arm due to a brown recluse spider bite. But in spite of it all, Ron and I married on July 4, 1995 at sunset on Padre Island beach, in front of two huge bride and groom sand castles, and six smaller sand castles representing our children. My granddaughter handed out sparklers after the ceremony. Condo guests were leaning out of windows to wish us well, and everyone on the beach joined our festivities. He is still the sweetheart he was 48 years ago.

I was a young boy who had a crush on his grade school teacher, as many young boys do. But I never got over that innocent love I had for her. After going back to my old hometown, after 50 years, to attend a reunion of former students, I wrote a brief letter to my former teacher, Alice (not in attendance): "You were my second grade teacher, and at the age of seven I was madly in love with you. You taught me how to knit and bought me popcorn balls."

She responded, innocently: "What a welcome surprise your letter was, and what a flood of memories it unleashed! I do remember you. I loved all you kids with your shy, bright faces, and your innocent seven year old's dreams. I've hoped that all of you had happy, successful lives. You know, I was sixteen, hardly more than a child myself then. I look back on my years at West Grammar School as happy and hopeful, in spite of the world in chaos and the war escalating quickly.

"It was thoughtful of you to write. I enjoyed the parade of memories your letter brought, though I couldn't remember where in that little town I would have bought popcorn balls. Then I remembered that the Home Economics class made and sold them. I learned to knit when the church ladies taught some of the teachers to knit sweaters to send to the soldiers in England.

"Tell your family hello for me, and tell them that I remember you as a very sweet little boy!"

But that was only the beginning of this reconnection. Here is the story:

The year was 1943, in a Mississippi town of 300 people. It was a time not long after the flood that inundated the entire Mississippi River delta basin drainage area; the waters washed the topsoil from the fertile farmland in the mountainous regions and deposited it in the Delta along the river basin. Immediately following the flood came the Great Depression, which left the people in the mountainous regions no recourse but to move to more fertile areas, since farming was the only means available for providing a livelihood for their families.

The practice of sharecropping developed—an arrangement whereby a family would live and work the land, the landlord would furnish the tools and seeds, and each would get half of the income when the crop was sold. My family and Alice's family lived as sharecroppers. We were quite poor, with no electricity, no central heating, no running water or indoor plumbing. The kids worked in the fields too, even the seven year olds like me.

The stereotype of the townspeople was that sharecroppers were shiftless, lazy, and unintelligent, and would never be good for anything except to work the land. This background will help you understand why I was fearful of the world when I was away from my mother at school.

In addition to those hardships, the United States involvement in World War II was upon the country, causing the children like Alice and me to have serious concerns for the survival of our families.

I attended a school five miles away from my home. We had to get up each morning before dawn, walk three miles along a gravel road (which got very muddy even in light rain), and then arrive at the bus stop just about daylight. My first grade teacher whipped us kids if we came to school with mud on our clothes, and for lots of other reasons. We were traumatized with fear of her. In addition, the bigger boys liked to scare little boys like me. So I hated going to school, I cried every morning getting on the school bus, and I learned very little in first grade.

At the beginning of my second grade year, a young lady (Alice), who had lived 30 miles away, came to our community to teach. She was beautiful (yes, even seven year old boys notice those things) and exhibited nurturing comfort and maternal warmth. I fell madly in love with her, and was jealous of the attention she received from the young men in the area.

As an adult today, I am aware of the press coverage of teacher/student sexual affairs, so I want to be sure that you understand that there was nothing improper about our relationship. Alice was friendly and understanding, my protector, very patient with lots of enthusiasm, and I started looking forward to going to school.

Alice's sister lived on a farm just down the road from where my family lived, and she became my mom's best friend; her husband became my dad's best friend. On days when the road was not muddy, the school bus would bring us as far as my house, because the road was graveled to there; on those days, Alice would ride the bus to my house and wait for her brother-in-law to pick her up, with horses and wagon, for the last mile of muddy road to their house. I was excited when Alice would be at my house—more time with the lady I loved.

Alice held me back in the second grade, so I had two years with her as my teacher. But the war grew more intense, and after 2 years of teaching, Alice joined the Navy Reserves and left town. I was heartbroken; I wrote one or two letters to her, such as a third grader might write. As time passed and I grew up, I still had fond, loving memories of Alice—of her beauty, her friendliness, her understanding, and my desire for her to be in my life.

Over the years, when my family moved away, my mother and her sister kept in contact by mail. Sometimes her sister would write about Alice, and my mother would tell me about that.

In 1993, I got her address from her sister, after attending a 50 year school reunion, and wrote her a letter. We wrote to each other several times a year after that. I made plans to visit with her after her divorce became final. I rented a car at the Los Angeles airport and drove to Alice's house. She greeted me with a warm, friendly hug. I brought pictures with me—of me when I was young, of my family, and one of a cotton gin that her grandfather had built and mine had bought. She showed me pictures of her family and of her from the days of our past. With these pictures, we bridged the space of time.

We talked into the night. At one point, she said something and then added, "I can say that to you because I know you will understand, but I don't know of any other person out here in California who would understand what I'm talking about." Such is the strength of our shared roots.

The second day we took a drive and visited with some of Alice's friends. That night as we got into the car for the ride back to her home, I said to Alice, as I had said before, that I loved her as a second grader. And I said that I had thought of her often and with love over more than 50 years, and that she is still the most wonderful woman for me to love. Her reply this time was, "I believe that now; I do believe you now." We held hands as we drove to her home on that warm November night.

The third day we had dinner at her house with her daughter. We talked more about our families, and the lifestyles back in that time, that place. That night as Alice turned from placing the coffee and tea cups in the kitchen sink, I was standing in front of her; I reached for her and put my arms around her and brought her body to mine. Our lips touched, and in that moment we knew that our relationship would never be the same, that it would impact on the rest of our lives.

The emotional fear of the moment, of rejection, was overcome by my urgency to act, to show Alice my feelings. I sensed that my advance, my embrace, and my kiss would be welcomed, and to my delight and relief, Alice's approval of our love has become our lifeline to much fulfillment and happiness.

Before that moment, we had never been romantically associated, only in my heart. Today, the soul mate understanding, the commonalties of our basic backgrounds, the achievements and economic status we have each secured as adults, and our need for expressions of love are the supports for the foundation upon which our love grows. The effortlessness of a love that is not controlled by egos, love that allows free expression of oneself and is enriched with each disclosure. The difference in our ages does not exist in our minds. I see Alice as the beautiful young lady I knew 55 years ago. I feel as though I got older and Alice got younger.

As we travel to various places and visit her relatives who knew me from my youth, the fabric of our past connections are woven to become a comforting blanket securing our love. We are married and will live out the remainder of our lives in bliss.

I wish to contribute to your stories of reunited first loves but wish to add some caveats as well.

Gary and I have been married almost 1 year following a 3 year, long distance courtship. Each of us had been in a marriage at the time of our meeting; mine was 35 years but beginning to disintegrate following a secretive fling I had with someone I met on a business trip to Europe, and his after a deteriorating relationship of 12 years. I was invited to a high school reunion where he and I both had attended 8th and 9th grades. I had no idea whether he would be there, but he was knowledgeable of my plans and made it a point to attend. Both of us had lived most our lives in states far from where we went to school in Maryland—I in Oregon, he in Arizona.

Our short years together in school were interrupted, first by his one year's attendance at another school far away and then my family's move to another state when he returned to our high school. Our paths did not cross following our 9th grade year. It was his infatuation following 40 years that initiated the affair and my delight in a totally different lifestyle which held allure for me.

Our paths to the present were very different. Gary had had many long term relationships, both in and out of marriage. I married the man who lived next door to my apartment. Gary is a very intelligent man, perhaps a bit too restless to have pursued a college education to which he had access; I have a doctoral degree in mathematics. I was brought up in an intact family; Gary and his siblings were reared by their grandparents after their mother had been deserted by their father when they were all very young. I was reared in a very strict Baptist tradition where any aberrant behavior was unacceptable. Gary was reared in a more permissive environment where pursuit of life's pleasures was promoted. He experimented with drugs, both marijuana and cocaine, and led what I would consider a fast lifestyle of wild partying and women.

His family all lives in the area. I moved away from my friends, family, and career to marry him. I thought that during our 2 year courtship, I would have learned to deal with his past, and indeed, drugs had become a thing of his past. However, he has just recently come home more drunk than I had ever seen or known of him and certainly contrary to any expectation I've come to expect of his more recent history.

He has been very willing to listen to my trepidation and concerns; and I'm committed to the love we know. I just want to say that the strong attraction, born of an early naiveté and innocence we both knew, has its challenges. I will be seeking a counselor to help me deal with the differences we have experienced in our lives and help us both to understand how we deal with those discrepancies. I must say that Gary and I share a devout faith which has grown for him since our connection.

These lost loves can be full of passions of all sorts, but at the same time full of pitfalls. I hope that my story is not the only one you've received that illustrates how a long ago passion is rekindled yet brings with it challenges of significance.

I am a fifty-five year old man with a wife I love, a precious nine year old daughter, AND a newly found lost love. Please try not to judge me, as I am experiencing enough pain over this as it is.

Thirty-five years ago, I had to make a decision. My steady girlfriend moved with her family to Baltimore and I lived in Syracuse. Although we promised ourselves to each other as she boarded the plane, I had no idea how to be faithful to a promise like that as a sophomore in college. We had no plan and no money to make those promises become reality.

So with no real concept of fidelity, after she left I resumed seeing a young lady who had captured my heart the summer before (when my girlfriend was away working as a camp counselor). I had stopped seeing her (a stupid move) when my girlfriend came back in the fall. After my girlfriend moved to Maryland, we again had a beautiful two months together, and thoughts of my steady girl began to fade fast. I fell in love with this girl in a way I have never forgotten and have never felt since. We were innocent in our conduct, but sincerely and deeply involved with each other in a close and trusting relationship. We made out like young people do, but never crossed the line into a sexual relationship. I wish we had.

Then the phone call came, and my life took a sharp turn: my girlfriend had left carrying an extra passenger from our sad goodbye the day I put her on the plane. What was I going to do? I called my Dad, who told me to join the Army and run away. But my Mom got me to think about my responsibility to the child and the mother. I decided to do the "right thing."

I went over to my sweetheart's house to say goodbye and to apologize; I was heartbroken. Then I left for Baltimore.

I married her and had three children, finished college, and went to law school. But I NEVER forgot that girlfriend—really my first love—and I have missed her every day of my life since then. I do feel that to wish for things to have turned out differently would be almost like denying the existence of my children, whom I wouldn't trade for the world. But that doesn't take away the longing and the pain of missing for so long someone I felt was so right for me.

The marriage was rocky from the start, but we both shared a commitment to our children, so we made it over the ups and downs. We were friends and lovers, and comforters of each other's souls when we weren't tormenting each other instead. I made the mistake of telling her about the girl I left behind to marry her. That was not wise, but I wasn't wise then, and for damn sure I'm not now either. We hurt each other often. We did not learn how to give ourselves to each other as married people do—at least I didn't, and I felt that she didn't in a lot of ways either. It was never a complete marriage, for whatever reasons. Fault is not an issue here; bad stuff happens to good people, and we both were.

My lost love went on with her life, of course, and became a nurse. She married a police officer, to whom she is still unhappily married. He must know this, but he doesn't seem to be paying attention. They have four children and live in Manhattan now.

I am an attorney in Baltimore. I called my lost love a few times and visited her once after she married, but I didn't know how to tell her how I felt. In fact, I didn't even understand then what my feelings really were. The second time I saw her, she was pregnant, and that cooled me off for awhile. I had no idea that she felt anything for me; each time I contacted her I thought that she was just humoring me because it was her nature to be kind. I lost touch with her twenty years ago, but I missed her all those years.

I divorced my wife, and eventually remarried. I was happy and this time I thought I was in love. In my forties, I had a daughter. My life steadied out for awhile. But I felt something was still missing, and I started drinking too much as my new wife began eating everything within reach and then going to Weight Watchers, Nutri-System, Redux, liposuction. Sex was good but no great love. Yeah, there was love but not LUUHHVV, and not in the same breath as sex. Anyway, I am still unfulfilled. I have a precious daughter who just turned nine; every day I ask her, "Who's the luckiest Daddy in the world?!" I AM!! But part of me still feels empty.

Then last summer I went back to Syracuse to attend an all-school high school reunion. My lost love sent a message to me via a mutual friend (hoping I would be there) that her class was having a reunion event the next evening, would I come by? So I went with my wife. I stood in the background—it wasn't my class's party—until I saw my sweetheart. Her face lit up. We spent a few hours talking, together with my wife, catching up on lost time. I looked her over from top to bottom—wrinkles, veins, gray hair, brown eyes a mile deep, white skin, red lips, and soft voice—and I lost it all over again. I went to her class picnic in the park the next day, with my wife, and daughter (then eight) who met her then nine year old son. The kids fell in love, too, and will be writing to you on their own in thirty years.

We went home, she to Manhattan and I to Baltimore, but we kept in touch through the kids sending pen pal notes. A few months later she called me to tell me straight out that she couldn't stop thinking of me, and still loved me. I about fell out of my chair. I told her how I felt, and several times since then. We are in love, and committed to each other. We thought this kind of love existed only in romance novels.

We are miserable too. I won't leave my wife, not yet anyway. I won't tell her about this affair, and I won't leave my young daughter. But I long for my lost and found love every minute of the day. She told me that she is mine, all I have to do is say it and she will leave her husband.

What do I do? I do love my wife. I wasn't trying for this to happen. I had not been unfaithful until this chance I never thought I would have, a love straight out of *Dr. Zhivago*. I will love this woman until the day I die, when I will say her name with my last breath. I won't ever shut this off again. If I am found out, the worst that could happen is another divorce (and I didn't say that lightly) and then I'd be with someone who loves me like I've always wanted to be loved, completely. But I know how painful divorce is for children; I don't want to act in haste.

So for the time being, and perhaps for a long, long time, we are lost loves who have found each other in our own way. She says she wants me in her life and will accept all that I can or will give to her. She risks her heart to say that to me, and I promise not to break it, as I know she will not break mine.

I have a lot to be thankful for. I know that I should be grateful for all that I do have and not be looking for more. But this came. It's here. I can't stop it. I love her.

Tonight is my 55th wedding anniversary, and I am writing to you after reading the *Dear Abby* column about your research, about how lost first loves can ignite old flames. Much to my shame, I am in that position at this time. We met again at a class reunion.

Our original romance began when I was 15 and he was 16. We dated for three years steady, then it cooled but was renewed a year later. He went into the service in 1941. I met and married my husband in 1946; we have six children, 9 grandchildren.

I didn't see my former sweetheart again until the school reunion. It was so obvious to both of us that we had made a mistake by not marrying each other years ago. His wife had died. Then and there we should have agreed not to contact each other until I was free, too. Well, it didn't happen that way. I am the one who arranged another meeting, and from then on, the old feelings returned full force.

My husband knows about this. I have been seeing a therapist and have talked to my two closest friends about my predicament. I am aware of my sin, very conscience-stricken about the whole thing. I have prayed, and chastised myself, but I cannot let go.

I have seen a lawyer to get details about divorce. I love my husband, but I haven't been "in love" with him for many years. He is one of the nicest men anyone could find, very moral and intelligent. We have a lovely home, lots of mutual friends, and we travel around the world together. People will think I'm crazy if I leave him. Will I? I am planning to, but who knows? I am one more married lost love who "shouldn't have."

We were sweethearts in Maryland in the 1950's. I can remember always watching Bruce—he was on the basketball team, and I was a cheerleader, and I used to hang around the boys' locker room, hoping for a chance to see him, in addition to our other time together. We did all the usual things, like talking on the phone for hours, passing notes in classes, and going to dances when his older sister drove us there. We had our disagreements like everybody else, but we were happy together.

At the end of my sophomore year, when I was 16, my life tragically changed. My family's home exploded and burned while my father, three siblings and I were inside. My father died later that day. We were relocated to a town 150 miles away, where I attended a new high school, and I never again saw Bruce or any of my old friends.

Bruce and I each married and started families and never had any contact at all until 1988, when he came for a school reunion. We talked only briefly and without much success in communication. But from that point on, he was in my head and I kept in closer touch with his friends to find out about him. I heard that he suffered a heart attack, and I also heard that he was divorcing his wife. I thought about calling him, but I never did.

Our next school reunion, in 1993, was the right timing for us. He came with the intent of finding out if I had remarried after my divorce. When he found out that I was single, he knew he would stay in town another three weeks to see if our relationship could be renewed. The first time I saw him, Friday night at the reunion, settled it for me. As the evening wore on, we kept eyeing each other, and I later found an excuse to invite him to go for coffee with a group of old friends who just didn't want the reunion party to stop. As we talked and tried to eat, feelings were there for both of us. I invited myself to attend a hot air balloon liftoff the next morning; I just couldn't take the chance that he wouldn't invite me first.

Next morning he picked me up on his Harley motorcycle and off we went… never to be apart again. We spent the next three weeks together, talking and catching up on our separate lives. To have him walk back into my life after all the intervening years and say, "I have been in love with you since high school" has been a humbling experience for me. Within a few days, I knew that I was still in love with him. My feet weren't on the ground for weeks!

He returned home to complete his divorce, then came back to me. We are living together now, until we get married next year—his son and daughter are both getting married this year. We are back in our old hometown.

Nothing could be better than what we have found together. There is no way to explain in words the emotional satisfaction that has come around for me and I know for him, too. He has enhanced my life to the point of disbelief. Our love has been so right that there have been no questions about what we should do or where we should be. It's just all there.

I am 63 years old, a retired professor with lots of hobbies, activities, and projects to keep me busy. My wife, Barbara, is a retired teacher. I re-met her at our 10th year high school reunion. We have four children, all married, and we look forward to all of the happy family events in the future. My wife and I enjoy traveling together, dining out, walking, talking, visiting friends, and many other fun things. I love her very deeply and we are happy together.

At the reunion, we reminisced, laughed, danced, joked, and were married nine months later. She is the best thing that ever happened to me.

Barbara and I organized and ran our 40th high school reunion. I wrote a personal note to my first love, Karen, on one of the notification forms, saying it would be nice to see her again after 40 years. We had been sweethearts during our sophomore and junior years. We dated one or two times a week, met in the auditorium early every day before classes, held hands between classes, went to dances, movies, hiking, skating and biking, and hugged and kissed a lot whenever we could be alone.

Karen's mother forced her to break up with me after graduation, ostensibly because of a couple of situations when I was not totally truthful in our relationship. There were, however, other reasons why I thought her mother didn't like me, such as socioeconomic differences. We continued surreptitiously to see each other during the summer while Karen was a counselor living away from home, but filial obedience prevailed and we said a tearful goodbye at a drive-in movie theater one night in late August. We were both going off to separate colleges, dutifully observing the parental prohibition; I was reluctantly resolved to the idea that there could never be happiness with a disapproving parent.

My next four years at college were unhappy ones which I prefer to forget. The next six years were considerably better, and then I had the good fortune to reunite with Barbara.

Karen sent in her payment for the 40th reunion, whereupon I became concerned that our meeting at the reunion would be somewhat emotional and embarrassing to me; so I called her on the telephone one night a few weeks prior to the event to suggest that we meet for lunch the day before the reunion. She agreed and we talked on the phone for awhile. I learned that she had been married and divorced twice.

The two of us met for lunch in the lobby of the hotel where she was staying. We hugged and kissed and spent a couple of hours reminiscing. Although she had gained some weight and looked very little like the 16 year old girl I had once known, her voice and mannerisms were the same. The 40 years intervening between that night at the drive-in theater and the day of our reunion were temporarily erased. Our meeting was a very pleasant interlude. Of course we met again the following night at the high school reunion where we spent a little time talking together, but our advance meeting was the one of importance, one of those treasured things in life.

Since that August reunion, I have written to her a few times and she has sent return letters. I sent her some photographs and original letters that she had written to me 40 years ago. There is an unspoken acknowledgment that we cannot reunite because I am happily married. It is improbable that we will ever come together again, except perhaps at a future high school reunion, because I love my wife Barbara with a love that has grown from a lifetime of sharing together, of raising children, and of experiencing all of the trials and happiness afforded to two committed partners in marriage.

I know that I have always loved Karen, the 16 year old girl, and I know I will take that love with me to my grave. But Karen can only be a "second alternative"—I know that sounds cold, heartless, and foreboding. I will continue to write to Karen about once or twice a year; I want to know how she is, and yes, I want her to know that I care.

Walt and I met in our high school freshman English class over 50 years ago, in a Deep South city. And we went steady until the summer after we graduated. We studied together, we learned to dance together, we swam together, we played together, we experimented with food together, we watched out for one another, and we talked and talked and talked, exploring the meaning of life. Walt says that I perpetually asked him, "Do you really love me, or are you just in love with being in love?" I don't remember that, but it sounds like something I would ask.

As dawn came on many sultry Southern summer mornings, I waited on the front steps of my home for Walt to come by, delivering papers, just so we could kiss.

Walt was interested in guns. He taught me to target shoot, and we joined the Junior National Rifle Association. He loaded his own ammunition and I watched, afraid he would hurt himself.

I wanted my ears pierced and I persuaded Walt to do it, using a big needle, a thread and a bar of soap behind my ear. All went well until a week later when, in his arms with my head on his chest, the loop of thread in one ear caught on a shirt button and pulled a slit almost through the ear lobe.

And together, both of us virgins, we explored all of the physical intimacies between a man and a woman, and we found that we were good at it—unabashed, freewheeling, passionate, mature lovemaking.

But part way through the summer after graduation, I left him. Why? I don't know why, but maybe I felt the need to try my wings, to get away from my family, to avoid going away to the university that was my father's alma mater, to explore other men. And so I cried, "Walt, let me go!" He was stricken, but he did.

Later in the summer I met someone else, a young man in the Army, married him after a whirlwind courtship, and moved away from my hometown.

Walt has told me that he nearly went crazy that summer. That he couldn't contain himself, that he cried every night for months, and on into years. He blamed his mother for our breakup, and to get away from his family, he married a younger woman several years later, when he was 21. They were married for 10 years and had six children together before the union ended badly, with pain and anger.

Walt's accomplishments are considerable. Without help from his family, he worked his way through college and dental school. He still practices dentistry, in partnership with one of his sons.

After his divorce, Walt married again. He is still married to this woman today. However, he never lost track of me. When I moved back to my hometown five years after my marriage, he knew I was there. And he knew when I divorced my husband and remarried, he knew when I became very ill, and he knew when one of my daughters, in school at the same high school that Walt and I had attended, dated one of his sons. That was when I learned that he had carried me in his heart for all those years, because when I was introduced to my daughter's date, Walt's son, he said, "Oh, I know who you are. My father has talked about you a lot."

Ten years ago my husband and I sold our business in my hometown and moved to Nevada, and Walt lost track of me for a while. My husband and I divorced, and I have been single for eight years.

Two years ago was the 50th anniversary of our graduation from high school and an alumni committee organized a reunion. Walt, who was well-known in our hometown, was contacted by the committee. He asked them to let him know if they located me. The reunion committee did locate me, and they asked if I would mind if they gave my email address to Walt. A few days later I received an email message that said, "50 years have passed. You're still in my heart and on my mind. Please contact me. Walt." My heart almost stopped. I responded quickly.

What has happened since is amazing, just amazing! We began to correspond by email in November. By mid-December we had explored our marital, work and family lives thoroughly, by email, and I was asking him how could these feelings have grown so quickly, and where was this relationship going? By early January I was thanking God for bringing Walt back into my life; by February we felt that our relationship was destined. And in March I flew to my hometown and we saw each other and held one another for the first time in 50 years.

The evening when we first came together was powerful. We had agreed that we wouldn't have sex when we first met, that we would touch and hold one another and kiss, and get to know each other again, and that's what we did. We held each other and the years dropped away. And we talked and talked and talked.

The passion in this newly-remade association was greater than anything we have ever experienced before. For myself, I spent those first months in a quivering, aroused state of sexual excitement every time I talked to, wrote to, or even thought about Walt. I glowed with such heat that people I know stared at me and commented. Strangers smiled at me on the street, and friends told me that I am beautiful. I was 68 years old, and not that beautiful, but the glow was from the inside.

Now, our relationship has changed. Some of the sexual urgency has gone. Having experienced one another, we know that we like each other, that the closeness of our friendship is still intact (and growing), and we want and need to be together. But Walt is married, and has no plans to become unmarried, for reasons that are good. We are in contact daily. We talk on the telephone once or twice a day, and email daily, also. We have become expert at carrying on major discussions in that way. And we send clippings and books and cards and notes and packages back and forth by snail mail. One of the hardest things is our inability to touch one another when we need to, neither in love or passion, nor in comfort or compassion.

What continues to be wonderful is that we're very dear friends and confidantes. We have and continue to benefit one another by filling several needs that each of us have. He has the mature attention of the girl who left him all those years ago, and hurt him and probably changed his attitude toward women for the rest of his life. I have the emotional support of a loving man in my life, and a generous and attentive man, at that. Walt pushed me back into the church several years ago (I was working on it, but couldn't quite get there), for which I will forever be grateful.

We share lengthy conversations about books (we're both voracious readers) and he frequently sends his books on to me. We talk about politics (argue, actually. We're at opposite poles.) We commiserate with one another, give and take advice, speak VERY fondly of sex , and on and on. We each manage to keep busy and occupied, and we certainly never lack things to talk about!

We are two lovers who lost each other for many years. We were a couple for three years in high school, continuing on for another year when Richard was in the Air Force. As teenagers we were never sexually involved (were many of us back then)? We would have burned in hell for sure or our parents would have disowned us if we got pregnant, especially being Catholic, which we both were. Not that we didn't get into long passionate embraces, mind you; we just kept our hands to ourselves and our clothes on!!

When it came time to talk marriage, which we always planned on, we differed as to the type of wedding we should have and how and when it should take place. We were really too young to make those kinds of decisions and we ended the relationship on a "not too happy tone". We eventually each married, and later found out that we each thought of the other many times over the years.

Our 50th reunion was coming up. I felt a terrible need to get to the "50th," for only one reason: hoping to see "HIM" again. Maybe to just see that he was okay and that he didn't hate me any longer for ending it when I did.

I used to dream about him, but he was always somewhere where he couldn't hear my voice calling to him. I think it had to do with non-closure. Well, it took a long while to find out when the reunion was going to be and by the time I did, I had been offered a job in Yellowstone National Park, and I accepted it. I am a registered nurse, but semi-retired, so I spent time doing anything out of the line of nursing for the summers!!! HOW FUN. I did the national parks for 5 great years. I also do community theater and right before the reunion, I had been cast in a show called "Ballroom;" it was night after night of dance rehearsals, and my character was the Queen of the Lindy. Need I say more about how much dancing we did? One month later, I had a hip replacement —- the doc said there was no cartilage left. So no Yellowstone National Park!

I hoped against hope that I could attend the reunion, seeing that it was pretty close to surgery; my orthopedic surgeon said, "Okay, you can go; just be careful." Off I went to Massachusetts, but instead of floating like Loretta Young into the reunion, I walked in with my cane. Now picture this redhead trying hard to walk sophisticatedly and trying not to cause pain. There was a silver-haired, tall man smiling at me, and he took me into his arms and hugged me so hard—all the while I was wondering, "Who is this that I must have meant something to?" I didn't have a clue. Well, when he slapped his name tag onto his coat, I almost fainted dead away.

As you can well imagine, we spent a great part of the night talking and reminiscing and (maybe a little flirting) with each other. He got the photographer to take our picture, and it made the reunion yearbook! He left before the end and I was devastated. I thought about it over and over in the days to come; I still felt the same way about him as I did long ago. I could not imagine never seeing him again.

I found out later that he felt the same way. He left the reunion because he found that the spark was still there, and he didn't want to lose me by being rejected again; but on the way home, he experienced the deep sense of loss as I had.

He tried to find out my last name and address and phone number through the reunion committee, then called only to find out my phone was disconnected for the summer (he had forgotten that I told him I was going to Virginia for the summer). He wrote a letter and sent it to my address in Florida and of course, it took a while to reach me in Virginia, and by that time, he thought I did not want to communicate.

His letter was very gentle, telling me that he thought that we should stay in touch "at our age," because one never knows. He asked me to call and I did. We started to correspond by phone and letters, and to his amazement, he even learned how to use a computer at the library to send email. We kept in touch this way for a while and then he made arrangements to meet me in Virginia.

This was an unbelievable meeting. We kissed for the first time in 50 years, but we also found out how wonderful an intimate relationship can be. We stayed in an old inn, had a wonderful dinner (how can I even remember what we ate, but I do). If you can just imagine my thoughts—- I am really with my Richard!! We kept thinking we were in a dream.

The next time we saw each other was when I flew up and we went to Cape Cod for another delightful time. It is one of our favorite places that we, who had both come from the area, had never been to before together. After that, he came to Florida twice and then I planned to make the trip north in January; after all, it was my turn. I never used the second half of my round trip ticket. I drove back with him from New England after his decision to give up his job and his place there, and move to Florida with me. He said he couldn't lose me again in one lifetime.

We are married, since Valentine's Day of last year. When we planned to get married this time, we decided to keep it small, so we went to City Hall and got our license and told our story to the clerk. We were going to get married by a minister, who at the last minute could not do it, so we said, "Let's just go the City Hall at 8 am all alone." I wore the dress I wore at the reunion, and he dressed the same as he had, too. We had little flowers and guess what happened at this quiet time? Channel 2 News TV was there, having heard about our story (and of course seeing that it was Valentine's Day). They interviewed us and recorded the whole wedding ceremony, which they edited and played on the 5 o'clock news. They also came home with us to film the pictures of us in our yearbook from high school, and they interviewed my son—-all of which was on the news. So much for a quiet wedding!! The tape is wonderful.

We took a trip to 6 European countries for our honeymoon in April, and have been on a honeymoon of sorts ever since. We are in our 70's now and are extremely happy. I have 7 children and Richard has 3, all grown.

There have been hurdles to get over, of course, as people do collect baggage in 50 years; but today we are handling the relationship with love and respect that we really did not have as teenagers. Richard regrets the years that we were not together, but I feel that we are so fortunate to have the "now." Our days together are filled with so much. We are living proof that things can happen "Somewhere in Time."

CHAPTER 3

Family Matters

In 1997, I reported in *Lost & Found Lovers* that my research indicated that parental disapproval of the romance was the most common reason the first loves broke up. In many cases, parents actively manipulated the breakup. Occasionally siblings interfered and harmed the romances as well.

Some lost and found lovers are bitter about the past, while others are more philosophical and forgiving. Middle aged couples voice regrets to me about the years without their first loves—years of youthfulness, when having children together would have been possible. And they are remorseful about their divorces, as they reflect upon the hurt they caused their innocent children and ex-spouses, which could have been prevented if the lost loves had been allowed to stay together years ago. The Prince Charles, Camilla, and Diana triangle epitomizes the damage that can result when young couples are separated by parents.

Reunited couples who are parents treat their adolescents with special sensitivity. Because they remember their own romantic difficulties and understand the enduring nature of first love, they are reluctant to interfere with their teenagers' romances.

I hope these love stories will remind parents to take teen love seriously!

I met the love of my life in the summer of 1955. I was visiting my best friend, Debbie, when her boyfriend stopped by to see her. He brought his friend, Al—a tall, good looking boy with sandy hair and green eyes. It was love at first sight for me, and he told me much later that he knew I was the girl he would marry.

As the guys left that afternoon, Al asked me to go to a movie with him the following weekend, and I gladly accepted. He stood me up. When he called a few days later, he said his old car had broken down and his mother would not let him use hers. He had no way to call me because he did not know my last name, or Debbie's, either. By the time he finally got the telephone number and called, I was angry at being stood up and not too interested in talking to him. But I agreed to go out with him the next weekend. We had a great time, and Al still teases me about my refusal to kiss him on that first date. I told him, "I am not that kind of girl."

We saw each other every day that summer. He had already graduated from high school, had recently been discharged from the Army, and was working at a local factory. We arranged our dates around his work shifts. We went dancing and to local amusement parks and movies. It was a glorious summer. We were very much in love.

When I went back to school that fall, it was my senior year. My father told Al that he would not be allowed to see me every day during the school year, and if my grades went down he would not be able to see me at all. I made sure my grades were excellent and I was on the honor roll. When spring came, Al took me to my Senior Prom. My dress was pink and fluffy. He gave me a beautiful pearl and gold ring. I still have that ring.

I landed a good job with the telephone company. Al and I were delighted about that, because we knew that we would be getting married. Al was laid off at the factory, but Debbie's father gave him a job at his store. Al picked me up for lunch and sometimes after work. We spent every waking hour together that we could. He put a down payment on a house halfway between my parents' home and his mother's house. We envisioned a wonderful life together with two children. By spring of that year, it was time to become engaged and begin making wedding plans.

On Sunday afternoons, we often went to the home of his aunt and uncle. His Aunt Mary said she would invite Al's mother and my parents for dinner. Once that occurred, I could wear his engagement ring. It would be official. The wedding plans could be made. Al bought the ring and kept it tucked away until the time was right.

Al and I were not invited to Aunt Mary's home to attend dinner with our parents that Sunday afternoon. When my parents got home from the dinner, they said they needed to speak to me—I was told that I would never see Al again. The relationship was ended. There was no explanation.

I saw him for the next six months or so by sneaking out, but my parents made it increasingly more difficult for me to get away from home. They insisted that I call them when I was at Debbie's house, or anywhere else, and they gave me unrealistic curfews. It just got to be too difficult. Al never knew that this was going on.

Finally I met a young man at work and began dating him. My parents had grown tired of dealing with their adolescent daughter and knew that I would return to Al if I could, so they thought this man was the perfect solution. They wanted me to marry him, and I did as I was told. I had four wonderful children with him; they are now grown with children of their own. During all the years they were growing up, I often thought of Al. I checked each new telephone book to see if his name was listed. It wasn't. I wondered if life had been good to him. I also felt guilty because I had walked out of his life without telling him what was happening in mine.

Five years ago, Al telephoned my mother; he was wondering how I was. My mother would not tell him my phone number, nor did she take his. But she did tell me all this a few days later, and that was all it took. I contacted a company that conducts computer searches, and they found him for me. Rather than calling, I decided to write to him; that way if he chose not to answer, it would be easier. Three days later, I received his phone call.

His voice had not changed one iota in those forty years. He told me he was married, with three children. We decided to meet just for lunch, at a quaint little Italian restaurant.

I remembered that Al had always arrived early for dates, so I arrived early, and there he was. Our hug felt as if we had never been apart. Forty years melted into oblivion. We walked to a park to sit and talk. A wedding was taking place there.

Al asked me what I wanted to do with this reunion. I told him I did not want another forty years to pass before I saw him again. He agreed, and told me that he never stopped thinking of me. Everywhere he went, he always looked for me. And he said he always loved me and always would. But he is married.

I have talked to my mother, since this meeting, to find out what happened at his Aunt Mary's house that Sunday long ago. My mother said that Al's aunt told her that she should not allow me to marry into that family, because I deserved better. Al's mother was an alcoholic, but my parents had already known that. And Al never drank. Neither Al nor I believe my mother's explanation, but she is the only surviving person of the group in attendance that day.

Al and I love each other dearly, and will savor the moment. Here we are in the midst of the same feelings we had when we were young, and again our relationship cannot progress. At some point, we know that there is a good chance that our times together will have to end.

I wear the gold watch and the ring that he gave me all those years ago. Al still has my engagement ring. I have never seen it.

Barbara and I met at a fraternity rush party in October, 1974. I was a sophomore, 19, and Barbara was a freshman, 18. Barbara had been invited by a fraternity brother and decided to check out the party. When I came down the stairs and into the party room, Barbara was sitting on a sofa in the middle of the room. I came around the end of the couch, our eyes met and we just gravitated towards each other. We spent the entire night talking, until it was time to walk her back to her dorm. It was as if we had known each other forever, in other lives, that was how comfortable it was. I was never entirely comfortable talking to girls, but with Barbara, it was the easiest thing I had ever done. We had a great time together, had a great good night kiss and started dating.

I had just broken up with someone, and once she found out someone else was interested in me, she wanted me back. Being young, somewhat inexperienced and very flattered, I made Mistake Number One and broke up with Barbara for this other girl after 2 weeks. One night, this other woman and I had concert tickets, and so did Barbara (with a group of her friends). Seeing Barbara at the concert, I realized I had made a terrible mistake and broke up with the girl.

A few days later, it was Thanksgiving, and as we both lived in New Jersey, we all met at my house and drove back to school in Washington, DC together. Barbara and I spent the majority of a 7-hour ride in traffic back to school in the back seat kissing. We were back together, starting a wonderful two year relationship. We spent all our time together, hanging out, going to parties or to hockey games. Barbara would watch me play goalie on my college hockey team and cheering me on at fraternity intramural sports. I didn't have much money, so the nights out to dinner were few and far between, but my Barbara didn't care; she just wanted to be with me, and together we made our own fun. We were virtually inseparable, informally living together in my fraternity house, which was common at the time for people going out a long time.

The first time I made love to Barbara was the first time I made love to anyone. As easy and effortlessly it was with talking to her and being with her, this too was so natural and wonderful.

We were madly in love and dated for two wonderful years. We enjoyed an amazing physical relationship as we were extremely attracted to each other, got along wonderfully, had a lot in common, rarely fought, and overall were very happy together. However, it was my first serious relationship and despite being happy, I started to listen to my parents and some of my friends, who would ask me if I was sure this was the girl for me.

My parents wanted me to date others, and they would talk about it whenever they called me. Barbara had made a passing comment one time when talking about our future. She joked that if I couldn't get a good job in my field, we could always open a pizza parlor. It was a joke, but my parents took it to heart, and then unleashed a barrage that she would not push me, would not make me a success, that I was not motivated because of her laid back disposition. (Years later, after we reunited, my brother confessed to me that the pizza parlor story was still talked about. Even more humorous was my mother commenting to me after Barbara and I were married a year, that she and my dad had been in a very busy pizza restaurant and that it probably wouldn't have been so bad after all.)

Anyway, all of this pressure from my mom finally got to me, and I started dating someone else behind Barbara's back when I was home for summer break. I finally told her that I thought we should see other people but continue seeing each other also. Barbara went along with that for one last date and then we never saw each other again. I never told Barbara the real reason I was breaking up. I wouldn't lie to her, so I told her that since we never fought, I needed a more "challenging" relationship. This fateful decision was to be the worst one of my life. What I regret even more is that Barbara was hurt so very much. Since our relationship was pretty close to perfect, she just assumed that we would most likely get married one day. The breakup more or less came out of left field, so Barbara was devastated.

I, however, thought I was doing the right thing, and went on with my fraternity life. My mother was happy that I was now planning to play the field. Barbara never had a hard time attracting other guys, and proceeded to parade many men in front of me in the hopes to get me to realize my mistake. Sadly, I was too ego-filled and proud to say that I made a mistake, but I was always aware of who the guys were. It never ceased to bother me when I knew there was another guy in her life, even when I was already dating the woman I would eventually marry, my rebound relationship. Ironically, not only did I not really play the field, but my parents hated my first wife because of her strong will and controlling personality.

Barbara, on the other hand, tried to move on by dating as many men as possible in a vain effort to find love again. It took two years before she met a law student whom she eventually married. She loved her husband, but never in the same way that she loved me. I had gotten married a year out of college and Barbara got married a year after she met her husband. She had four children over the 18 years of her marriage. Her husband had a quick temper, and the love had totally gone out of the marriage five years before reconnecting with me.

I had also been very unhappily married. My wife was verbally abusive, but I stayed in the marriage and had two children. Frequently, during almost 20 years of marriage, I would confide to friends and coworkers that I was unhappy. I began to find solace in movies that had a second chance theme, or a plot about a new chance at happiness.

Over the years, Barbara had contacted me twice. The first time was four years after her marriage. She had received a college alumni catalogue and my phone number was listed. We had a short phone conversation, mostly talking about mutual friends and their respective lives and children. It was another nine years before we came into contact again, this time by email. Barbara did a random search and found an email address for me at my job. As timing would have it, I was moving out of state in one week and only a few friendly emails were exchanged. Barbara had just moved into a huge custom built home and was trying to act the part, saying how happily married she was. Since there were never any overtures on my part, she assumed I harbored no feelings for her anymore.

Another five years passed. Barbara's marriage was over; she had told her husband 18 months previously that she no longer loved him and wanted to separate. He begged her to give marriage counseling a try, which they did, but there was nothing left to save.

About a month earlier, on a whim, she once again did an Internet search for me. Having found me once again, she emailed to say hello. It had been five years and although her marriage was over, she had no reason to believe that I wasn't happily married. However, this time, instead of pretending everything was great, she confessed in an email on the second day of contact that she would be ending her marriage shortly. That was all the opening I needed, and I asked if it was okay to call her. Barbara said yes, and I picked up the phone. All of those 23 years apart fell immediately away and the love that was always there exploded into reality. We both knew in that first phone call that our strong feelings were never really gone, just repressed over the years, mostly by me. Barbara knew that she always loved me, but had no choice but to move on. I, on the other hand, had pushed aside my feelings in an effort to make the choice I had made all those years ago. So, when the feelings resurfaced for me, they were overwhelmingly strong, and nothing could keep us apart again.

After the contact and phone call with Barbara, I leaped at the opportunity to truly be happy, and told my wife it was over. Many of my friends asked why it took me so long; they could not understand how I remained married for so long.

So, after six weeks of emails and phone calls, Barbara and I planned to meet, to see if the attraction was still there. I flew to her hometown, and we met at the hotel where I was staying. Although she was excited to see me, she told me later that she was nervous that I would no longer be attracted to her; she had gained weight since college, and having children and aging had changed her body. I was also heavier and now had gray hair.

We were both extremely excited and never more nervous in our lives. However, with one look, we knew our fears were unfounded. Neither of us cared about the changes in our physical appearances; the foundation of love was already there. We were immediately comfortable with each other and still very attracted to each other. We knew within minutes that we definitely wanted to be together forever. When we finally made love, it was so romantic and passionate, like something you see only in movies.

After seeing each other, we both started divorce proceedings so we could be married.

Barbara and I were married in September, 2001, a little over a year after we reconnected. Her kids loved me from the first time they met me, but mine still aren't happy that I moved away, even though they do see that I am now happy and a much more loving father because of it. I talk to them every day and try to visit with them every six weeks. There are still issues with dealing with ex-spouses. It is not an easy road, but worth it.

We now work together in the mortgage business. We're together 24 hours a day, but we still can't wait to get upstairs to be alone. Our relationship is definitely not the norm. We've now been married over two years and it isn't going into that "let's calm down" phase yet. We love being together and our love gets stronger every day. We feel it is an enviable kind of relationship, a real "true love" story.

Tom and I met at a McDonald's when we were 16; we fell in love instantly. He asked me out and I was on Cloud 9. However, on our very first date, he was extremely late, with no phone call. I was ready and waiting, pacing and ready to cry. My dad, being the protective father he was, was upset because I was upset. He advised me not to wait for Tom, but I couldn't leave and take a chance on missing him. Finally Tom showed up in his Pontiac Lemans and I was off on my first date with him, much to my dad's dismay.

I can't remember what we did on that first date, but I do know I fell in love with him and it wasn't just a crush. When we were together, time flew. We would go to the park and lie on the ground, look up at the stars and dream our dreams of the future together. We were inseparable. We gave our virginity away to each other and we pledged that there would never be anyone else. We were scared and we both cried.

Our favorite song was "Don't Go Breaking My Heart," by Elton John and Kiki Dee, and we would sing it to each other all the time. Through our years apart, whenever I would hear that song, I always thought of him.

My parents were going through a separation, and I was left to live with my dad. One day I forgot I was to go straight home from school as he had instruct-ed me to do. I was with Tom having our pictures taken together, for part of his senior picture package. After a huge argument with my father, he told me to choose between Tom or him. How could I? I loved both of them, yet Tom was my world. I chose Tom.

All my life, I had felt unwanted by my mother, so I couldn't go there. She had me when she was only 16 and always told me that I had taken away her child-hood. I was her punching bag and sounding board all my life. You can under-stand why I took refuge in Tom— for the first time in my life, I was truly loved.

I called Tom and he came back to get me. My father would not let me take anything with me, and told me that if I came back to get anything, he would have me arrested. Tom's parents took me in as if I were their own daughter. They helped me get a room at the YWCA, and Tom or his parents would come and get me there and take me to school. There I was, a senior in high school and vir-tually homeless. Through this ordeal, Tom and I grew even closer. I felt like he was the only one who really loved me in the whole world, and he truly did. I worked at McDonalds, went to school, and paid rent to the YWCA. That's a lot for a 17 year old girl!

Later on, I moved into his grandmother's apartment. After a while, though, the stress of trying to graduate, make a living and just survive, started to take its toll on us. We began to fight and argue constantly. My whole world started to fall apart and I felt like I was totally alone in the world once again. I moved back with my father.

I was told constantly that if I ever came home pregnant, I would be dis-owned and my parents would beat the hell out of me. Guess what? Yes, it hap-pened. Tom and I were fighting now nonstop and I didn't know what to do about the pregnancy. So when you are 18 and afraid of being beaten once again, you turn to the unthinkable. With me afraid of my parents, and Tom afraid to tell his parents because they are devote Catholics, we turned to the worst imag-inable thing: we decided to terminate the pregnancy. That whole day we fought, neither of us wanting to do that, but in our young minds we thought this was our only alternative.

On the way home from the clinic, I felt hurt and abandoned, guilty and unworthy. I started to hemorrhage, and my father found me passed out in the shower. He asked me what had happened, and I told him I couldn't tell him, because I didn't want him to hit me. He looked up towards Heaven and asked, "Oh my God, what have I done?" He told me we would have to tell my mother and, although I begged him not to, he told me we were eventually going to have to tell, because something was seriously wrong with my body for me to be so sick.

When she found out, my mother started screaming at me and asked why I didn't come to her for help. My dad told her to shut up, that both of them were the reason I didn't confide in them.

Before we went to the hospital, my mom called Tom at work and told him I was going into the hospital and he had better meet us there. He didn't. He was scared. He'd been attacked verbally by my parents so many other times, he couldn't go through it again.

I remember waking up in the recovery room and asking for my mom. I told her I was sorry and not to blame Tom, that it wasn't his fault. But they put Tom down all the way home and, unbeknownst to me, they had threatened Tom that he had better stay away from me, or they would tell his parents. I could never understand why he wouldn't talk to me afterwards. It hurt me more than words can say.

For 22 years, I have cried over Tom and the baby I never had. That baby was conceived in total love; the baby I never got to hold and cuddle or even say that I really did want it.

I became a Catholic two years ago. This was something I wanted to do; I needed God in my life and the Catholic Church opened its arms wide to me. At my first confession, I told the priest about the abortion and that I still loved Tom, had never gotten over the pain of losing both of them. The priest told me I needed to put closure on this and he told me to name the baby. So I named her Jane. I called the baby a girl because in my heart I know that is what she was. And all those years, without communicating with each other, Tom also believed it was a girl.

Last Christmas season, I finally made a break from my parents, who still tried to control my life, even at my age of 40. Then I prayed to God for guidance and called Tom's mom to ask for his phone number. When I called his number, I was shaking. No one answered; I got the answering machine and left a message saying that I was calling to wish him and his family a Merry Christmas and I just wondered if we could talk to catch up on each other's lives. I left my phone number and I figured if I heard from him that would be wonderful; if not, I would accept that.

A couple of days went by and then I got my answer. I was trembling. I told him that I had felt the need to put closure on the baby and that the priest had suggested that I name her. I told him the name I choose was Jane. He asked if he could choose the middle name, and of course I agreed. I apologized for the hurt we went through as kids and I asked him if he thought about it as much as I did. He answered, "Every day." The following day he called again, to say he had decided on Marie as the middle name and asked if the last name could be his, because she did have a father.

They say the cycle of abuse can carry on, from your parents to your own children. My children, however, have had total love and respect. They know about the abortion, I guess because I never want them to be afraid to come to me with anything. Tom's children also know. We both learned a lot from that terrible ordeal.

The same day that Tom called to tell me her middle name, he asked if he could come see me; he wanted to go to church to light a candle in her name and, together, finally ask for forgiveness. The closure has lifted a lot of pain from both of our hearts.

Tom and I still love each other. I called him at a time in his life when we could get back together and have a second chance at love. This is such a blessing. My parents do not know about this reunion, and I guess I really don't care. Unfortunately, they live in the past, and they are still good at placing blame.

Tom and I have found, after 22 years of searching, the love that was sitting right in front of us when we were kids. It was always there; we were just too young and immature to notice.

Our wedding date has been set, and I am looking forward to being with the man I never stopped loving.

My first memory of Barry was when our Hebrew School class walked across the bridge from New Brunswick to Highland Park, in New Jersey. We were on our way to Freddie Katz's Bar Mitzvah and, since we were religious and couldn't ride on the Sabbath, we walked together in the rain. The old wet bridge with railroad stakes holding the planks together left an indelible memory, and so did Barry. I was 10 and he was 12.

We hung out together at the local YMHA, always in a crowd. There were about 10 of us, boys and girls, and we joked and kidded in our prepubescent bliss, not even realizing that we were flirting. The routine was to go to the "Y" after school, go to Hebrew School, and then always attend synagogue services on Saturdays. The males sat in the main sanctuary, and the females sat upstairs in the balcony. We girls could watch the boys without them knowing. I did a lot of daydreaming during services. My fantasies all included Barry.

We amused ourselves with kickball, volleyball, and spin the bottle parties until one day it occurred to Barry and me that we were attracted to each other (15 and 17); we began to go to the Sunday night YMHA basketball games, always followed by a dance. We still traveled in the crowd, but he and I paired off at the dance, after which he walked me home.

We dated exclusively for about four years. Part of that time, Barry was in the Army (during World War II), and I only saw him when he came home on a leave. I really loved him and he loved me. We planned a life together—until his parents interfered. You see, I was the child of a Jewish mother and a Spanish-Catholic father. Barry's parents were both Jewish, as were all the kids in our crowd, I was the different one. His parents insisted that he stop dating me, since my family was a mixed marriage and considered undesirable, almost marked. My brother and I to this day speak of those really hard times when we were excluded from many activities because of our heritage. Even though our mother was Jewish, we were not accepted by the local Jews.

Barry let me know the hardships he underwent to see me. He had to lie and sneak until both of acknowledged the futility of our plans. We decided to part and date others. I went through a long mourning period after suffering that loss and never quite got over it. He had already been discharged from the service and was attending Rutgers. My family had started a new life in upstate Massachusetts, but I kept meeting the same problem of discrimination with other young men, until I found my first husband who defied his family and dated me despite their protests. We married in 1949; Barry married 4 years later.

Six years later, my husband and I and our 2 children moved to Wisconsin where I reinvented myself. I was 26 years old and no longer a reject. In fact, I was quite sought after as "the big city gal with lots of savvy." I had another child, and I was the mother of three lovely children—but not with the man I truly loved.

We moved back East, and I attended several of my high school reunions. I usually met Barry there. I still felt the same about him, and I went to every reunion so I could see him. He or I never called or wrote. We didn't want to disturb the fates. But we had many of the same friends, favorite haunts, songs and foods. Sometimes he and his wife, and my husband and I, and all our shared friends got together. That continued for years.

In 1963, we moved to Chicago, and 2 years later my husband died. I was 36 years old, widowed with three children, and without any skills but mothering. I could barely breathe without having a panic attack. I had never been so fearful in my life.

In 1970, I met and married a widower with 2 children. We moved to California 5 years after we married and I again started a new life, as a student. At age 41, I enrolled as a freshman at State College and I earned my BA and MA degrees, took five years off, and then earned a Ph.D. in Clinical Psychology. At that point I had been married for 20 years, and I left my husband. My five children were all on their own, three of them were married, and I was ready to set myself free. I wanted a true love and a new life.

I bought a condo, sent my friends new address cards, and Gloria from New York called to tell me that Barry's wife was critically ill with cancer. I called immediately but she was already in the hospital, never to go home. Within a month she was dead. I called to support my first love and spoke to him hours on end. He was devastated by the loss of his wife. He had been very dependent upon her during their 35 years of marriage and parenting two sons.

Barry came to California for a visit, at the urging of some of our mutual friends from our home town. A few months later, he came back to California, and this time he stayed with me; our love was still there. I helped him through his mourning and bereavement.

After we had lived together for three years, we entered a contest we heard about to win a Fantasy Wedding. I wrote a 500 word essay explaining what marriage in the 1990's meant to me, which was the topic that the contest was based upon. Well, we won! We competed internationally with 85 other couples. Our essay said it all: we were finally able to marry, despite the prejudice we had met as young people, and were free to live as we chose. We won a champagne wedding reception for 200 guests, and the gowns, shoes, headpieces and tuxedos for the entire wedding party. Plus flowers, cake, invitations, music, balloons everywhere, and a honeymoon in Maui. We were on every TV station in the nation and in every newspaper—and our home town paper in New Jersey put us on the front page using our high school yearbook photos.

We made up for all the years of separation with the celebrations, but it was all just a plus. Our love for each other is more sincere and devoted than ever. We did all of our growing up while we were apart and returned to each other fully mature without any of the youthful hang-ups. We have both grown to appreciate each other more each day, and we pray that we have many more years together. We will celebrate our tenth anniversary on August 18, surrounded by family and friends: my five married children; his two sons, one married and one single; and my eight grandchildren. The eighth is 3, his granddaughter, but now we share them all. We are truly blessed.

We were preteens in the 1950's. We came from a small town in Iowa, and met in church. By the time we grew into teenagers, we had become a steady couple, inseparable. We still went to church together, and we also went to the same high school where we could study and eat lunch together, and enjoy all the things teenagers did in the early Sixties. We spent hours listening to all the records in my record collection and attaching personal meanings to the songs. He was my best friend and confidante. If you saw Frank alone, he was either on his way to my house or on his way home.

Because we spent so much time together and loved each other so much, my dad had suspicions that we were much too close. One night when Frank came to visit me, my dad met him on the front porch and told him he was no longer welcome at our house, and was never to see me again. Dad told him that he was not good enough for me and that if he did try to see me, he would take legal action or send me to live elsewhere. Frank's family had already moved to another school district, so we couldn't even meet at school.

Frank came from a close family and felt he had to abide by what my father told him; he didn't want to come between me and my parents. He also believed that my father meant every word he said (which was true). After that, I was grounded and chaperoned everywhere I went. I was not allowed to go anywhere other than to school without my parents. They checked with the school every day to make sure I was there. I was totally lost without Frank. I had lost my very best friend as well as the person whom I loved. I grieved for months, listened to records alone and cried.

Frank went on with life by keeping busy at his school. He tried to fill the void that was left by marrying when he was young. I never got over him. After high school, I married a friend of his, but his memory always haunted me.

A few years after I married, we moved away, and I hoped that I could forget that painful chapter in my life and start anew in a new state. But whenever I went back to my hometown, I would secretly search the town, hoping to see him. There was an uneasiness inside that always gnawed at me, even though I felt that he probably had forgotten about me.

About 15 years after we moved away, my husband and I stopped at Frank's business to say hello to him and to his father who also worked there. It was brief and awkward and difficult to talk. I went away thinking that my visit meant much more to me than it did to Frank. Much later I learned that he had the same butterflies in his stomach that I did.

Years later, I returned to my hometown for my 30th class reunion. This time I entered his store alone, telling my husband to find something else to do for awhile. I recognized no one. I asked a young man if Frank still owned the business, and was told indeed he did and that the lady behind the counter was his wife. I told her that I was in town for a reunion and that Frank and I had been high school friends; I had dropped in to say hello. As fate would have it, he was in the back of the store, even though he seldom came to work on Friday afternoons.

Frank came out, and as he walked towards me, his face showed his shock. I tried to make a joke—that he probably didn't remember me—because he was at a loss for words. He finally said my name, and there were those beautiful blue eyes melting me again. Time stood still, and I found it difficult to breathe, let alone carry on a conversation. But I did find out that he had begun a new business, related to the business I was in. My company finances a type of equipment he was looking for, and I offered to help him purchase it, left my business card, and rejoined my husband.

I returned to my job the following Monday morning. Frank called and told me he had always loved me. When I moved away, and when my parents died, he had no idea where I was or how to find me, until I left my card. We talked on the telephone over the next two weeks, and then he came to visit me. Within a month, he had moved here.

When we got back together, there was no "getting reacquainted" time—it was as though he had never been gone. The bond we had formed 35 years earlier had never been broken. Each of us had loved the other enough not to want to interfere with the marriage and make a problem, but this time the love was bigger than both of us. We forged ahead and divorced our spouses.

We married in a beautiful ceremony for which we had waited 35 long years.

September, 2000. A grief-stricken man in his late twenties came to my office at the university, to tell me his lost love story and to seek comfort. As he told it to me, punctuated by long periods of sobbing, I will tell it to you:

He introduced himself, and told me that he was a university graduate with a degree in business. When he was 26, he had come from a small Muslim country to study in Sacramento, because his cousin lives here. And he fell in love with a fellow student; they were inseparable for 3 years. She was his first love. He explained to me that because he was an observant Muslim, he couldn't "date" in his home country.

He and his girlfriend assumed that they would marry, but he refused to tell his parents about her. He had an older sister, he said, who was unmarried, and by custom she had to marry before him. To tell his family that he wanted to marry would have put undue pressure and guilt on his sister. So it was his plan to wait, and hope his sister married soon. His American born Muslim girlfriend did not share this custom, and this cultural difference widened between them. She became tired of waiting, lost faith that their marriage would ever happen, and after 3 years, she just hung up the phone on him one day. And that was that… for her, but not for him.

He was unable to put the grief of losing her behind him. As he sat in my office, he alternately talked and sobbed. He had trouble with his emotions, but not with his English. It was perfect.

He told me that he had been suicidal and wanted to die when she left him, but the one thing that held him back, the one reason he did not do it, he said, was because of my book, *Lost & Found Lovers*.

"It was like a beacon, a candle out there."

He had come to meet me, just to thank me, because my book meant so much to him, giving him hope that his lost love might return to him. At that instant, all my work on that book seemed worthwhile.

The year before, on June 19, his birthday, his coworkers gave him a cake—at that time he worked on campus for one of the administrators—and told him to blow out the candles and make a wish for something he really wanted. He blew out the candles and wished that he would die and not have to see another birthday, not have to live without her any longer. June 19 rolled around again 3 months ago—he lived, but the next day his father died. He felt in some way responsible for that.

He saw his lost love once again, by chance, in a parking lot on campus. He noticed that she wore an engagement ring. She noticed that he still wore the watch she gave him, and told him that he shouldn't wear it anymore. No, he would never stop wearing it, he replied, and would never stop loving her. She did ask about his sister—still unmarried. Then she walked away. The next day, the second hand of the watch stopped working, and he saw meaning there, too.

His lost love had married, a month before he came to see me.

He had decided to return to his country within two months. There was nothing for him here now, and his newly widowed mother needed him—he is the only son. He said he would take his place in government there, as he had always been expected to do. He then mentioned that his grandfather had been the governor and his father was the minister of education. I asked which state/province his grandfather headed. "The governor is the head of the whole country," he told me, "like a president."

His political importance did not become evident until this point in his story. He was not there to impress me. His father died in office, so there would be an upcoming election. He would go back and run for his father's district, to preserve the family name in those towns and places named after his family. If the opposition won—if he did not run for office—the places would all be renamed and his family's position lost. The other party did not want him to return, of course, and he said they would fight hard. His mother had always groomed him "for this" (it was her father who had been governor).

Somewhere toward the end of his story, he mentioned that his grandfather had been assassinated in office. It was 1971, an uprising against the government. I asked if he would be in any danger, and he paused a while. "Yes," he said. "But times are more settled now than in 1971; I don't think that will happen. My mother has long prepared me for this 'death with honor,' if it comes."

But it was his love that consumed him, not politics. His cousin had warned him not to get involved with an American woman, that his place was running the country, and he had to go back. He didn't listen; she is his soul mate. He thought it would all work out somehow, as soon as his sister married. She was now married. But so was his lost love.

Now that his sister had married, there would be pressure on him to marry someone there, he explained to me. This distressed him greatly. "I cannot do that; it would be too cruel to the woman, to marry her when I love someone else."

If he told his mother the truth, and if his sister found out, the sister would feel a terrible burden of guilt. He was unwavering that he had done the right thing; his sister had to marry first. He would stall, he said, but that would not be easy. With his family's political legacy, and his American education, he was "a good catch." Already eight families had offered their daughters. There was no joy for him in his popularity, only dread. He broke down in tears again.

No one else understood his feelings, he complained. "They tell me, 'Move on.'" He emphasized that he was grateful that I understood, and grateful for my book that gave him hope that they will reunite someday—if not in this life, then in the afterlife.

He promised me that he would keep in touch, would write to me from his country every few months. But if there were ever a long period of silence from him, I would know that "something happened" to him.

He stood up, thanked me again for writing the book; it helped him more than I could ever know, he told me. He shook my hand, then left.

He wrote once, just a note to thank me for our conversation and to wish me well. I never heard from him again.

I have found my lost love after 14 years and am the happiest I have ever been in my life. My partner and I are victims of interrupted love due to the fact that my parents were adamant about us not being together when I was 21 (I am 35 now). I knew back then, as I do now, that this was the person I was supposed to share my life with… my other half.

I got married when I was 23 after a 2 year courtship, to a man my parents approved of. He was a good man, a decent man, with many admirable character traits. We moved away from the small town in which I grew up, and within 3 years we had a child. I left my job at the age of 26, and joined the ranks of stay-at-home mothers. I remained in distant contact over the years with my lost love and visited briefly to catch up when I went back home to visit my parents and family. My lost love was in a new relationship and seemed content in many ways. I knew, though, when looking into those dark eyes, that I was still "the one." Nothing ever transpired between us due to the fact that we were both committed to other people.

My child became ill, and I found myself traveling on a powerful and life changing journey. Over the next 6 years, I dedicated myself to his recovery. Today, he is functioning at an age appropriate level, and I believe he will go on to live a normal life with the same advantages as his peers. Hard work, hope and faith are very powerful things.

Unfortunately, during this time, my husband and I became distant and our relationship became strained. We shared no intimacy, love, or caring for each other. It was as if we had become strangers... or two friends sharing the same bank account. I feel the one thing that kept us together was our son, even though he had also become one of the reasons that started to pull us apart.

Once my son started to emerge from this debilitating disorder, I saw a light at the end of the tunnel. I just wanted to be free to be me, with my own sense of who I was... finally. I just wanted to live the life I was intended to live from the beginning.

I was approached at this time, out of the blue, by my lost love. I should tell you that my lost love is a women, and this caused the controversy that surrounded us being together when I was younger. My parents are extremely religious and this was totally against their beliefs. At the time, I did what they wanted, because they said it was the right thing to do and that I would "grow out of these feelings." That never happened. I was so unhappy for many years. The only distraction from this unhappiness was my child.

My lost love, Sherri, came to me while I was visiting my family and asked if I still felt the love we once shared so long ago. I was afraid to speak. We had not spoken of this in so many years. She told me that she still loved me deeply and would gladly give up the life she had made in order for us to be together, finally. I was speechless, because this was not something I was prepared to hear. I needed time to think.

The next morning, I prepared to catch my flight back to my husband and son. As I headed to the airport, I pulled a U-turn and drove to see her at her office. When I walked in, I saw in her eyes everything I had always wanted and needed in a human being, and I said, "I still love you, and I am ready now." We hugged and then proceeded on a path that would change our lives forever.

I decided to end my marriage. I went through so much guilt knowing I was giving up a good man, but I did come to the realization that a good man is not necessarily the right man. I decided to finally build a life with my child and my long-lost partner, Sherri. My son loves her dearly and Sherri in turn loves my son genuinely. We have purchased a home together and we move in at the end of August 2004. I am so excited. We all are! I live in Vancouver and remain here due to the fact that my husband wishes to remain active in our son's life. My husband still keeps in contact with me, and we are developing a much better relationship as friends. Sherri lived in Calgary. She left her family, her job of 14 years, her pension plan, sold her home that she built herself, and sold off most of her belongings, and is on her way to me. She has given up so much to ensure that my son and I stay where we are for my son's best interests. She is such a wonderful and loving person.

I think many people are like me, and give up their desires and dismiss their feelings in order to please others.

I guess you've probably heard the Willie Nelson quote, "Ninety-five percent of people aren't with their first choice; that's what keeps the juke box playing." Well, I've got my first choice.

Our love story is about parental interference. It isn't an Ozzie and Harriet kind of thing. Our lives have been messy, with some tragic moments, and our family histories have some pretty dysfunctional characteristics.

We had just started dating in the spring of 1972. We met at a school dance. Arlene had been dating a close friend of mine a year earlier, and I had been enthralled from the moment I saw her. I was very shy in those days. When I got home, I wanted to set the stage for more dates and started to tell my mother, so I could use the car, because we lived 30 miles from town.

My mother (now deceased) was formerly Arlene's teacher and absolutely did not want us seeing each other. Arlene was from the "wrong side of the tracks," and people picked on her at school. Within a couple of weeks, my mom even went so far as to set me up on a surprise blind date with an ex-girlfriend and she scheduled follow-up dates right on the spot. At the time I was mortified, embarrassed, and too shy and confused to say anything. Arlene thought I had lost interest, because I didn't know what to say to her. I'd get tongue-tied around her and was naturally ambivalent about seeing someone else at the same time. To make matters worse, I lived far out in the country and couldn't get to town very easily, if at all. Even telephone calls were long distance. Inside I was seething. I thought the ex-girlfriend would dump me pretty quickly, so if I just played it cool, the whole thing would blow over and I could resume with Arlene. Eventually the ex-girlfriend did dump me, but only after duping me into rescuing her from a bad home life with stories of abuse and getting married to me. By the time she dumped me for her druggie friends, it was too late. Boy was I gullible!

In the meantime, Arlene drifted into a bad crowd, dropped out of school, got married at 17, moved away, changed her name, and was severely abused along the way. Her first marriage, like mine, lasted less than a year, and then a real predator found her. After months of beatings, her mother went to get her out of a hospital after she had nearly been beaten to death. Somehow I knew something like that was going to happen. Whenever I thought about her, it would make my eyes tear up (sometimes it still does).

I couldn't talk about it to anyone. In thirty years, I probably mentioned her only once or twice, and never really told the story, but as soon as I could, I started looking for her; but her family had moved away. It was really hard to find her, and there were times when I thought she was probably dead or that I would never find her. Now I know why it was so hard. Her real name wasn't the name I knew, because her natural father abandoned her as an infant. Arlene didn't know about her birth father until she was a teen, and she had never told me. By the time I found her (by luck, she posted her name on Reunion.com), she had been married three times, the last time to an abusive alcoholic who is still fighting her for custody of her children. Nothing she told me was a surprise. I understood why she moved two states away, with her sons, one of whom is very emotionally troubled because of his father's abuse. She took a job at the Vet school, so she could take college classes. She worked in the fields putting out cattle feed in all kinds of weather. The sun had aged her, and her hair turned white.

When I found her, I was happy just to know that she was alive and well. I was on Cloud Nine. It didn't matter to me whether she was interested in me or not. That's not why I wrote to her. I just wanted to know how she was doing, and I was elated just to know that she was okay. I had worried about her all the time because she was so timid and shy. Losing her the way I did was like watching a small child wander into traffic on a busy street. In fact, in May of 1983, I had a very memorable nightmare that woke me, bolt upright in the middle of the night. It was so intense that I never forgot it. The only way I can describe it is that I felt the presence of evil. I woke up in terror, like I was about to do battle with some fearsome intruder. I was so afraid that I went to the kitchen and got a chef's knife as I inspected every room in the house. I was shaking. At that same time, her husband was threatening her with a shotgun, pushing it into her face and using it to beat her. I am generally not a superstitious person, but I can't help but believe that I sensed what was happening.

Arlene and I share unpleasant family experiences. We're both children of abusive alcoholics, and each of us has played the role of Enabler to our previous spouses. My mother ended up spending the last years of her life in mental institutions, variously diagnosed with manic depression, or schizophrenia, or both.

She died five months before my son was born, at the age of 57, after suffering from cancer. Arlene's abusive stepfather left her mother and the family went separate ways shortly after we stopped dating. My father has been in AA for over 15 years, and is very contrite and caring now.

I can honestly say that no one ever loved me as much as Arlene. We were the only attendees at our wedding. Arlene was divorced when I found her and I was ending an extremely unsuccessful series of marriage counseling sessions. After a quiet divorce, Arlene and I were married in secret. We really didn't think anyone else was interested in celebrating with us.

Despite the dismay of everyone in my family, the shock of my colleagues at work, the strain of maintaining a long-distance relationship with my son (which is going very well), and the risk and difficulty of making a new career in a new state, I am happier now than I have ever been. Fortunately, my ex-wife understands and is actually supportive, but most folks think I've lost my mind and some are overtly hostile toward us. Some of my relatives actually sent Evangelists to "save me" from Arlene, whom they call "that woman." They harassed me with emails for a couple of months while I waited for my divorce. My colleagues here think I'm a bit odd and don't really know what to make of me.

Arlene and I are trying to have a child of our own, although we're a bit old and it doesn't look like that will happen. I guess that it's been a tough path for us, but it doesn't matter. For the first time in my life, I feel whole in the most profound way.

I live in New Zealand. I just reunited with my first love after over thirty years. Despite all the years apart, the feelings we have for each other have never dwindled. They seem to have lain dormant, and are now re-igniting as never before.

He was twenty-one and I was eighteen when we last saw each other. I was madly in love with him, and he with me, but we never ever told each other. You didn't back then. Besides, I was engaged to someone else whom both my parents wanted me to marry. I could not go against their wishes.

My family was poor and very hardworking. It was decided that they could educate my sister with a university degree, and later my brother if he wanted it (he had a choice). It was deemed that I should marry well. So it was arranged. I married into a wealthy family with a big formal wedding.

But ten weeks prior to the wedding, Dennis came to my house. He was a frequent visitor, as his brother and mine were pals. Both of my parents were out, and he could see me alone. We sat in the family room, I between his feet on the floor and he on the couch. He told me how he felt about me. I felt his tears in my hair. I never told him how I felt; I was under oath not to tell by my mother. He held me in his arms and kissed me. I have never ever forgotten that kiss. I have never forgotten the love I saw in that poor tortured face.

On the eve of my wedding day, my mother had friends to tea to see my gown. When they had gone, I cut it short to above the knee. Her first view of this was as I walked down the aisle the next day.

My chosen husband was gay—one never spoke of such things. The wedding was soon annulled. To keep gossip to a minimum, I was encouraged to move to Australia, where my name was changed and my family disowned me. I remarried and had two daughters. That marriage ended in divorce. I have since reunited with my family and returned to New Zealand. My father ran into Dennis two years ago, and we began writing immediately. He is single again, too.

It is as if time had stood still. We have each made a commitment that we want this to work. We never thought we'd meet again. It is a miracle.

This all started back in the summer of 1978, in the rural Midwest, when I was sixteen and she was fourteen. We were at the county fairgrounds for a 4H meeting. I knew her brother from playing little league baseball, but I never really noticed her until she pinched my butt while I was working at the fairgrounds setting up display tables. She was a freshman and I was a junior in high school and after that day, we were always together. She was my first love.

She lived with her grandparents, because she and her mom did not get along at all. She was the oldest of eight children. Well, she got pregnant, and her mom moved her to Texas to get her away from me. She had an abortion. While we were separated we talked on the phone constantly. My burger flipping job paid for the $100.00 a month phone bills and for my old hot rod. By this time I was eighteen and she was sixteen and still very much in love. I finished high school, and packed two suitcases and $150.00 and hopped on a Greyhound to Texas. Her mom was furious that I was there but understood why I left the Midwest.

After another six months or so, her mom packed up the whole family again and moved out to California, and again I was left behind. We kept in touch. Then her mom threatened my life… she said she was going to hire a biker gang to keep me away if needed! Well, after that I didn't go to California right away, and my lost love met someone and got married two years later. That was the last time I heard from her… until five months ago.

Almost twenty-one years had passed, and I got this call on my cell phone at my office and I knew from the area code that it was from my hometown. It was my lost love—my found love! I knew the voice, but I did not know quite who it was until I talked to her for a few minutes.

I am married, for thirteen years. I served in the military for more than ten years and I have my own business in California. And this call just stirred up all those old feelings that I have had for her and never really had for anyone else since, not even for my wife. My true love has been married twice and has four children and is now divorced.

Now, I had thought about her over the years, wondering what happened to her and how she was doing. On a recent visit to my hometown, I had left my business card with my cousin. I had no idea that she had moved back to her grandparents' old home. It took her three weeks to get the courage to call me after getting my business card from my cousin. She was planning a trip to California to see her family, and asked if she could see me and meet my wife. Wow… you can imagine the emotional roller coaster I have been on since!

That night, I told my wife that she had called, and I felt that I had to tell my wife everything about my lost love relationship. I told her things I have not told anyone, ever. But my wife did not feel comfortable meeting her, and I said I would not see her.

There was only about a week before her trip, and I could not stop thinking about her. I called her back and we talked… I mean for hours. It was like we were back in high school, just talking. We had twenty-one years of catching up to do, but even so, this easy reconnection was unbelievable to me. My heart was pounding and so was hers. We both felt the same: that we had been cheated out of a life we could have had together. So I did something I never thought I would do; I went to see her secretly when she arrived in California.

I gave her a short hug, sat down, and started talking. She brought pictures of her family, and I did, too. But it was still there, our love for each other never left either of our hearts. Before I left, we went out to my car and sat there for a bit while it was raining. I wanted to cry… We talked more and shared a very long hug… my life had been changed.

I went home, and for a while after that visit, life felt like it was still keeping us apart—my marriage, my business, and my standing in our church. But I couldn't help how I felt about her. We have spent hours talking to each other on the phone since this reconnection started. I cannot stop thinking about her. Man, was I in a mess, or what?

I felt like I was crazy. I wanted to drop everything and run away to be with her. And then suddenly I knew: maybe it does sound crazy, but I HAVE to be with her. So, in just a few hours, I plan to be home with my lost love. I am so excited to be going home, yet I am seeing the impact of my choice on those around me here.

My wife is nicer to me now more than ever… I was expecting her to be nasty about this. My business partner is scrambling to "not let three years of my life go down the drain." It looks like I may not have as much money as I thought I would have to make this move… and none of this is stopping me from going home to be with my lost love.

I have been called "cold and scheming," not caring about anyone else but me… No one here understands why I want to be with my lost love, neither do they expect us to have a lasting relationship. No one here thinks I feel any remorse for hurting them… but I do. It's hard to believe it was just over 5 months ago that my true love first contacted me. Man, what a ride!

So I have packed my belongings into a rented U Haul, leaving my condo and most of my things for my wife, and tomorrow I leave for the Midwest, to be with my first love, to live back on the family farm in my old Midwest town. I am going home.

Back in 1963, when I was a sophomore in high school in Houston, Texas, one night I spent the night at my girlfriend's house and met her younger brother, Joel. Although he was only a year younger than Carole and me, he was two years behind us in school (his birthday was in November, so he had to wait a year to start kindergarten). Despite the slight age difference, we hit it off immediately and for the next seven months we spent every spare moment together, walking hand in hand around our neighborhoods, hanging out at each other's houses, plus hours and hours on the phone. Carole used to carry notes back and forth between us, because Joel was still at the junior high. We were totally and completely in love. We never fought, and he loved me so much that even though we had plenty of opportunities, we never went "all the way" because he respected me too much for that. But, oh my God, did we make out!

The following fall, he had a serious talk with my father and told him that he wanted to marry me someday. Of course, we knew it was a ways off in the future, but it was enough to make my parents very nervous, and they started putting pressure on me to break up with him and date other people. I know their intentions were good, but when I did finally break up with Joel (November 22, 1963, the day Kennedy was shot) my heart absolutely smashed. I know I cried literally for months after that.

We went our separate ways. I went to college, and Joel finished high school. We saw each other a few times while I was in college, but I always thought that he didn't care that much about me anymore, and he always thought that I was getting on with my life and didn't have time for him. I think he didn't ever realize exactly why I broke up with him. Neither of us talked about our true feelings.

It was "The Sixties." I became rebellious and promiscuous, got into the whole hippie thing, and didn't have any kind of serious relationship for my whole four years of college. After I graduated, I moved to Denver, met a speed freak from San Francisco, and for some ungodly reason married him. The VERY DAY I got married, I received a letter from Joel, who was now in the Army, proclaiming his undying love for me and begging to see me. My heart just broke—if the letter had come even one day sooner, I would have gone to him in a heartbeat, because I realized by then that he had been my "true" love.

I don't remember if I wrote him back—if I did it was just to let him know I was married. The speed freak and I moved to San Francisco in 1969 and blended into the "scene." Years went by. Predictably, the speed freak and I split up after a couple years and I went on to have a lot of "boyfriends," and a lot of acid trips. I didn't hear any more from Joel, although he was never completely out of my mind.

In 1975 I remarried and we moved to Alaska to be near my family who had moved up there in 1969. In the early '80s, I located Joel's sister, and we corresponded for a while. She told me that he was still in the Army and was married with a couple of small children. I was married with a couple of small children, too, so I never made an attempt to contact him.

My marriage broke apart, and I remarried in 1985 and went through years of struggling with addictions and alcoholism, but a lot of good times, too. Four years ago, he got clean and things settled down a lot.

Then for some reason, shortly after New Year's Eve 2000, I got an urge to get in touch with my old classmates. I think it was the whole Millennium thing, plus an awareness that I'm "not getting any younger." I went on the Web and located some of my graduating class and ultimately tracked down Carole. From there it was just a step to Joel. He had divorced his first wife, and was in a 10-year marriage.

One day I got a call from him at my office, and I couldn't even believe how it felt hearing his voice. He sounded just the same as 37 years ago when we used to talk on the phone late in the night. Well, even though I knew it was dangerous, we started writing and talking on the phone periodically, and as it turned out, he had never fallen out of love with me. He said he had heard that I was in California in the early '70s, and that each time he visited there, he'd walked the streets looking for me.

Before I knew it, I was taking a solo vacation to visit Carole and Joel and many of my old Texas classmates who regularly get together. It was like we had never been apart at all. Joel's wife was at a convention in Miami, so he and I spent the first five days I was down there together. When she came back, they had a huge fight and she told him to pack his bags, which he did. He stayed with

Carole for the rest of the time I was down there. All I could think about was being with him, and my husband was the furthest thing from my mind. It was almost like he didn't exist.

I went back to Alaska and left my husband. Joel broke up with his wife, and lived alone in Houston, waiting for his divorce to come through. He said he would never marry again, but we were married last summer.

And guess what? My ex-husband found his long-lost love, too!

I can't believe Joel still loves me so much. He is the only lover in my 54 years who never did anything to hurt me, who always treated me well. We both love to cook and to garden. We have the same spiritual beliefs, and ideas about how to handle money, how to celebrate Christmas, how to do everything, really. We are both interested in archeology and have an attraction to East Indian culture. Our politics are even the same; we both hated the Vietnam war. It's completely mind-boggling to me, when he was the straight-arrow Army man and I was the flower child, how we could have come back around at this point to be so alike.

First love is the best—I don't interfere with my daughters' love lives. And I really wish my parents hadn't interfered with mine!

My first love and I were boyfriend and girlfriend from the time I was 16 until I was 22. We were very much in love in an innocent and good way. We were top students. He went to college in Wisconsin and I went to an Ivy League college in the East. When I was 19, I transferred to his school to be near him. For two years we saw each other daily.

His father died suddenly during my lost love's senior year of college. My father immediately began to exert immense force on me to break up with my guy. The pressure was that my first love would have inherited the gastrointestinal condition that killed his father and that I would be left alone. My father was very much the boss in our household. He was the "smart one." How could he be wrong?

I broke up and had a brief (thank goodness) engagement to a foolish fellow of whom my father approved. Two years later, at age 25, I married a wonderful man. We have been married for 30 years. However, I never forgot my first love.

In August, I came across him while doing some research related to my work. In the process of doing a computer search, I found a journal article by someone with my lost love's name. Even odder, the article had nothing at all to do with his work; it was just something he had once written out of interest. I contacted him and we have been corresponding regularly since then. It's just like an ongoing, delightful conversation.

He, too, is happily married, which pleases me. He is very conservative politically while I continue to be more liberal. However, we are both committed to traditional family values. There is no way we would ever consider meeting one another. Both of our spouses know about this correspondence and have even become involved in it. It is largely an intellectual exchange of ideas, but there is a great deal of feeling as well.

My first love does in fact suffer from the health problems that my father predicted so long ago, although there are better treatments nowadays and he has taken precautions that his father did not know needed to be taken.

Okay, so mine is a standard story up to this point. But there is one compelling issue that is haunting me.

I have four children and he has five. My second daughter is very involved with a wonderful young man. She has had boyfriends before, but this is the first one she seems very serious about. They are both computer engineers in Seattle.

Everything should be wonderful—and it is, except for one thing. His father has a chronic disease for which there is a distinct genetic predisposition. My husband is a physician and thought of that right away. He did some research of his own and found that this disorder occurs fairly commonly in people who have afflicted first degree relatives. It is quite disabling in many cases.

My daughter has no idea that this is a problem. She wouldn't think of it. My husband has promised me that he will never raise the subject with her, because it is too painful for me and he is a loving and sympathetic man. I have never forgiven my father, who passed away five years ago, for what he did to me. My lost love has no idea of the truth of how or why I left him—he has guesses, but they are all wrong, and I will never tell him. Only my husband and my mother know the whole story.

I think the issue of how early memories and experiences are reactivated when one's children are facing the same problems is very interesting. My father was trying to do something that he perceived would be in my best interests. However, I cannot violate my daughter's spirit in the same ruthless manner.

Perhaps it is best not to interfere with our children's romances, because first loves—and resentments—may last forever.

CHAPTER 4

Casualties of War

Another common reason why first loves separated was that young men and women were in the military and were relocated. Their tales spanned the globe as the troops were called overseas in times of war. Some of these couples fell in love during World War II. They are in their eighties now and are reuniting, finding renewed love in their senior years.

Other war separations occurred when parents moved their families out of war-ravaged countries. Although it was urgent to take the children out of harm's way, young sweethearts were tearfully torn from each other.

And some men and women who served their countries during times of peace were still torn apart from their sweethearts, or their "military brat" children were.

When we think of war, we usually think of battlefield casualties. For some people, the casualty of war was the loss of their one true love.

I was finishing high school in 1943, and he was a dashing lieutenant on temporary assignment in Biloxi. Like many young couples in those days, we fell in love quickly. We never made formal plans but we knew we'd marry.

Rod was transferred. He wasn't permitted to give me the details of where he was going. He just let me know by sending a bouquet of roses, seventeen red and one white. While he was in Europe, he wrote often, over two hundred letters in all.

One day as the war was nearing its end, he attempted to disarm an antitank grenade, but it exploded. It left him blind with serious injuries. He visited me on leave after his hospitalization, but I never realized how emotionally affected he was, trying to cope with his injuries. He wrote me a goodbye letter to spare me the burden of his problems and what he thought would be a bleak future.

I went on to marry, have three children, and later divorce. My lost love married and had two children. He overcame his disabilities and earned a doctorate in history; he was a college professor for more than thirty years. His wife passed away five years ago.

I always wondered what happened to Rod, and he wondered about me the same. He knew I went to the University of Kansas, so he searched for me through my college alumni directory. One day the phone rang and a man asked me if I was the same Betty from Biloxi. It was Rod's brother. He set up a telephone call between us.

We started talking several times a day. We exchanged letters, and on Valentine's Day I sent a batch of cookies with a letter in Braille. I got a hold of a Braille writer through a local man I know who is blind. I didn't want anyone to read that letter but Rod.

By April we met again for the first time in fifty years, but it was like no time had gone by at all. He gave me a gift, a music box that plays, "As Time Goes By." It was our song.

We have now been married for five supremely happy years. Since we have been together, it's been like a dream, and we can still hardly believe our good fortune. Even though I did not know where he was or anything about him for fifty years, it didn't take us long to know we should never have parted in the first place.

We grew up in a small town and were in the first grade together. But we didn't become sweethearts until after high school, when I enlisted in the Army. While I was in the service in Alaska, I began writing to her. Then when I got a furlough, I went down to see her, and her mother said she was out with someone else. But we kept writing and when I returned home in 1941 we got engaged.

Then Pearl Harbor got bombed, and I reenlisted. Lucille drove me to the bus depot in my Model T Ford the day I left town; I left the car with her, and we said our tearful goodbyes.

I saw action in North Africa and Sicily, and later was part of the D-Day invasion at Normandy. I came out of that without a scratch, wondering why some people are killed and others are not. Maybe it had something to do with Lucille praying for me back home. But I didn't know she did that until I found her again, wouldn't have guessed that. I thought she was pretty angry at me, because

I had already broken our engagement—well, she was!

While I was lying in a British hospital from injuries in France before D-Day, and thinking I'd be crippled for life, I sent a letter to Lucille saying I had gotten married. It wasn't true, but I didn't want her to be sitting back home worrying about me.

When I got back to our town after the war, I looked for her, but she had moved away, and her parents had moved away, too. No one back home knew where she had moved, only that she had gone North. And there's a lot of "North" in California.

I almost found her once; I found the right town and was told she was a teacher; but I went to the grammar school where no one had ever heard of her. She was teaching at the high school.

Eventually I married, and so did Lucille, but neither of us ever had children. Somehow word had gotten back to our hometown that I died during the war, but I didn't hear that rumor. Lucille did, though. When she went to a class reunion, it was printed in the Memory Book, so that made it final for her!

Years later, in 1989, when I was retired and a widower, I looked up an old buddy who showed me the Memory Book. I was very surprised of course to learn that I was dead! But I also saw that Lucille was living in Cedar Oaks. I didn't know where the heck Cedar Oaks was, so I got a map and headed North. That was 1990.

I went to the Cedar Oaks City Hall and asked about Lucille. A clerk told me she always had lunch at a nearby Mexican restaurant, so I headed over there. She wasn't there, but I found out she lived right across the street, the other side of a highway. I got her phone number and called her. Lucille told me later that she didn't want to tell me over the phone that I was dead, so she just told me to come over.

It was the foggiest day you've ever seen, and it took me awhile to cross that highway. Lucille by that point was legally blind, so she couldn't see me. I had to prove who I was. After all, she believed I was dead. So she asked me to answer a few personal questions. The first one got me in the door. The second one got me on the couch. After I told her where and when we had been engaged, that did the trick, and we got friendly. About a week later, we were reengaged, and a few weeks after that we got married, 49 years after our first engagement. We are both very grateful for our good fortune. I am 86 years old now, and Lucille is 85.

Boris—the father of my first love (Laura)—was a Russian nobleman with a big estate near Smolensk. When the October Revolution began, he was in the White

Army, fighting very actively against Communists. Luck was on the Communists' side, and in 1920, when the Whites were surrounded in the Crimea, Boris escaped with the help of the English Navy and settled in Malta.

Soon the Communists announced amnesty to all those White officers who would like to return to the Motherland if they would give an oath not to fight against the Soviet Republic. Nearly 100,000 of the officers returned to Russia, but these men were immediately arrested and shot to death. Boris managed to escape; he had not trusted the Reds. He fled to China, and that's where he met his future wife, my first love Laura's mother, Katya.

Also in 1920, when the civil war in Russia reached its peak, another family experienced the upheaval of war. Reverend Peter (my grandfather), my grandmother, and their children lived in the Ukraine. Since 1918, this town was a real battlefield. Communists, Whites, Anarchists, Greens, and simple bandit gangs fought against each other to take possession of this region. There were fierce battles every day, and often the town was seized by all these gangs alternatively: in the morning one could see red flags, in the noon black ones, and in the evening green flags over the local City Council building.

My grandfather, Father Peter, gathered all wounded men and treated them, regardless of their politics. One day, gang leaders found wounded men from a different gang in his house; they dragged out the wounded soldiers, and my grandfather, and put the wounded men against a wall for execution. My grandfather could not bear to watch, and he died of a heart attack.

Soon hunger came. It was so horrible that all the roads were filled with swelling corpses. Grandmother and the children would have died, too, but were saved by chance: my grandmother's brother was a French Consul in China. With the help of the Red Cross and United Nations Relief Association, the Consul managed to take us out of our nightmare, to China. One of the boys in this family, Alex, became my father.

Another family forced to leave Russia was Serge's family. When the revolution began, he emigrated to China, because the Communists were executing all White officers. His daughter later married Alex, and in 1937 I was born.

It was in Tsingtao, China, where my parents and Laura's parents became good friends. We children met nearly every day at parties, picnics, and at the yacht club. Laura's brother, Dimitry, became my closest friend. But even though we all met at the Russian school every day, it wasn't until 1953 that I suddenly saw Laura differently. It was her 14th birthday, and I fell in love. I knew that my feelings were reciprocated when she began to spend much more time with her brother ("to look after him," she explained), who took part in all my adventures, so we met every day. Since we were brought up with old fashioned manners, we never spoke about our feelings.

In that same year, however, the Mao-Tzedung Communists arrested Laura's father, Boris, when they found out that in the 1930's he had helped Chang-Kai-shek's army. As a result, in 1955 Boris was forced to emigrate to Australia; the Reds forced him to sell his house, setting the least value on it, and for a few months before their family's departure, Laura's family lived in our house. Those were the happiest days of our lives!

But soon everything was over. Her family left for Australia, and my family returned to Russia (Stalin's terrors were gone). But from the moment we arrived in Russia, we realized that nothing had really changed; communications with friends abroad were restricted, so I could not even contact Laura.

All through those long years, Laura's amiable image was before me, and I never forgot her.

Then something incredible happened—the USSR collapsed!! I began to make inquiries about Laura. That wasn't easy, because nothing worked (phones, mail), and everything was in chaos until some order was restored by 1996.

Laura also began to make inquiries, and she found me in 1996. I invited her to Russia, and in August, 1996, we met in Moscow after more than 40 years of separation!! In spite of our ages, we fell deeply in love, just as we had been as teenagers, impassioned by each other. Three months passed in a moment and she had to return to Australia.

Soon she sent me an invitation to visit her. I got a visa and arrived in Melbourne. We married shortly thereafter and realized that we never knew before what real happiness is! Now we know that we will spend the rest of our lives together.

My mom was born in New Brunswick, Canada, and during World War II, she lived in Nova Scotia for a brief period. There she met a man named John—her nickname for him was Paddy. He was a British soldier. They went on a couple of dates, nothing spectacular. My mother believed that she should never get involved with a soldier, because she might never see him again. She moved to Toronto and worked in a war factory. Apparently John put an ad in a Toronto newspaper looking for her, but did not get any answer. He later found out that she had married, and so he went back to Britain when the war was over.

My mother met my father on a blind date, and married him two months later. My parents had six children. My father died in 1985.

A number of years after Mom was widowed, my brother received a phone call from a private investigator who was looking for my mother. Apparently the only information he had to go on was my mother's maiden name and that she lived in Nova Scotia. He pieced together that she was born in New Brunswick and somehow was able to contact her relatives there. The relatives gave him my brother's name, and my brother gave him Mom's telephone number. My mother was contacted by the private investigator. and she found out that someone was trying to find her and that he lived in England. He did not give her the name of the person. My mother had no idea who this person was but agreed to talk to him.

A couple of months later, John called my mother and reminisced about the times they were together. There were many phone calls and letters between them. He also sent current pictures of himself along with some taken during the war. He sent her plane tickets and my mother traveled to England to see him that summer. This came as quite a surprise to my brothers and me, since my mother was not one to do anything without someone with her.

She spent the first week in England with John and his sister, then four weeks in Spain at his villa and then one week back in England before she came home. John had never married. He told Mom that every time he met someone all he could see was her. He loved her from the first time he saw her and he never forgot her. They went for many walks together. He remembered so many things about my mother. He wanted to know about her sister, with whom she had been living in Nova Scotia. He talked about many things that my mother had forgotten.

She was so happy when she came back home. He had been so kind to her, and bought her lovely presents, too. She was acting just like a teenager! He had been concerned about her health, encouraging her to rest. And she had been concerned about John—she even quit smoking while she was in England because John had a lung problem. (My mother had been a heavy smoker, begun soon after she married).

My mother and father had a good marriage, and after my father passed away she grieved long and hard and was ready to die herself. But after she met John again she was full of life.

John planned to visit her in Canada the following summer. My mother was 75 years old at the time. Two months after her trip to England, on a September weekend, she passed away in her sleep.

My brother told John about her passing; he was quite upset and felt that her death must have been his fault, because of the trip. We assured him that our mother had come home so very happy and had not been that way in a long time.

John passed away the following April. I believe he died of a broken heart. And to think my mother said that you should never get involved with a soldier because you never know if you will see him again.

I was born in Viet Nam, at the time the country was dividing in half. Like thousands of other families who didn't want to live under the Communists, my family immigrated from North to South Viet Nam to seek freedom. During this transition, my parents got separated. Being a French army officer, my father had a duty to fulfill; we never learned what happened to him. I was just an infant at the time, so I never knew my father.

I guess these experiences took some toll on me. I remember very clearly how frightened I was of people around me, and just about anything could make me cry. My mother was never home; poor thing, she had to work so hard to take care of me, my sister, and my brother. She hired a maid to take care of us in her absence. I felt so alone. I had no friends and I didn't want any.

I was doing very poorly at school as well. French was a hard language to learn and I hated it. I hated the nuns who told my mother that I was just plain lazy, despite the fact that I loved to read, I loved music, and I could draw well. I also embroidered beautifully and made lovely hand crafts. I wondered why nobody saw my good side.

My mother moved me from one school to another, hoping that a new environment would motivate me to do better in school, but nothing helped because I could not learn the language. I had to repeat third grade. This made my mother very angry at me, and it made me crawl deeper into my shell.

To make matters worse, my mother remarried when I was eleven years old. I did not like my American stepfather right from the beginning, and he didn't give me any reason to like him, either. We had many conflicts with each other, and I always ended up getting spanked. To me, he was a mean and wicked person. Many times I thought of running away from home, but I didn't have the courage.

A change came when I turned twelve and was starting sixth grade. I got up enough nerve to ask my mother to let me go to a Vietnamese school. She agreed, only because my stepfather wanted us to learn English, and English was taught there as a second language. A whole new world opened up to me. School was no longer a nightmare; I began to get good grades and I made a lot of friends. I even loved my teachers. I joined the girls' club, got involved in writing for the school newspaper, and even was the class president at one time. My friends and I often got together to study, bake, and go to Catholic church. We went to movies, parties, and shopping.

When I was 16, I fell madly in love with a 20 year old college freshman who had lived next door to me since I was a baby. We dated for about a year. It was a very intense relationship, and I always thought and hoped that we'd get married after he graduated from college.

These happy times didn't last very long for me. I was seventeen when my stepfather came home one day and announced that he was going back to the States—he sensed trouble because of the war—and of course we as his family were going too. I will never forget the sickness I felt in my stomach that day. I wanted to say something, but I couldn't do it. My world was coming down. All I could do was cry, and all I could think of was the boy next door, with whom I had fallen in love.

June 14, 1972, was the turning point in my life—the day I left behind all of my friends, all my happiness, and most of my heart. My boyfriend and I stayed up all night the night before I left, talking and comforting each other. We made a lot of promises to each other, which neither of us kept later on. We wrote to each other a few times and then stopped; this was definitely out of sight, out of mind.

When I arrived in this country, I cried for days before I decided there was nothing I could do to change what had happened, so I might as well pick up the pieces and start over. The language barrier made it hard for me to adjust, and I really had to struggle to adapt to the new place, new culture, new environment, and new people.

Two months after we arrived, my mother told me I should look for work to help the family. I got a job in a factory. Little by little I learned to accept the new life. I even got very wild, and I quit school. I started to go out to nightclubs, started smoking and drinking. I lost all my moral standards and religious beliefs. What a change from a shy, quiet, and frightened child to a wild, outgoing, uncontrollable teenager. My parents had absolutely no control over me.

Now seventeen years later, like the American saying, a lot of water has passed under the bridge. A lot of things have changed. At 35 years old, I have a different perspective on life. I settled down, got married, and had a family. I regained my religious beliefs. I stopped smoking and drinking. And I entered college. I have come a long way.

But I obsessively think about the boyfriend I once had in Viet Nam. I didn't think I'd ever see him again after the fall of Viet Nam in 1995. But through his sister who lived here in the States, I was able to keep track of him. I heard he got married, a few months before my own marriage. He and his family escaped from Viet Nam and came to California in 1980.

When I got the news, I went to see him. The minute I saw him, all the old feelings came back; all the love and pain that had been suppressed in my heart all those years resurfaced instantly. However, I kept my feelings to myself because I didn't want to hurt his family or mine.

Eighteen years have passed since that meeting, but I can't get him out of my mind. I dream about our past. I yearn for his touch and long for his kisses. Although we were not sexually involved then, I fantasize about it now. We have seen each other a few times since then, but never alone, and each time brought up emotional distress for me. We only live about 90 miles apart.

Six months ago, his father passed away. I went to the funeral and saw him there. We talked quite a bit; after the funeral we went back to his brother's home to visit. This time both his wife and my husband were absent. His brother reminded us about our past love and expressed how much he had wanted us to marry each other. He blamed my stepfather for breaking us up. My lost love didn't have a lot to say. I died inside.

Since that day, my heart and soul are with this man. (My marriage is long over, but we stay in the same house for the children.) I think of him every minute of the day; I can't sleep, I binge on food, I go to bed with his image in my mind and wake up with it. So many times I have picked up the phone and then put it back down. I want to see him and talk to him so badly that it hurts.

You see, I've never told him that I loved him, and I don't think he ever told me that he loved me, either.

I was so surprised when I read about your research. We thought we were the only couple experiencing this phenomenon and we discussed the mystery of our longtime attraction to each other many times.

Larry and I started dating in the fall of 1967 when I was a senior in high school and he was a year ahead of me, expecting to start college. Although we were totally in love with each other and planned to marry, there were several obstacles in our way. For one, I was determined to stay a virgin until marriage, and he was very popular, with many temptations. So we broke up a few times during our sixteen month romance.

Even so, I was head over heels in love with him. He said he felt the same way and we planned on getting married eventually. My parents were not fond of him, and planned to move me across the country, from New Jersey to Oregon, with the hope that our romance would end.

Well, he messed up his student deferment and was drafted in June of 1968; he left for boot camp on the morning of my high school graduation. I cried the whole night before graduation. My parents just LOVED that!!!

While he was stationed in North Carolina, he came home every weekend to be with me. We consummated our love on November 23, 1968, the only time we did IT because we were so afraid of pregnancy!!

He left for Viet Nam in January, 1969. Before leaving, he broke up with me because he "didn't feel that it was fair" to keep me waiting for him. I would have waited. I wanted to wait. I looked forward to it. It angered me that he made that decision, and I suspected his motives—I didn't see him after that.

My family moved us to Oregon in July, 1969. My first love and I wrote to each other on and off, but eventually even that stopped. I later heard that he passed right through Oregon after he was discharged, and I was devastated that he didn't get in touch with me.

I married my husband in June, 1975. The morning of the wedding, I fantasized that Larry would rescue me just like Benjamin in *The Graduate*. Remember how Benjamin storms into Elaine's wedding and runs off with her, in her wedding gown, riding on the motorcycle? I thought of that ON MY WEDDING DAY!!!!!!! And I was (and still am) in love with my husband. I can't understand that.

Larry was the only man I have ever fantasized about. I am not bragging to you, but I know that I am still attractive—many young guys are among our friends and I get a lot of attention from them—but Larry is the only other one for me.

I heard that he got married in 1973—to a girl who looked a lot like me.

On Christmas, 1982, I sent a Christmas card to him at his office. And a month later, he called me!!! He said that he was so surprised that I contacted him, that he drank a whole six-pack on the train on the way home that night. He said that I would have been "THE ONE" if I had stayed in New Jersey. I was overwhelmed by my reaction. He made me so HOT just talking to me!!!! After that, he called once a week for about a month and then... .NOTHING! I was so confused and disappointed.

I didn't hear from him again. I was trying to put all thoughts of him in the back of my mind, to lock him in there and to rarely take him out. But I thought about him frequently over all those years. VERY FREQUENTLY.

Then in 1996, he called me!! He was in Portland on business and wanted to see me!!! I was amazed at my strength, but I was firm and said that I was too busy. I feared that if I saw him, I would lose my head and make a fool of myself. I couldn't risk that. Of course, I regretted that decision later. He stirred everything up again and I wondered what had been on his mind to prompt him to contact me.

Six months later, he called again—a business trip to Portland. And this time, I agreed to meet him...

He had changed. Aged. I DID NOT recognize him!!! At first, I was so disappointed. I had kept myself in shape and looking good... JUST IN CASE (In the back of my mind) I ever saw HIM again. He had really been my inspiration. Amazingly enough, though, after a little while, I did not care how he looked.

When I looked at him and realized that he was LARRY, nothing else mattered.

I saw him during three afternoons over that visit and it was all platonic. I even took him to our beach house where we were alone, yet he didn't approach me. So, I figured that we would remain just friends and that he had no ulterior motives. When I saw him on the last day, he gave me his office number and said that I should call anytime and OFTEN. We kissed good-bye on the lips. Nothing else.

I was confused by the feelings I was experiencing afterwards. I called him a few days later, after I awoke from a very erotic dream about us. I asked him if he had ever dreamt of me and he immediately said, "All the time. I have thought about you every day for the last thirty years."

WOW!!!!! What were the odds that my dream would EVER come true? We were just in shock to discover that we both felt the same way. Shocked!!

We talked several times a week after that. He came to Portland last year, and we spent almost every day together. We DID it and it was wonderful!! The best!! We were both so amazed that we were so comfortable with each other. So at ease. We seemed to connect so deeply. As someone said in your book, *Lost & Found Lovers*, we ACHE for each other! ACHE.

He is coming again next month. We are so excited. Where will this go? We can never be together; we would hurt too many people. We fantasize about having the freedom to enjoy a relationship in the open. I think we expect to carry on this way for a very long time. All in all, I think this is so sad. So sad.

What happened to me?? Why are our feelings still so strong?? Why him? Why me? He had had many other girlfriends, but he was my only boyfriend besides my husband. And my husband and I are basically happy; I have no complaints about him. We have fun together, and share a wonderful sex life. (Sometimes thoughts about Larry enhance my sexual appetite.) Larry is not happy in his marriage but knows he will never divorce.

Dr. Kalish, it is so good to talk to you about this, since I have not told a soul. We are so amazed that your research shows that this is some type of phenomenon! Thanks for listening!!!

Ten years ago, in my one of my high school classes, we were told to write to "Any Soldier" in the Persian Gulf War. I never thought I would get a response or that anything may come of it. To my surprise I received a very nice letter from a person named Mike. We corresponded for awhile and I noticed that I was becoming attracted to this person, and yet I never met him. He surprised me one day and called me, and the connection became more meaningful. We continued writing and calling each other for about a year and a half. Then in January, 1992, he flew in to meet me. I was so scared; I tried leaving the airport, but my friends wouldn't let me. I asked the airline desk if he was really on the plane. They couldn't tell me. So, my friends told the airline people "our story" of how we met. When his plane arrived they announced it and said: "And yes, Mike Miller is on the plane."

I ran to the bathroom, so nervous, and then got the courage to go back out and wait. Nobody came off the plane who looked like the picture he sent me. Then the flight attendant came out and they were pushing him in a wheelchair—everyone was in on the joke but me!

Our meeting was so magical, I felt an instant attraction. The whole week he was here, we connected so well, it was like we were soul mates. We never spoke our true feelings to one another. I fell in love with him, but I was too afraid to admit it. When he left that day, a piece of my heart left with him. I cried so hard. He flew back to the Navy, and we talked for a few months, but we somehow lost contact with one another.

I always thought about him, and wondered what happened to him. I always held a special place for him in my heart. I always had the regret of never telling him my true feelings. When I was with him, he just made me feel complete like no one ever had. I wondered, if we met again, would things be different?

Christmas, 2000, I was sending out Christmas cards. I came across his mother's old address, and I thought, what the heck, I'll send him a Christmas card. It was bothering me not knowing where he was, and if he was okay and happy. A month went by, and I knew he had to have received it, because I never got it back. I gave up all hope, but on New Year's Day, 2001, he called. It was just like we had talked yesterday. We clicked so well. We caught up on the news in each others' lives…

He said he had a 14 month old child, and a girlfriend whom he was having problems with. She was away for the holidays when he called. So when she came back, Mike started getting stressed. I could tell. One night our true feelings came out. He said he had always loved me, and that I was his first true love. He said he always did and will continue to hold a special place for me in his heart. I started crying because I had always felt the same way. I said to him that things may have worked out differently if we would have said this 10 years ago. I was going to fly to Texas and visit him, but I told him he should try to work things out in his life first. I told him I cared about him, and I wanted him to be happy.

He told his girlfriend about me, and now they are working things out. I wanted so badly to see him just one last time, for closure or to see if we really are soul mates, if our destiny is being together. I guess I am three years too late. I don't regret finding him again; I am happy that he is okay. And he will always be remembered in my heart. The hardest part is letting go.

I'm writing to you following the recommendation of Mrs. Sylvia Breslev, a family investigator with the Government Department of Children and Families here in Boca Raton. She succeeded where many had previously failed in trying to locate me and reunite Miss Debbie Albertson and myself after almost 10 years. Our story is long and at times, almost too bizarre, but I shall give you a summary here.

I met Debbie on April 14th, 1990, during a cocktail party aboard my ship, the Royal Navy Antarctic Survey vessel HMS Endurance, when she put into Fort Lauderdale following a 6 month deployment to the Antarctic region. I was then a Lieutenant in the Royal Navy and my task onboard was the Senior Pilot of the ships' LYNX helicopter flight. Debbie and I immediately felt a strong bond and enjoyed 4 days of amazing happiness. Our feelings upon my departure were almost indescribable…

Debbie visited me in the UK the following August, just prior to my appointment to Denmark as an exchange officer with Royal Danish Navy. Unknown to me, on May 5, 1991, Debbie gave birth to our daughter, Ashley, who Debbie continued to rear single-handedly while working in the Miami area. She relocated to Lake City some 4 years ago, to be nearer to family support and for a career change.

Meanwhile, her continued efforts to contact me failed. I left the Royal Navy in October, 1992, originally intending to emigrate to New Zealand; instead, I remained in the UK and eventually joined Her Majesty's Coast guard in 1995. The Royal Navy refused to relay any personal mail to a former serving officer, until Mrs. Bretoni intervened, via the British Embassy in Washington, and managed to send a registered letter to me in Cornwall, England. That was an amazing day to receive such news!

Thereafter, Debbie and I resumed communication, and I spoke with my daughter for the first time over the telephone—quite a daunting event for an 8 year old girl!!

I flew to Florida in February of last year for a 2 week visit, which predictably, was all too short. However, on 23rd October I returned to Florida, this time for good. We wanted to try and see if we could make it work as a family, and after some 5 months we all knew that this is totally right. We all seem to be flourishing with a our new situation and happily I can say that Debbie and I are to be married on April 14th, 11 years to the day after we first met… ..It promises to be quite an occasion!

My 75 year old mother has taken her first flight ever to visit us and is sched-uled to return for the wedding. Sylvia, the family investigator, has become our close friend and will attend our wedding. We have discussed on several occasions how to express the awesomeness of the turn of events that brought us back to-gether. Debbie says to me, "I'm living a fairy tale." We found your web site — someone needs to know our miraculous story.

CHAPTER 5

Media Matchmakers

Years ago, young people began dating (or "courting," as it was called during the World War II years) after being introduced by mutual friends, or perhaps after meeting at a friend's party (as my parents did). Maybe they sat next to each other in high school or college classes, or found each other through a school club or a religious youth group. Of course millions of couples continue to meet in these ways.

But now it is also commonplace for people to use media and technology to meet new partners and to reconnect with former ones. Personals columns in newspapers, singles' profiles on dating web sites, search engines and web sites to find classmates, video dating services, lunch date and speed date match services, and even reunions on television shows have all become ways for modern couples to connect. Still, sometimes an old fashioned telephone directory or a radio will do the trick. Here are a few examples of what these new (and old) techniques and technologies have contributed to love.

Lily and I were both seventeen when we met, though she was a year ahead of me in school. My family lived in San Mateo, in the Bay Area near San Francisco, and Lily's lived in Turlock, a small farming community. That summer, her family and mine just happened to go on vacation, during the same two weeks, to Pine Crest, a resort area with a lake. My family stayed in a cabin, and Lily's family was camping. This was in 1951.

My brother, a friend and I went down to the beach one day and were throwing a tennis ball around in the water. Lily was there with her cousin. Well, that tennis ball hit Lily right in the eye. That's how I met her. We've joked since then that she was moving around, trying to get hit, so we could meet.

For two weeks, Lily, her cousin, my brother, my friend, and I hung out together, and soon Lily and I paired off. We went to outdoor movies, walked along the wooded paths, things that people do at that age. At the end of the two weeks, our families were leaving. We walked one last time through the dark path in the woods and said our tearful goodbyes.

We lived very far apart, so couldn't see each other after the vacation. But we corresponded for a year. Nothing romantic, just newsy letters.

The following summer, our families went to Pine Crest again, but it wasn't the same. We hung out together, but there was nothing romantic whatsoever. I didn't know why it changed between us until recently, after my reunion with Lily; she told me that her family, being from the country, had the idea that city boys were loaded with money, and she felt that she couldn't keep up. So no point in starting something she couldn't handle. My family wasn't rich, but that's what she thought.

I met my wife during my last year of high school. I graduated from high school, and went to college. Between my junior and senior years of college, I married. We had two children and 44 good years together, before she passed away.

Lily married three or four months before I did, and also had two children. She lived in Woodland. I moved around for awhile with job changes and wound up in Turlock, of all places, Lily's hometown. But at that point, I didn't know if she lived around the corner or around the world.

Writing has been one of my hobbies. I wrote a World War II book, memories of growing up during the war, that is autobiographical. Two years ago, I submitted a short section of this book to the *Modesto Bee,* for publication in their column "Our Turn" that runs every Sunday; they showed interest in it, but they kept wanting revisions—change this, change that, cut the words. So finally I said, "I quit. I can't reach the standards you are demanding." But the editor said she'd be in my area the following week and she wanted to take a photo of me.

Earlier, for my own benefit, I'd written a story about my brief summertime romance. When the editor came to take my photo, I showed her this story and she liked it very much. So I gave her this one. But I had to do the same edit, re-edit, rewrite on it as on the first story I'd submitted. I joked to the editor that I was cutting so much of Lily that she was becoming anorexic!

The column ran on September 29, 2002. At that point, I had been widowed for three and a half years. I'd written frequent letters to the editor, and my name was not a common one, but Lily never contacted me, so I thought maybe she didn't want to be found. I wasn't thinking of remarriage, but I thought maybe this story would flush her out. I only used her first name, and no specific dates. I didn't want to embarrass her in any way; and I didn't want impostor trouble-makers phoning and saying, "Hi, I'm Lily." One woman called and asked if I had written about a Lily Thomas. But that wasn't her.

Turns out that one of her old Turlock boyfriends just happened to read the article that day; he doesn't usually read that section. But he saw my column and something clicked. Maybe my Lily was his old friend. He knew where she was because she'd kept in touch with her classmates.

Ray called her; he said, "There's the strangest article in the newspaper… could this be you?" He read the article to her over the phone. That night at 9 p.m. my phone rang, and there she was. But I asked her what her last name had been—that wasn't in the newspaper. I was leery of crackpots wanting to have some fun. But she was my Lily. And she was single.

I have muscular dystrophy, so I couldn't travel to her, and she lived 2 hours away. But two weeks later, on Columbus Day, she came for a visit. We hit it off like fifty years hadn't happened. We married October 4, 2003. At our age, we figured we didn't have time for long engagements.

Her grown children were accepting, but mine were leery. They had their old dad pigeonholed, my future all mapped out. And I had absolutely not been looking to remarry. A woman actually came over to "borrow sugar" once, but I put an end to that. No plans whatsoever to remarry. I figured I had a wonderful marriage, and so now nothing.

But Lily was something special.

About 7 years ago, I read the *Dear Abby* column that mentioned your book.. Got your book because my husband of 27 years had run off with his high school $#@%&! I wrote to you and told you about this experience, and you sent me a very nice personal letter.

The book went by the wayside, and now, ever so much later, I have found my very own lost love! My high school boy friend, free at age 55, got in touch with me by email after no contact for 35 years. He had heard about the Re-union.com web site and actually paid the membership fee just to find out what I had been up to. When he saw I was divorced, he got in immediate contact. We emailed 4 or 5 times a day for 2 weeks, then started having hour and a half nightly conversations on the phone, plus emailing.

One month after first contact, a miracle happened: last Thursday he came from Washington to New Mexico to visit me during my spring break (I teach first grade). We had 6 days and 5 nights of an absolutely rewarding reconnection. He's moving here in 15 days and we are going to be married. We can't believe the love and concern we have for each other that has been missing in previous relationships, even marriages, and never want to be apart again. He was tickled when I told him about your book, and that we're not the only reunited lovers (even though it seems as if we are the only couple in the world).

Thank you for studying this phenomenon and for believing in true love. I hope your life has become as happy as mine, and my darling man's. Luckily, I had already planned on retiring this year, and he's very close to the same.

This story begins in 1956 and it continues to this day. It starts with us together and ends with us together. I just turned 59, my lost and found love is 56. We met, in a tree, when she was 12 and I was 15. It was love at first sight. We were the first love for each of us. It was that white hot, all consuming, first love that just grabs you and won't let go.

I know, I know, 12 & 15? What did we know about love? All we knew was that when we first kissed, it shook us down to our very souls. It was something that neither of us fully understood at the time, but over the 3 years that we dated and went steady, there was never a time that we didn't feel the same with every kiss as we did with the first kiss: butterflies, weak knees, heads spinning, hearts racing. We never became intimate beyond some heavy petting and a lot of heavy breathing during the three years we dated.

We always assumed that when we got out of high school we would marry at some point after we graduated. But during my junior year in high school, my father, a minister, decided to accept a call overseas, and I broke up with my Lost Love. I went over the night before we were to fly out and took back the locket that I had given her three years before. I spent the next year and a half overseas and never wrote her. After I graduated, I came back to the States and to Atlanta to try to find her. She had moved. I turned the city upside down trying to find her but to no avail. So I went off to my freshman year at college.

Every time I was back in town I would try to find her again. Found some mutual friends but they didn't know where she was. I finally ran into her sister and she told me that my Lost Love had gotten married the week before and had moved to the West Coast. It broke my heart. The pain got so bad that I dropped out of college and joined the Army. Spent two years in Europe but still couldn't get my Lost Love off my mind or out of my heart.

When I returned to the States, I vowed that I would find my Lost Love no matter how long it took. So I started my search. But how to proceed? I didn't know her married name, and had no idea where she lived, but I tried everything I could.

In the meantime, I met a young lady at college; we dated for 7 months and decided to get married in the summer of 1965. Over the following 35 years we had two children, the oldest a girl and a son two years younger. My marriage was what you would describe as rocky. We split once for almost two years and everyone, including the therapists, said, "You have to get back together and raise your kids together." Bad advice, but we did it anyway. But I never forgot my first love or lost my love for her over the 40 years we were apart.

I had a picture of her that was taken in 1960 and I have it still today. I had kinda put her in my subconscious, but then I would hear a song, usually "16 Candles," which I gave her for her 16th birthday, or would smell her perfume, or something else would happen that was one of those "trigger points" that you have and the memories come flooding back and you find that you still love your first love as much as you did the last time you saw her 40 years earlier.

I still looked in phone books for her any time I would visit a new town while traveling for my job. Never did find anything.

Then I discovered the Internet. What a great tool!!!!!! I started with every on-line phone book, email address book, high school records, alumni associations, anything that I could find that might contain her name. Nothing… until about two years ago when I found Reunion.com. I registered, hoping that she would find the web site and maybe find me. Nothing. This went on for two years.

There wasn't a week that went by that I didn't try at least six sites to see if I could find her. In the meantime, I ended my marriage.

On February 19, 2001, I received an email from Reunion.com, asking me to check out their new format on the web site and also that my dues were due. So I paid them and checked out the new format on the web site. I noticed that they had a new search mode where you could search by name instead of by school, so I typed in my lost love's name. It came right back on the screen! I just sat there looking at her name for at least 20 minutes. My heart was racing, my stomach was tied in knots that would have made a Boy Scout proud; butterflies, sweaty palms… I couldn't even make my fingers work on the keyboard to go any further. Now the thought comes to mind, "Now what the hell do I do?"

I decided to go to her web page and see if it was really her. Graduated two years after me… yes, that was right. Same name that I knew her by… okay. But now what? I found a box at the bottom of the web page to send a message. But what should I say? So I got creative: "Hi, I think I know you. Did you used to live on Delaware Street in Atlanta between 1956 - 1960?"

I sent it with my email address and waited, and waited, and waited and waited. I must have checked my email 100 times that afternoon. Nothing. Checked 200 times the next day. Nothing. The third day, nothing. So I decided to go back to the web page and see if I had missed anything, now that I was a bit more rational than I had been when I found her name. I found that I had missed her married name that was listed at the top page. GREAT, A NEW CLUE!!!!!!!!

So I started with the web phone books, email address books, all of those things again. Found a ton of listings with the last name and some with the first initial. Called all of those, nothing. Went across the entire country, up the West Coast, across the mid- section, then the East Coast, finally nothing left but six southern states. So I put her last name in the state I live in and the one next to me. Her name popped up right on screen. Her husband's name, address, phone number and hers listed separately at the same address. Couldn't be that easy, right? I printed out the information and sat there trying to work up the nerve to call. What would I say if her husband answered? "Hi, I'm your wife's long lost high school sweetheart... is she in?" Right.

So for the next seven days, I tried to make the call but never could. I was now on the roller coaster of obsession that Dr. Kalish's web site talks about. No email, couldn't get up the nerve to call, why hadn't she replied to my email, should I send another one, WAS I CRAZY??????? All of this happened between February 20 and 27th.

I got to work on the 28th, opened my email and the second one down was a reply to "I think I know you." After ONE HOUR of sitting there looking at my screen, hands shaking, heart racing, pulse pounding (and I thought it was bad before), I finally got up the nerve to open it:

"Hi, I think I know you too. I'm the girl that you took back your locket from 40 years ago and disappeared out of my life. Where have you been, are you married, do you have any children, where do you live, where do you work?? Please write and let me know how you are."

Now I'm almost in cardiac arrest. IT IS HER, I'VE FOUND HER. So now what? Always that question, you know? Well, like some one said, one step at a time... yeah, like in a minefield.

So I sent her a reply giving her a short history of my past 40 years since we had parted... married 35 years, two kids, 1 grandchild, worked in the financial field and lived 120 miles from her. Back it came, her information... married 31 years, 4 kids, 3 grandchildren, worked in financial field, divorced.

We continued to exchange emails on a daily basis. Two days later, I received one with an attachment. When I opened it, there was a picture of my first love that had been taken two years prior. If I had had any doubts before I saw that picture, that erased any of them. I could have picked her out of a crowd of 1,000,000. She looked the same... older, but the same as she did the last time I saw her 40 years ago. Then later that day, another email: "Why were you looking for me? How did you find me?"

Well, to me, the only thing that I could do was to answer as truthfully as I could. What I was going to answer her might kill the entire reconnection, but I had to be up front and truthful with this. There was no other alternative.

"I have been looking for you for over 40 years. I loved you then and I love you now as much as when I left you. Why do you ask?" Then I told her how I found her.

Back came her reply, 15 minutes later: "Because I have been looking for you for over 40 years, too. I told my husband honestly that you are the only man that I will ever truly love, and that if I ever found you I would divorce him, and if you wanted me I would marry you in a heartbeat."

My roller coaster left the tracks and went into orbit. A week later she wrote and said that she wanted to meet me and see once and for all if what we said we are feeling was true love, a fantasy, a memory or what. She had to know if it was real. Could we possibly feel the same love after 40 years? So I agreed to meet her, but I wanted to meet in a private place, not a restaurant, or a park, but somewhere we could be alone. So she decided on a motel in a town half way between the cities where we live. I agreed to meet her at a place we both knew and we would go to the room from there. When she drove up beside me and we exchanged glances, we both just smiled and I followed her. We parked and went up to the room.

Nothing had been said, we had not touched, not even hands. We got in the room and I sat on one corner of the bed and she on the other and we just looked at each other. All of the fears we had had about seeing each other (I had put on 80 pounds, gray hair, scars from surgery,; she 40 pounds, gray highlights in her hair), but neither of us saw any of that. The lights were on but all we saw was the person that we had last seen 40 years ago on that fateful night.

She looked deep into my eyes and said, "If you don't kiss me, I'll die." So I did, and it was like 40 years just melted away. The feelings, butterflies, white hot passion, love, the taste of her lips, it was just like the night that I left her. But the intensity had had 40 years to boil and condense and grow and become something that was so much more than that night so long ago. All that I will say is that we parted nine hours later with the promise that we would see each other again as soon as it could be arranged.

After we have spent 8 days together in the first 87 days we have been back in contact, we planned our wedding, for the 9th of June, 2003. And so we were married on that day.

It truly amazes us how God has lead us through all of this. The signs that were put in place, some of them over six years ago, that finally lead us to each other. Things that unless you know the whole story, would not mean a thing until you connect them to the events that lead us to reunite.

Dr. Kalish, your book, *Lost & Found Lovers*, and your web site gave us the strength to believe that this was truly not a unique situation, and that there are millions of us out there who reunite successfully with their first loves. To all those people who joined your web site message boards and posted their questions, problems, doubts, and fears… to those who are still waiting to hear back from a lost love… and to those who have started to doubt after the initial rush from reuniting, together we come to Lostlovers.com and pour out our souls and hearts and find an understanding group that knows what we are talking about and can discuss our feelings without fear of being put down, especially at our ages. Not many people understand. But as my daughter said, "Dad, if you have a chance for true happiness, don't miss out on it." Children can be wiser than adults sometimes.

Since our reunion, and our marriage, we have grown more in love with each other than either of us thought possible. As we grew to accept that what we had was truly real, it became more and more obvious that we had to be together. We have discovered the happiness that started 47 years ago and has withstood the test of time. We have come full circle and the love that we have for each other is something that grows more precious with each passing second.

There is nothing like waking up next to the one you love in the morning and going to sleep holding her in your arms. I hate that we lost so many years of this wonderful feeling but we are determined to make up for lost time. We just got back from five days in Atlanta. Went back to the old neighborhoods where we grew up together, first met, first kissed, and went to some of the places we dated. Boy, talk about memories!!!!!!!! It was a great trip and we intend to do it again next year.

Oh, and the locket I took back in 1960… when we got together the first time I replaced it with a double heart, a small heart with diamonds inside a larger heart on a beautiful chain. She never takes it off.

God, what a feeling of joy. Brings tears of joy to my eyes just thinking about it. UNBELIEVABLE!!!!!!!!!!!!!!!!!!!!!

My heart skipped a beat when I read your interesting letter, "Flirting With a Memory," in the Circuits section of The New York Times.

In March of this year, I went to a newly posted web site about my old high school—a tiny, coed boarding school in Vermont. There I found the email address of my boyfriend from 26 years ago. We had been close friends as teenagers and then had a serious romance when we were in college. But we lost touch after graduation and went our separate ways.

We began a feverish email correspondence. He is divorced. I am unhappily married with 3 young children. Our love rekindled its old flame by the second or third letter. In 6 months, I received about 900 letters from him, and I sent him about 600. We began speaking on the phone after about one month. We are geographically separated, but met up face to face in September.

We spent a heavenly 48 hours together—a time filled with comfort, deep affection and the most tender love. We were kindred spirits. Neither of us had been a "cheater" before. I've always considered myself a person who would never consciously hurt another human being, and that meant not having affairs.

Then reality set in. We began a spiral into a helpless, hopeless sorrow. It ended very badly, with much yoyo-ing, seesawing, and a very unmerry merry-go-round ride.

Intellectually, I find it very interesting; I am curious as to how many other email love affair disasters you have uncovered in your research. Emotionally, I am a wreck, my heart utterly broken. He was the boy I let get away, but I KNOW he and I would have been far better off if we had never reconnected. I hate my computer!!

Donna and I lived in New Hampshire, and we were as madly in love as 7th and 8th graders as people could possibly be. This was in 1967. We were sure it would last forever—and it appears it did, with an all-too-long interruption.

Being 13 and 14, we were not sexually active, but long bouts of necking, anywhere we had the chance, were the next best thing at the time. In June of 1968, my family moved to the state of Washington. The problems my father was addressing, when he decided to move the family, were not known to me at the time. All I knew was that in June we were told we were moving, and in July we were gone. Poof! 90% of my possessions were left behind and 100% of my childhood friends, memory places, schools and the town I grew up in—and worst of all, my first love and I were torn apart. I had crushes and sweethearts of a less serious nature before, but never like I felt with Donna. It seemed to me that the world had ended and a new one had begun. I was given a nice going away party by Donna and then it seemed as if I drove into another life. The world behind me had a dark curtain across it and it followed my family across the country as we drove. Each mile brought me both closer to the future and further from the past.

I wrote Donna, but she did not answer. We went back as a family two years later, for Christmas, and I saw Donna briefly, but she had a new boyfriend by then and was not able to see me much. But our meeting showed that the fire and adolescent passion between us was still there. My family left again after a week, and the excitement of flying in one of the first 747's, and being grounded in a bomb scare and search, served to distract me. As far as I knew, I was never going back.

I was a rebellious teenager and a general pain in the ass to any and all adults. My extended adolescent adjustment carried over into early adulthood. In high school, I dated and had a couple of steadies in sequence, but I felt a deep, unidentified, emotional torment I could not understand. I frequently felt things with such passion that it surprised even me, and in matters of the heart I was very intense.

I joined the service, and in the first year I married my last steady from high school. I thought that I loved her, that I knew what love was, but now I can see that for all the years I was married, and before that, all the relationships I was in, I always held part of me back. I could not give my all, because it did not feel right.

I had been married for 8 years when my spouse decided it was time to have a child, so my daughter, Suzanne, was conceived and born. I was the first person to see her face, and in my heart I made a commitment to be there for her until she was grown. I had my moments of doubt, as when my spouse was diagnosed with a mental illness and we went through some roller coaster rides. But with Suzanne on the scene, I was going nowhere. We weathered 24 years together.

Over the years I had wondered what had become of Donna. In the mid to late 1970's, my brother had been to see Donna and her first husband, with whom we had gone to school; so I knew she was married and living in the area. In 1988, I was in Boston for a professional conference and rented a car to drive up to New Hampshire. I spent a day looking for Donna and other classmates I had known. I found an older couple, who had known me and my family and had been our neighbors. Strangely enough, the woman knew Donna and worked in the same company as she did, but I did not know that until many years later. I was within one degree of separation and did not even know it. So 15 more years passed.

While I was working on my high school's 30th reunion committee on a computer web site, I realized that I could access all the schools back East from my childhood. I put in the high school that I would have graduated from with all my old school mates and of course, with Donna. I found her listed, and sent an email. I checked every couple of hours for her reply. I received her first email back to me—our first direct communication in 33 years. We began an email exchange that grew to 4 reams of printed exchanges in about a year. I cannot fully explain or describe the incredible swelling in my chest, the electric and emotional shocks and almost ecstatic state I was in. Email would arrive and I would be overcome with intense emotion and passionate sensation as I read and responded to her writing. It took me only 2 weeks to get to the point where I knew I needed to talk with her and that I had to see her. When I heard her voice for the first time in all those years, I said, "You're real!" I was so happy to speak again with her. We would talk for hours at work by telephone, and Instant Message for hours at home.

I told myself that I had to see my hometown again, smell the smells and see the places, but of course the focus of my planned trip was that I had to see Donna. I could not believe the depth of emotion and passion that I felt for her. I thrilled to hear her voice each time we spoke; I lived for the next time we would speak; and then I could wait no longer—I had to see her. I visited in May for my 48th birthday, a present for myself.

Donna and I met at the T station in Cambridge, MA. After a tense 2 hour wait—she was at the escalator head of the station, and I was outside in the passenger pickup, and each of us was worried that the other had stood us up—we met in the running embrace you see in the commercials or cliché movies. Donna ran to me and I caught her and buried my face in the side of her neck. In that instant something my counselor had cautioned me about happened; my therapist who accompanied me through the emotional reawakening of my journey had warned me that I should go carefully and tread lightly.

With my face in her neck, I did not hear anything or anyone, but instead I inhaled deeply and said to Donna, "It's you. It's really you!" My brain had never forgotten Donna's scent, her natural one as she wore no perfume at that moment. I had reconnected with my heart and felt as if I were no longer a "boy interrupted." I felt such a surge of passion and joy that I was dizzy. We walked to her car in the car park, steadying each other and talking and touching like we had never been separated. We had agreed to do nothing that caused either of us any regrets, in particular, no sex, as we were each still married. We were just visiting, talking, traveling, and becoming acquainted again.

Donna was generous with her time and agreed to travel those old roads and paths with me—to see my old home, schools, and places of my childhood; she showed me the homes of her life since I left, and told me her story in the segments that each place evoked. I smelled the forests and roads wet after a spring rain, heard the thunder of home, the whippoorwill's calls, the katydids, the moon through a humid night sky. I was home, in every way but one: I was still connected to the West Coast.

I had told my wife that I was going home to see what I was going to do. I had been gradually reawakening at midlife and was determined to make purposeful choices for the future rather than be driven by others' ideas and needs. I had been reading a book about midlife and found it to be very enlightening. I saw that I was not alone in this journey and many of my experiences were shared by other men and women. I had the realization that we must each choose to take responsibility for our lives from midlife onward, or someone else will choose for us.

I decided during this visit that I would move back East after my daughter, then a Junior, graduated from high school, with or without my wife. In July, I filed for divorce due to issues unrelated to my reconnection with Donna. My daughter and I visited New Hampshire together in August; she is very supportive of Donna and me. Susan's attitude has been, "Whatever makes my Dad happy, will make me happy," an attitude that belies her 18 years, and reflects her maturity. Donna's son, age 26, has felt that way from the beginning, too. The support of the two most important people in our lives (apart from each other) has been a blessing.

I visited New Hampshire again in October, January, and February (again with my daughter). In April, Donna traveled to Washington to visit us. My daughter stated that she would be willing to move to New Hampshire at any time, but I was adamant that I would not do to her what was done to me—she would graduate with the students she had gone to school with for 11 years. After my daughter graduated, I fixed up the house for sale. Donna purchased a townhouse in New Hampshire (her divorce was final), and we moved there in late August.

The electricity we feel when we hold hands, or even when we are just near each other, is beyond description! I have never loved anyone the way I love Donna, nor have I felt as loved as I do now! I have never felt this sort of passion. The physical intimacy that we share is something I have never experienced before. Oh, sure, we had sex with our previous spouses, but never like this!! It is as if we are truly one, soul mates connected in all possible ways. I had heard of this, but wondered if anyone ever really felt this way. Now I know.

My brother lives in Boston and believes Donna and I are the strangest couple he has ever observed. Not for personal qualities, but for the amiable nature of my relationship with Donna's now ex-husband. So much has happened that has proven to us that we are meant to be together, our likes and dislikes, our spiritual values and needs, our color preferences, even our brand choices and our temperaments—we believe that we have been fated to be together, as bizarre as that may sound. We wonder if our lives are knit together across time and perhaps lifetimes. We are so deeply in love, across 35 years, 3000 miles, and now after 18 months of email and long-distance relationship, it seems even stronger. The word for us is Kismet, or fate. Every sign pointed us to this love being of paramount importance to us, for our completion of our lives' journeys and paths to actualization.

We spent some time on the "what ifs", wondering if my father had not moved, would we still be together. The what ifs cannot be changed, though, and while the years have had good times and bad for both of us, we each have a child who we would not have had if things had gone differently.

We were married on September 27, 2003—a long overdue union finally completed! Donna asked Susan to be her Maid of Honor. My daughter accepted happily, and we were pleased to be able to include her in our special day. We were married in the Meeting House next door to the Parsonage in which I lived while we dated all those years ago—yet another circle completed.

Dr. Kalish, it was so very nice to find your web site, and to know that this is not as uncommon as we originally thought. Donna had begun seeing a counselor last December, because she was concerned that she was either losing her mind, or going through a midlife crisis (her ex's theory). To her counselor's credit, she said it was neither; she said that, although the fact that Donna was reassessing her life could be attributable to age, it was not why she loved me so very much.

Thanks for listening to our story—we love telling it!! I believe there is a deep spiritual connection between us, and the Universe feels right again. It has not felt right for me since 1968. I have my life back and my soul is traveling a better path.

Hi, Dr. Kalish. This is Mary and George. We both wanted to tell you our love story. Mary will go first:

Fifty-five years ago, my family had just moved to Detroit. I attended the Easter service at the church and saw a boy sitting alone in the back. He had the bluest of eyes and was the most handsome of guys, and he was looking back at me. At that moment, time stopped for this seventeen year old girl; my heart was beating so fast and loud and hard that I could hardly take a breath. Love at first sight! I am sure I did not know then that it was truly a moment which I would never forget.

That young man, nineteen years old, invited me out for that evening. That was the beginning of our "love affair." We were inseparable after that for nine months.

And then he went away. He just quit his job and left town, and nobody knew where he went. The word went all over church that he had "run away." Finally we found out that he moved to Canada and joined the Royal Canadian Air

Force. In all the intervening years, I always told people that he ran away from me, but later I found out there were problems at home.

With all the passing years, a lot of details have been forgotten. But I clearly remember running into his mother at the grocery store a couple years later. She told me that she was going to his wedding in a few weeks! I knew I had lost out. I spent the next six weeks crying every time I was alone.

After the United States got dragged into the war, I met an Army officer and married him. That marriage ended in divorce. When George was in town to see his mother, he came to visit me a couple times. And once his wife called me to tell me he wanted a divorce; I told her that was news to me, and that she should be talking to him about it, not to me. He came to visit once more after that, and we even made a date for New Year's Eve, 1951. But I never heard from him again.

A few years later, I married a man I had known for five years. I had three children and was very happily married, until my husband died of lung cancer. But beneath the surface all those years was George. It was nothing that could have been obvious to anyone. I just looked at his old pictures now and then while I was rummaging through old stuff. And songs of that era always evoked memories of him. He was the one who never went away—MY FIRST LOVE!

I was a widow for fifteen years. Just worked, slept, ate, and played in my garden. I often wondered how George was doing and if he ever thought of me. One day, though, I turned on a talk radio station. They discussed an investigator who finds lost persons. I grabbed a pencil, wrote down the number and got right on the phone. I made an appointment to see her for that very afternoon, and I gave her whatever information I had about George and me.

By the following day, she had found him! She told me that she had called him, that he was divorced and delighted that I wanted to find him. It took only four days from there for him to drive to see me. He stayed for a week, then went back home for a doctor's appointment and to move a trailer-full of things back to me. We were married right away. And, as we started our lives in the teenage years as first loves, we will end our lives together as first and last loves.

My first love always had a special place in my heart. Even though I went on and had a successful life with a good marriage, no one ever knew of that secret love—only me . Now it's not a secret anymore!

Doc, this part's from George:

In 1950, I went to Detroit to visit my mother. We had some very good mother-son chats. In the course of one of these chats, she brought up the subject of my old girlfriend, Mary. She stirred up in me the feelings I had about Mary, which were not the kind of feelings that a married man should have about another woman. Being a proper person, I did my best to put these feelings on hold, if not trying to bury them completely. Mom gave me Mary's address and, being a typical man, I put this piece of information in my billfold where it remained for months.

However, that fall I was in town on business with nothing to do. I went to visit Mary. This visit made me realize exactly what my feelings were for her. I made up my mind that I was going to divorce my wife and then talk Mary into marrying me. At this time she was married, too, and her husband was in Korea. It seemed obvious to me that she was not happily married, and I anticipated that, once I was a single man again, she would also get a divorce.

I went back to Chicago and faced my wife with my desire to get a divorce. Once the shock settled down, she filed for a no fault divorce, and it quickly became final.

I took a few days of leave and drove to Detroit to see Mary and talk about our future. But before I had the opportunity to tell her that I was a single man, her mother informed me that there was no way that Mary would ever divorce her husband. This naturally was a big blow to me and, as a result, I kept my desires to myself and just enjoyed a few days with Mary. She did not know what had actually happened that November until many years later.

I returned home and soon discovered that I was too much of a family man to live alone. And I missed my daughter more than I ever thought I could. Around Christmas time, I decided to give my marriage another chance. We remained together until 1989.

It was then that my wife told me she was leaving me. We separated again after forty-eight years of marriage, but we remained friends. I helped her out as needed and we occasionally had dinner together.

After a few years, I moved into a retirement home in Nevada. There I had a nice room with a bath, and a good dining room with excellent meals. I thought I was set to be a bachelor for the rest of my life. I was enjoying life there—making friends, playing cards, going to the senior center, and visiting with my grandchildren who lived nearby. Last but not least, I was doing my share of fishing.

On one of those excellent fishing days, I didn't get home until 9 pm. There was a message on my machine that I could not quite make out. Someone had called and asked me to call a certain number, but I could not determine who or what number. I found one of the other tenants who had better hearing than mine, and we were able to determine the number. I called and reached someone in Detroit; it turned out to be a private investigator who found me in a computer search and wanted to know if I knew Mary. She wanted to know if she could give my telephone number to her. Naturally I said yes. Mary was my first love and I had never stopped thinking about her. The investigator said that I would be hearing from Mary in a few minutes and, although it was only about ten minutes, it seemed like hours.

When she finally did call after those interminable ten minutes, we talked for a hour. I found out she had been widowed fifteen years ago and she found out I was divorced.

After four more days, I left to visit her with my head in the clouds. I arrived on a beautifully sunny day. Mary was standing on the front doorstep. Not only did I recognize her immediately, but my mind was made up as to what I wanted to do, that I would do everything in my power to accomplish what I wanted, and I wasn't going to take "no" for an answer. Even after forty-three years, this was when life began anew.

We talked and talked and talked for about four days. Then I made plans to go back to Nevada for a physical exam, and to pack up my belongings and return to Mary.

Because I knew her husband had died of lung cancer, and because I was a pack-and-a-half-a-day smoker, I knew that certain changes in my lifestyle were necessary. Mary had said nothing about my smoking, but I knew in my heart that it would bother her to see me continue. So, after my physical, I took the pack of cigarettes out of my pocket, crumpled them up, and tossed them in the wastebasket. Since then I have not had another cigarette. I also knew that Mary was against drinking alcoholic beverages, so I even quit drinking. Don't get me wrong, I'm no saint. I just had the insatiable desire to have Mary for my wife.

I rented a U-Haul trailer and moved only what I felt was appropriate and necessary. I made one stop—to pick up a plain gold wedding ring.

The next day, I was glad to be back in what I intended to be my new home. Just about the first thing Mary greeted me with was the fact that she had two things for us to do that day: first, we were to be at the courthouse at 2 pm to get a marriage license, then at 3 pm we were due in the judge's chambers to get married. Bear in mind that I had not proposed marriage to Mary, and she had not proposed to me. It was just an indisputable fact that this was going to happen, and there was no point in normal formalities.

So we dressed up in our Sunday-go-to-meeting clothes, and Mary's daughter came by and took our picture. But the daughter thought we had dressed up to go out to dinner. No one was told what was going to happen. Well, things happened just as Mary had planned, and we came home as Mr. and Mrs. We had our wedding dinner at a Chinese restaurant nearby.

Once we were married, we told our families what the score was. They all seemed a little (!) surprised, but they all accepted the fact.

After a certain amount of time, we found room in the house for most of my things. I was introduced to the yard and garden. It was beautiful; Mary sure has a green thumb. I got her permission to do some of the lawn mowing, but the garden was for her labors, not mine.

Life has continued to be a huge helping of marital bliss. I am enjoying every minute of it and trust that Mary is, too. Perhaps in another year or so, I'll write another chapter of this tale. But for the present, let's leave it as is.

My parents moved away from the Bronx on February 10, 1967… my 14th birthday. That was the last time I had seen my first love, Frankie.

I first met Frankie on Sherman Avenue off 167th Street, in the Bronx. We were playing in the fire hydrants and we were both 13. We hit it off right away and were inseparable for the rest of the summer. We would hang out in the neighborhood, but our special days were spent at Orchard Beach. We had to take 2 buses each way to get to the beach. We would catch the bus on the Grand Concourse and take it to Fordham Road. From there, we would take the second bus to the beach.

Our biggest decision in life at that time was whether or not to catch that second bus on the way back home or buy a chocolate cone at the beach. The bus ride was $.20 at the time. We always opted for the chocolate cone and the long walk on the Grand Concourse from Fordham Road. That meant more time for us to spend walking with our arms around each other, hand tucked in the other's back jean pocket.

Summer soon came to an end and due to a teachers strike, school didn't start again until October. Frankie always seemed to cut class but he would walk me to school and be waiting for me when I got out so he could walk me home.

We were kids and we loved to play but we were also discovering the new feeling that came with puppy love. Frankie taught me how to "tongue" kiss, as we called it in New York. Here in Texas, it is called French kissing. We never took it further than kissing and Frankie would give me an occasional hickey which would infuriate me. I'm sure my Dad wondered why I was sleeping in turtleneck Barbie pajamas in the middle of summer!

Frankie always protected me and treated me like his little princess. The craziest thing we would do would be to walk through the "Shuttle," an abandoned subway tunnel located somewhere near the old Polo Grounds. This abandoned subway tunnel was pitch black and curved so you could not see from one end to the other. Frankie and I would walk through there, hands held tightly, never knowing what would happen. One day I got hit in the head with a rock. Frankie lit his lighter and there were homeless people living in there. When I think about it now, we could have been killed in there and our parents would have never known where we were.

Walking the "Shuttle" is still the scariest thing I've ever done.

My parents did not tell me we were moving to Lubbock, TX until one week before the move. I remember Frankie and I hanging out in Joyce Kilmer Park off of the Grand Concourse & 161st St. on our last night together. It was the day before my 14th birthday. We were both just devastated. The next morning Frankie was waiting while my family loaded up the car and had our trailer in tow. I can still see Frankie standing in front of my building on Walton Avenue, crying as we drove away. Who could ever have imagined we would end up where we are today?

We were devastated by my family's move to Texas. Even though Frankie and I continued to speak on the phone and write to each other for 4 years, we eventually moved on to other relationships. I wrote Frankie in September 1974, informing him that I was getting married in May of that year. Frankie married someone 55 days before I got married.

In 1999, I did an email search through InfoSeek for Frankie and I found someone with his name at throgsneck.com. I knew this had to be Frankie, because Throgs Neck is a part of the Bronx! I sent an email stating that I was looking for a "Frankie who grew up in the Bronx in the '60s and we used to go to Orchard Beach and walk on the Grand Concourse. If you are my Frankie, please email me at… ." The very next day, I receive a reply from Frankie. He said he had been looking for me!

We emailed for 2 days, spoke on the phone for 8 more and then Frankie rushed to JFK Airport and hopped on a plane—no clothes or belongings, just a Yankees pendant, 2 Yankees shirts (for me) and all my emails tucked under his arm. He had to catch a connecting flight in Dallas, so I figured if he could do this for me, I would fly to Dallas and surprise him. I immediately went to the airport, caught a flight to Dallas, and ended up having a 2 hour wait for his delayed flight. While waiting, I struck up a conversation with a couple waiting for the same flight. I told them about the reunion about to take place. They got all excited and couldn't wait. And they told other people.

I sat down in some seats in line with the passengers de-boarding. As Frankie walked off the plane, I fell in stride to his right (as teens, I always walked on Frankie's right), placed my arm through his and started walking with him. His eyes got HUGE. He said, "Linda?" and gave me a hug and a light kiss on the lips. He pulled me off to the side and really kissed me. A crowd of people started chanting, "Go Frankie! Go Frankie!" He looked at me with some confusion and I explained who they were. When Frankie kissed me, I knew those lips in an instant. It was like we had never parted.

We flew back to Lubbock and Frankie was due to return 11 days later. The plan was that he would go back to New York, close down his business and move to Lubbock. You see, he proposed to me the night before his flight; he said he couldn't leave me. We rescheduled his flight for a few days later, so I could accompany him to New York. We did just that, rented a truck and moved him to Lubbock. On my 46th birthday—32 years to the day that we last saw each other, we were married. I walked down the aisle to Judy Garland singing "Somewhere Over The Rainbow."

Frankie and I realized we had to go through hell to get to heaven. We have a saying, "everyday is Christmas… every night is New Year's Eve." We are truly each other's soul mates. We will soon have our 4th anniversary. We also will both turn 50 years old this year. Thank you for letting me share my story. Even now, I still am amazed at it myself.

So, back from a glorious week with Ruth, and I do not know even where to start, except to recall a statement from one of your research participants in your book: "I am writing because Nancy Kalish understands." I have read the book thoroughly, many times in fact; the initial reads were difficult, as much for reading through the tears as the wealth of emotional content. But now, after all the highlighting and notes in the margins to jog thoughts and years of recalls, I hope that I can offer a succinct and cogent narrative of what has transpired.

First, let me sincerely thank you for your efforts and state that I would not have been able to continue this quest without the help and support of your research and writings. You gave me renewed hope, as I read and reread the participants' stories. I was going to give up looking for her in the year your book was published, but then I realized I was NOT unique; this is a reality for so many people, and one where the statistical results are skewed to the percentage of reunited lovers who remain together.

In the summer of 1963 in Boston, I was playing guitar at a local coffee house and one of the girls in the audience really caught my attention. I was 18 and ready to go to Boston University, and she 19, already in college in Connecticut. Her name is Ruth. We dated through the remainder of the summer, laughed hysterically at everything (especially ourselves), and grew to love each other deeply. We tearfully had to part to go to our respective schools but remained in constant contact when my parents gave me what I needed most in school—a telephone credit card!! They did not understand why I asked for this, until after they started receiving the bills, each month up in the hundreds of dollars. They really could not complain, though, because I was not neglecting my school work and was working at the same time. But they did not like it (at least my mother did not).

We had not at that time been lovers at all; were both virgins and had grown up in middle-class families with good values and mores. But my family was dysfunctional due to alcoholism, with which I had to deal all through high school, raising my sister so the Social Services would not be called in by one of the neighbors. I grew up before my time.

The phone calls became insufficient, so at the end of the first semester we started an alternating weekend sojourn where she would drive from Connecticut to Massachusetts and then I would visit her the following week. She had a car, and I did not, but that didn't stop me; I picked up rides to get me within half mile of her campus—there is a God! We grew closer and closer, exploring our own sexuality to the point that on Homecoming Weekend, we passionately deflowered each other. She shared with me recently that no one in her life was as gentle and caring while at the same time passionate. The emotion of that sharing is such that I still lack adequate intellect to explain to anyone. School went well, and we looked forward to the summer together at home.

Well, that was when it hit the fan. My mother did not like her, and her father did not like me, due to the seriousness of our situation. My parents were attempting recovery but were still drinking, and some situations became nasty. My mother took my mail. We allowed our parents to drive us apart. I met someone late in the summer and by midterm, I was married. I now realize that this marriage was my attempt to achieve certain things: one, to hurt my parents by saying, "You caused me to lose her… now I am going to cause you to lose me… ;" and second, since my sister had gotten a little older and had the support of some of the older nieces and nephews, I had to establish an assurance that I would never have to return to that level of responsibility or to view the ravages of their addiction. I introduced my wife to my mother, left and never returned until well after college. Guess I showed her, right? NOT! I lost what I now realize is the most wonderful relationship in my life. True, full, honest, intellectual, a love of the arts, a sincere level of sensitivity and compassion. My mother's initial response was, "You married out of your zip code." Out of my zip code, mind you! I was divorced within 18 months and had lost contact with Ruth, who had graduated. Her father passed away, and her mother had moved out of state. There were no siblings.

I graduated and went to Vietnam where I served four years and 18 days. I was caught on a night patrol and served as a POW for 7 months. Ruth told me that she never dreamed I was in Vietnam and she was glad she did not know; she would have died watching every newscast.

When I got back to the States, I kept checking all the leads I could find. I did not know a lot of her friends in school, because we spent all the time to ourselves. I did find that she had possibly moved to Hawaii and had a gallery there (she had been an Art major). But nothing checked out.

I remarried, had a son, did well at work and socially, but still had a "void" that nothing could fill. Too much work led to another divorce, and I remarried again about 4 years later (well, at least I keep trying)… but still that "void." All during this time, I continued to seek her, to no avail. She did not register with her Alumni Association, and all other name checks of similar names were dead ends. I admitted defeat—which is not something I do readily. My spirit was broken. That was 1997—and then your book came out, and the Internet became a factor.

In 1997, my only child was killed in an hit and run accident and my life was shattered, including my current marriage, due to the stress of this loss. It was the only thing in my life that was a greater loss than losing Ruth, and after getting some grief counseling for a year or so, I realized that I had to find her. During 2001, my sister passed away at 45 and I was even more determined to correct what I had mishandled many years ago.

I sent emails to all the people in her class (150+) who I could find at Re-union.com; most were dead-ends, because she never communicated with them at all. I tracked all the galleries in Honolulu, found nothing. And then I heard from a college friend of hers who was a librarian, and when I told her my story through many tears, she said, "I live on the computer… I love it… I know it… we shall not be denied." Six days later, on November 18, 2002, she called me with three possible names and numbers in the Seattle area. I emailed a gallery, and with no response called the number. The owner said she was her old partner, but they had split and were involved in a litigation; but she forwarded my email to her when she read the sincerity of my inquiry. She said, "I may be mad at her, but I'm not mad at you… and you have gone through a lot."

No response the next day (November 19, 2002!!!!) and I could not wait, so I called. All I had to hear was the voice on the phone and I knew, and I said, "Are you sitting down?" She heard my voice, which was always something special to her, and she knew, and responded, "I am now!" It took me 5 minutes to get a modicum of composure and extract a coherent thought, but all went well after that in the conversation. She had sent an immediate response, but as technology would have it, it was floating in the "Net;" when I terminated the call, it was there in my Inbox—a sweet encore to a wonderful talk. I think it was intended that my first contact with her again would be by voice—oh, to hear her laugh!

In our exchange of emails, the most difficult thing for me to read was how much I hurt her as to how I ended our relationship. Then she said, "All you had to do was ask and I would have married you—no reservation." I felt briefly again, broken. My failure in judgment had cost us both deeply. But the more we talked, all became well. I still know she has been the only person I could discuss anything with, without fear of judgment or her thinking any less of me. We both agree that the most important thing in our lives is to be happy and follow our dreams. She was elated to hear that I have continued to play guitar, recorded and still find joy in it. I took my guitar when I visited her, and there were many teary times.

The passion was exciting yet humbling, caused many tears, more discussions sitting in front of the fireplace at night, reading poetry to her which she had not had done since we parted. We fell in love all over again—like the lady in your book who met her love in the airport "… and the 35 years just melted away… " Whew, when I came up the steps at the airport and saw her, I thought I was going to pass out; I have never felt that eruption of emotion—even when I was released from Vietnam. It was a bountiful week. I met her grown daughter (Ruth has been divorced many years, and said she had no need to get married if not to me).

I also found out that she spent years looking for me, but all my family was gone too and she ran into dead ends. Well, one of us was successful, and we are both happy beyond our wildest dreams. If the love is right; it will always be there. I believe that now beyond any thought known to mortal man.

Nancy, you hold a special place in our lives and in my heart, next to Ruth, for without you, she would not have returned there. Thank you… thank you… thank you!

September, 2000:

My recently found long-lost-love, Sharon, and I read your book cover to cover in 2 days. It was an amazing read, and what was so cool is that I found the book at Barnes & Noble only weeks after we reconnected. A very fortuitous coincidence! We were so surprised to find that the majority of couples you interviewed had such similar experiences as us—especially the parts about how fast everything seemed to move once we reconnected, and the incredible intensity of the emotions involved. We had been separated physically for 21 years; the last time we spoke had been 18 years ago.

The way we reconnected is that I wrote a book, and in the acknowledgments I wrote, "Thanks to Sharon for being there when it counted the most." A mutual friend copied that page and mailed it to her, along with my current address.

She wrote to me on June 7 of this year, and within 2 weeks we were emailing back and forth. Once the email "bond" was established, Sharon decided to call me. By the end of the first week of emails, she confessed she was falling in love with me all over again. I already knew I was in love with her, because

I had never stopped being in love with her, despite the 21 year estrangement (she dumped me in the original relationship). I went on to other relationships and even a marriage, but constantly thought about Sharon, fantasized, wished, prayed, dreamed, never suspecting something like this could ever possibly happen.

Anyway, we both filled out copies of your research questionnaire and sent them in. We hope that you will do a follow-up book, maybe to see where the couples are 5 years later or something like that. That would be interesting!! Thanks!

David C.

October, 2000:

Hi Nancy,

It's great to know that the thing with Sharon & I is pretty much the norm. We were talking just tonight about how (you'll get details on this later) when we reconnected and communicated via email (and then almost immediately by telephone) that when we planned to get together for the first time in 21 years it was going to be an all-day hotel room thing. I mean, it was just a given, without any discussion—we knew that's what we wanted to do. About the only discussion was her saying something like "I'd love to see you, but I don't think I could keep my hands off you," and me replying, "I hope you don't keep your hands off!" It wasn't like "let's meet for a lunch and check each other out and see if we're still interested." We knew we were still interested. Of course, as you already know, I knew how I felt for years, whereas for Sharon it was all a surprise, like "where the hell did these feelings come from, I didn't know they were hiding inside me."

We're meeting Friday this week. Then in two weeks we'll have 3 days & 2 nights together. The complicating factor in all this is that she is waiting for her son to graduate high school, so that there will be no major disruption of home life for him.

Oh, I'm telling details I should probably wait and put in the "story"! Forget I said anything! I have only finished half of the Sharon/David tale, but hope to have it ready tonight or tomorrow to send. Well, by the end of the week, at least!

I've enjoyed talking to you, and I hope we can keep in touch!

David

There were several email notes from David after that, as we chatted back and forth about films and books, but he hadn't completed writing his love story to send to me; after a few months, we lost touch.

In January 2003 I was looking for couples to appear with me in a mag-

azine article on rekindled romance. I thought of David and Sharon. I still had his email address, but when I wrote to him, my note came back undelivered. I knew that he was a book author—the book with the dedication to Sharon—and I had his full name, so I thought he might have a web site about his books, perhaps listing a new email address. I looked for him through search engines.

I found a web site about his work, but not about his books. I didn't know he also had a band and recorded some CDs. There was his photo, and under it, "In Memoriam." The web site said that David had died in a car accident. We had never met, but still, reading that was very disturbing and brought tears to my eyes. A couple of days passed, but I couldn't shake the sadness; I wrote a short note to two members of his band, who listed email addresses on the band's website, to send my condolences.

January, 2003:

Hi Nancy,

Thanks for writing and for your condolences on his death. He mentioned you and your book many, many times.

I met David in 1971. He was my best friend for thirty-one years. Through mutual friends, I'd heard about this guy in my high school who had the same interests as myself: movies and heavy metal. When we finally met, it was like brothers separated at birth reunited.

Throughout the three+ decades, we would crack each other up with jokes about obscure references to movie plot lines and bad actors that no one else would think was remotely funny, but we'd be in tears. We went through a virtual catalogue of teenage life experiences involving sex, drugs and rock & roll that I shared with no one else, and now my partner to share those memories with is gone, leaving me to try and desperately retain the images of the experiences we'd reminisce about…

It was quite emotional for me to read both your message and the original email he'd sent you. I am the "mutual friend" he referred to who sent Sharon a copy of the page from his book in which he thanks her.

For twenty years, I heard him express his regrets over and over that their relationship had ended badly. We'd be in the middle of a perfectly happy conversation and I'd see him get this sad, puppy dog face, and I'd say, "Oh no, don't start thinking about Sharon!" They were going to get married in their early 20's. He never got over her, and she was the true love of his life. When I saw his book and the mention of her, I made a color copy of the cover and the Acknowledgments page, and after receiving it, she told me to go ahead and give him her address. He sat with it for six months, starting letters he never finished, afraid she'd reject him all over again.

She eventually wrote to him around his birthday in 2000, and even then he called me up, too fearful to even open the letter for a day or two, lest it be hostile. I convinced him otherwise, and their two year reunion took off.

Their story is one of intense passion; it is funny, romantic, sexy and silly, ultimately a tragedy. I don't know if you're aware of the details, but David was out with Sharon to buy a new car. They had just left the dealer's lot in the new SUV, and were heading out to grab a bite to eat, when they were broadsided by a car running a red light. The driver of the car was seventeen years old. David died of his injuries, but Sharon was okay.

If all of this wasn't enough for Sharon to go through, the car dealership sued her to get her to pay the full amount for the car she'd had for ten minutes. The whole thing makes me sick to my stomach.

David had just sold his house and moved into Sharon's home—just days before the accident. He never unpacked.

I know I've rambled on quite a bit, but I have never felt loss like this. More than five months after his death, I still feel emptiness, sadness and anger virtually every day. David was the brother I never had. The fact that we managed to record one last time is fantastic, and I hope it will be a special piece of David that the world will be able to share with us. And thankfully Sharon and I have spoken almost daily for the past five months, sometimes for two or three hours. No one knew David as intimately as she and I did, and we relate to things no one else can understand. We take comfort knowing that he was the happiest man in the world for his last two years.

David felt very close to you, and intended to keep in touch and give you their story. He started writing the story, and then ran out of time, but intended to finish it later for you. He was so busy with work, Sharon, writing, music—he had lots of projects going on at once, in addition to his intense love for reading and movies. The beginning of his story is probably in his computer, but Sharon says the end is too sad for her to look. It's too bad you can't write the "happy ending" version of the David and Sharon Story that David was hoping for, but maybe there's still a story to tell.

My name is Amy. I met my lost love, Ron, during our freshman year in college in the dorms. I went to a party with my friends that involved crazy stunts, such as swallowing goldfish. Ron was there with his friends. The next day at the dorms, there was an envelope in my mailbox filled with goldfish crackers. I still have it, though they are crushed to smithereens.

He was my first love, and we were inseparable until the end of senior year. The interesting part of our relationship was that we wrote letters, notes, and illustrated stories to each other almost daily, even though at times we only lived right across the street. I saved every scrap from Ron, a talented artist and writer, from our days together and organized them in The Box.

At the end of our senior year, Ron broke up with me to pursue travels and graduate school. That was 1990; I was heartbroken. I always considered him my true love, and it was inconceivable to me that we would not be married and grow old together.

I saved The Box with the volumes and volumes of materials. We both moved on, I married, Ron was in long time relationship for 10 years. Neither of us had children. At one point, my best friend ran into Ron about 6 years ago, and I mailed him The Box. I thought he would be interested in reading all our old stories and letters. I also thought that it might be silly hanging onto those memories all those years.

Well, my former husband and I separated, on a Saturday night, after 10 years together. I was feeling extremely depressed when I arrived at work Monday morning. Unbelievably, the first message on my voice mail was from Ron asking how he could return The Box to me. (I am an attorney in California, and he looked up my work number at the State Bar web site.)

Something inside me said, "This is it," but it took about a month for me to screw up the courage to call him. The story was that he had just ended his long time relationship as well and was in the process of moving out of his house! He was going through and separating boxes in the garage when he came across The Box.

We planned to meet for lunch, so he could return The Box to me, about a month later. In the intervening time, we talked on the phone nightly for hours and emailed each other like crazy. Ron's powers of storytelling had not diminished, and I have saved every email.

As the time for our lunch approached, Ron posted a countdown clock on the Internet—I was crazy nervous. It was stunning to me that somebody I had not seen in 13 years was all of a sudden the most important person in my day.

Our lunch was to be at noon on Sept. 28, 2002. Ron showed up 10 hours early and stayed approximately 18 hours late. We both knew immediately.

Three weeks later we traded tattoos of our names and announced we were engaged. If you saw us you would know how out of character tattoos are for either of us. We bought a darling old house that is right on a park. A mutual friend from college, who was there the night we first met, obtained a minister's license online. And in our park, in front of a small gathering of friends, family and neighbors, under a beautiful tree in the rain, I finally married my true soul mate.

Our love now is truer, purer and stronger than it was even in college. It's like losing a loved one in death and by some miracle of God's, they are returned to you years later. You realize how precious they are and go out of your way to show them how much they are adored. I have never been treated as such a princess. We both are stunned at our compatibility and love for each other. And I mean truly stunned in every meaning of the word. We are 35 and 36 years old.

Talk about coincidence and reunions, this one is definitely worth writing about. Today I was reading a magazine and came across the article "You've Got Love (Again!)." I wasn't even going to read it at first, because I said to myself, "Their stories couldn't possibly be as great as ours;" but something made me go ahead and read it. Halfway through the first story about Ron and Amy [*their story is above*], I realized that Ron was a long lost friend of mine from my freshman year in college! It was actually somebody I knew! What are the chances of that? I emailed both Ron and Amy today, and they told me you suggested them for the magazine story; they gave me your web site address. I am really looking forward to getting together with them. If that wasn't coincidence enough, we share such an amazingly similar story of rekindled love—right down to the box!

Todd and I met for the first time when I was a junior and he was a senior in high school. We both grew up in a small town in Northern California, but attended different high schools two towns apart. Like any small country town, there wasn't a lot to do, and most every weekend was spent "cruising." Apparently Todd had noticed me in my sporty red car one weekend and asked a mutual friend to introduce us. Our friend told me about Todd, and although I had no idea who he was, I knew his car from the cruise. One magical—or should I say McMagical—day at the McDonald's drive-thru, I saw his car pull up behind me. We spoke for the first time in the parking lot and it was love at first sight—with a side of fries, no less!

I'm not sure what it was about Todd, but he was literally the man of my dreams. I had actually dreamt about him before I ever met him. We had one terrific year together, but sadly he had enlisted in the Army before we had ever met. Once he graduated from high school, he headed straight for basic training. We wrote to each other almost every day and spoke on the phone as often as we could. We hoped and prayed that he would be assigned somewhere nearby, with great hopes of it being the Presidio in San Francisco. We had spent one of the best days of our lives there.

On December 28, 1985 Todd and I drove to San Francisco and spent the day walking along Fisherman's Wharf and taking in all the sites and smells. I remember it like it was yesterday. We took a carriage ride, had a caricature drawn—which is proudly hung in our bedroom today—and best of all, we were so happy and in love that a total stranger issued us a kissing violation and actually thanked us for our infectious happiness.

Unfortunately, rather than being assigned to the Presidio, Todd was stationed in Korea. Once again San Francisco was the background to another memorable event, but this day would be the most difficult and heart-wrenching of our lives. I so vividly remember standing in the airline terminal, crying so hard that I ached, and watching an Army uniform-clad Todd board his plane. Time seemed to stand still and even though I was in a crowded airport, I felt completely alone.

That painful day would be the last time Todd and I would see each other for eleven years. My Todd Box has all the letters and cards he sent to me when he went off to the Army. He was in the States for a year then went to Korea for five years. The Todd Box also has a kimono, a glass figurine and a beautiful Japanese doll that he brought back for me. And for my high school graduation, he gave me a freshwater pearl necklace that if I wasn't wearing, stayed in that box with all our memories. And the best thing of all was his Army picture. Every so often I would take that picture out and pine over it! Boy am I a sap! Although we continued to write and call each other for months to come—I even pleaded with my parents to send me to Korea for Valentine's Day—the distance and our individual needs to grow eventually tore us apart. We never officially broke up; I just never heard from Todd again.

Todd spent four years in Korea and eventually moved to Los Angeles to attend University of Southern California. I spent my first year of college in Santa Barbara, then went to Cal Poly San Louis Obispo, and then headed to London where I finally began to grow up, take education seriously, and find my passion in Art History. It was in London that I met someone who I would eventually marry.

I remember going home to my parents after getting engaged and taking my box of Todd memories out of the closet. I must have stared at his Army picture for hours wishing so desperately that he would suddenly appear on my doorstep and tell me that I was making a huge mistake. I knew that was never going to happen, so I went on with my life and married as planned.

As fate would have it, my ex-husband and I moved to San Francisco, where our marriage slowly fell apart. After a last-ditch effort to work on our marriage failed—not even a trip to Thailand and Bali could bring us back together—I began to reevaluate my life and asked myself why I was staying in an unhappy marriage. I wondered what it would be like to be in a loving relationship that I knew would last forever.

Around that time I went to visit my parents again. Once again, the Todd Box came out of the closet. This time, however, it was different. I had a very intense feeling that something bad had happened to Todd. It was something I couldn't shake, so I was determined to find him.

When I went back to San Francisco, I began looking for him on the Internet. I had just gotten Internet access at work, and had no idea how to maneuver the World Wide Web, but after two days of searching, and some help from friends, I found him on an alumni web site. I didn't even know if Todd went to college, but I learned that he had graduated from the University of Southern California and was living in Los Angeles. I immediately called Directory Assistance and got his phone number. I was more than relieved when his answering machine picked up and announced that "Mark and Todd cannot come to the phone right now." He wasn't married!!!

Somehow I managed to leave a message and waited by the phone for his call. Two days later—which nearly killed me—he finally called. When I heard his voice for the first time my heart melted, and I thought I was going to pass out. Naturally one of the first things he asked me was why I had called him after all these years. I told him that the past Sunday I had a very strong feeling that something bad had happened to him and I had to know if he was okay.

After a long silence, Todd explained that on that day he took his box of Janelle memories out of his closet, and threw it away. Todd's box, in addition to my letters and cards, contained a book of poetry that I sent to him when he went off to basic training. I bought him a Blue Mountain book of love poetry and placed ribbons between special pages, and wrote additional lines and my own poetry throughout. He had spent the prior week looking for me on the Internet but couldn't find me, so he had given up. In fact, he had just registered himself on the web site where I found him, just in case I was looking for him. It was Fate.

I was so sad when I learned he threw it away. Back to the Internet I went. I contacted Blue Mountain, and shared my story with a lady there. After she finished crying, she found a copy of the poetry book for me. Now we have all our memories together in one place, and have added ALL the email correspondence from when we found each other again.

It was amazing when we began talking again. It was as if we were never apart. There was one problem, though. I was still married but didn't tell Todd that I was. I was so afraid that if I told him I would lose him again. My marriage was over; I just hadn't had enough guts to end it yet.

After talking on the phone and endlessly email each other for a few days, I finally had the courage to tell Todd that I was married. It was quite a blow, but he stood by me and offered his strength and friendship and gave me the courage to do what I should have done long before. It all happened so quickly, and within two weeks I had moved out and began a new chapter of my life. Todd and I continued to talk on the phone and email each other every day, and it was during one particular eight hour phone call that I nervously blurted out that I have been in love with him all these years. He admitted the same and flew from L.A. to San Francisco to see me the next day! It was incredible.

June 16th, 1997, there I was back at the San Francisco airport, this time waiting for Todd to arrive, eleven years later. When he stepped off the plane, this time in a suit and not a uniform, it was like we were the only two people in the airport. Time stood still once again. I have never been so nervous in my entire life. Would he still like me? Were all the feelings we were having real? Is he still the same person I knew and loved? Yes, yes, and yes!

We went straight to Fisherman's Wharf that day, and although Pier 39 had changed over the years, the love and happiness we shared had not. Everything was perfect, except once again, Todd was moving far away again! Thankfully not to Korea this time, but honestly if it had been, it wouldn't have mattered. I wasn't going to let distance separate us again. Todd was leaving in August for Harvard Business School. We spent every minute until then flying back and forth from Los Angeles and San Francisco, and we saw each other as often as we could once he started school. As fate would have it once again, he got a summer internship in San Francisco.

We were engaged that fall, and were married in the South of France. We will be celebrating our fifth year wedding anniversary this May.

I believe it is safe to say that Todd and I truly left our hearts in San Francisco. We just needed a little extra time to recapture them.

And on September 20th, 2002, we brought another little heart into this world. Sydney Claire Graves was born at 7:04 am—in San Francisco. She looks just like her daddy. Whenever I look at her, my heart melts.

To this day I still have "wow moments." I still can't believe I got to marry the man of my dreams! Who would have thought that a box could completely change your life?

My family moved to California in 1975. My dad was in the Navy so we moved just about every two years. Andy's mother moved his family just about every year in search of better paying jobs. We both moved to San Jose, California the same year and as luck would have it, Andie's mom stayed there for three years before moving on; so Andy and I were able to maintain a relationship until we moved, in December of 1977.

We both were in 10th grade. I already had a boyfriend when I met Andy in art class, but by October of 1975, I had broken up with him and started dating Andy. He was so sweet and so cute I just couldn't resist him. We were both into music and art and my family just loved him. I got along very well with his family also. His mother was the first single parent I ever met and she had a strong influence on me, in that she was okay with being alone and she was a very confident, vivacious woman. Andy told me that being around my family influenced him in positive ways, also, my father in particular.

My parents were very strict, so we didn't get a lot of alone time, but we managed to find ways of being together a lot. We used to ride bikes, go for long walks in the park near my house, and play music together. We talked for hours about everything and anything. Andy and I were both virgins when we met, and we were each other's first sexual partners. It was very positive for both of us, in that we were very much in love, and our times together were very loving and giving. I never forgot that, and through the years I would think about what a great time we had together. Andy would walk me home after school and then walk the mile back to his house. We rarely had disagreements, and Andy was always respectful of my family's rules.

In the summer of 1977, my father received orders to move back to Virginia. Initially, we weren't supposed to move until the summer of '78, after we graduated, but then the Navy moved the orders up to December of '77. We were both crushed at the thought of breaking up. My family offered to take Andy with us; they loved him too. Andy decided it was not the right thing to do, and near the beginning of our senior year, he broke up with me, his thoughts being that it would be easier to deal with for the both of us when the time came for my family to move. I was hurt and angry and I wasn't very nice to him at times, but he never lashed back.

In December when we moved to Virginia, I enrolled in high school, got another boyfriend, and graduated. During this time I wrote to Andy about five times, and then we just lost touch. I moved through a succession of relationships, but none of them ever stuck. They just didn't feel right. I have been married twice, have 3 children. Andy had a couple of girlfriends, but didn't really date until about two years after I moved. He's been married once for 9 years, has a 14 year old daughter.

He is a successful graphic artist. I have moved through quite a few jobs, my favorites were as a nanny and a legal advocate for battered women at the Family Refuge Center in Lewisburg, West Virginia. Several of my relationships were very abusive, which is how I came to work for battered women. That job helped me to work through issues from my childhood and even after I was laid off, I continued to work out these personal issues. When I ended my last relationship of five years with a controlling partner, I was very happy to be on my own.

After being on my own a couple of months, I happened to be surfing the Web, and saw Andy's name. Actually I had seen Andy's name a few years before but never thought of contacting him. The day I contacted him, July 20, 2003, I did so merely to see what his life was like. I wondered if he ever thought about me. It turns out he had and that he had attempted to contact me. He searched my name, found an article on a play I was in, but since my last name at the time was different, he figured I was married so he never contacted me. The day I contacted him, he was in the process of moving out of the apartment he was sharing with his current girlfriend. Their relationship had been struggling for some time, and Andy was just waiting for the right time to move on. He immediately emailed me back, indicating that he would love to get in touch with me. Nothing romantic, just friendly. We emailed for a couple of weeks, once again just friendly emails.

When I finally called him, we talked for about three hours and both of us were amazed at how easy it was to talk to each other, just like in high school. It didn't seem to matter that 26 years had gone by, it was just like we picked up where we left off. It was amazing to the both of us the similar patterns that our lives had taken. We both had daughters named Michelle, my son's middle name was the same as Andy's, we were both musicians, we still liked a lot of the same things. We have the same values, philosophies of life, and sense of humor.

After talking for a couple of weeks, we decided that we'd like to see each other in person, but neither of us had the money for plane tickets. I had heard about a reunions television show, and I thought about contacting them. I was amazed that when I got home and checked my email, the first thing I saw was from Andy, stating, "Hey, wanna be on TV?" He had been thinking the same thing that day that I had, only he saw the ad for Second Chance.

Neither of us could explain why we felt so compelled to see each other again, so we just accepted it and went with it. Neither of us was looking for a relationship; we had both come to a place in our lives where we were ready to be on our own.

Andy contacted Second Chance and they liked our story. We were both willing to put up with the cameras and the hoopla; all we wanted was to see each other. Andy is actually the one who contacted the show first, but since I actually contacted him first they decided to name me the "seeker." So the show was geared towards me because of that. But our show was different in that Andy was also a participant in surprising me.

A producer from the show flew to West Virginia, and a camera crew from Charleston was hired for what was supposed to be a day long shoot (it actually went for a day and a half). They came to my home and interviewed me and my children, and my best friend, for most of the day. They then followed me to work and filmed there.

I was not prepared for the flood of emotions that their questions brought out. I cried a lot. I had forgotten lots of little details, and looking at the old pictures and remembering those great days together, I was drained by it all. It opened up how much I had missed him, and how good those times were, especially in contrast to the years in between our reunion.

Andy was filmed prior to this at his home, and also with his daughter and his sister doing different things around the house.

They actually had over 30 hours of tape and edited it down to 24 minutes of air time. It was tiring, but they crew and producers were very professional and nice. They really got into the spirit of the thing. At some points, even the producer was in tears.

When it was time to go to Los Angeles for the filming of our reunion, we decided that I would stay with Andy for a week, instead of just the day that Second Chance had planned for us. The show would only pay for one night in a hotel, so I would have to stay at Andy's for the week. It was startling to the both of us how we trusted that everything would go well, even after 26 years. Both of us had been burned pretty badly before, we should have been at least a little wary, but somehow we weren't.

The day we finally got to see each other, I was driven from my hotel to the restaurant where we were to see each other for the first time. The plan was that I would wait at a table for Andy to appear and then we would chat and have a drink. What I didn't know is that Andy was already at the restaurant on stage where he was going to sing a song he had written for me. He called me to the stage over the public address system, and when I walked around the corner, there he was up on stage.

He started singing as soon as he saw me. There was no audience during the filming, other than the crew and maybe some people hanging around. When I first saw Andy I was overwhelmed. I could not stop looking at him. My heart was just bursting. He must have felt the same way because he couldn't finish the song. He jumped off the stage and hugged me really tight and didn't let go for awhile. Neither did I. It felt like I was finally home again.

While this was going on the crew was very good about being discreet. Never was there a camera shoved in our faces. Afterwards, the crew wished us well, and asked to be invited to the wedding. We actually hear from the producers and crew occasionally. They all said how touched they were by our story.

Then Andy and I went back to his house, and that week was the best week I ever had. We were so in sync with each other. We played music, made love, and talked for hours. I flew to San Jose with him for a family wedding, and both of us were amazed at how everything just seemed to flow. It was like we had been together for years. His family still liked me, and everyone said they hadn't seen Andy this happy in years. I flew home, not knowing when I would see him again.

His sister and sister-in-law bought me a plane ticket for our birthdays (both of our birthdays are in October, I'm 9 days older than Andy). I spent another week with Andy and his daughter and it was even better than the last week we spent together. We knew then that what we wanted more than anything was to be together always. We didn't know how we were going to do that but once again, Fate intervened.

When I got back to West Virginia the second time, I found out that I was being evicted. My house was owned by my ex-fiancé, and my having another relationship was more than he could take. So we decided that the kids and I would just move to Los Angeles. My children wanted to go, having always wanted to live in California. I have been here now for almost two months, and everything couldn't be better. We still don't have enough money, but it just doesn't seem to matter.

My daughter is moving out here at the end of the month; my son is already here. He and Andy get along very well, and I get along great with Andy's daughter Michelle, and the kids like each other, too.

Between the time the show was taped and aired, I was interviewed by my local newspaper and also on my local radio station. It was big news for a small town. I was already well known because of my band and my performances in community theater. We were both interviewed by the *San Jose Mercury News*. It was kind of cool being a "quasi-celebrity." Because there seemed to be so much interest in our show, Andy decided to put up a web page. It's had over 600 hits since the show first aired, and we've received email from people who don't know us personally but wanted to wish us well. What amazes us is how everyone keeps telling us how our story has "touched and inspired them."

Andy and I haven't had even the smallest argument, which is amazing because there's a lot of stress in relocating. What we love the most about being together is that we can truly be ourselves with each other—no hype, no walking on eggshells, no pretending. I love him just as he is, and he loves me just as I am. I have never laughed so much in all my years, I have never been so comfortable sexually with anyone like I am with him, and the music is just flowing out of us both. I've never been able to write songs, and with Andy's encouragement, I've written several that I really like. Andy has been writing songs for years, and it's great to listen to his musical journal.

We can talk about anything, there are no rules. There is no jealousy or possessiveness. This is the kind of relationship that we both have dreamed of having. And now here it is, and how cool that it's Andy, my first love and my last. We know that we'll get married some day, but neither of us is in a hurry. We just cannot believe our good fortune. We were 15 when we met; we are both 43 now. It's like the 26 years apart never happened.

What is really remarkable about all this, is that it has affected other people around us. It's like the happiness we feel touches others. We have been very pleasantly surprised by the support of our families, friends, and coworkers, and even strangers who watched the show and emailed us. All I can say is that whatever Powers that Be helped all this along, thank you!

I married my first love, Debbie, but she left me over religious differences in 1978 after we had been married for two years. In 1984, I phoned her, but found out she had remarried.

In 1992, when Debbie had been divorced for five years, she unknowingly answered my personals ad in the newspaper [*below*]. We married each other for the second time in December of 1993:

> Once upon a time, he lived happily ever after. A White Knight then went on a crusade for a Damsel not in distress. Full hair, six foot one inch tall, Prince Charming collects CDs, antiques, and adventures. Rapunzel, Rapuzel, let your hair down to candlelight dinners and full moon walks. No extra armor. Must love courting and jestering. Calligraphy preferred. Write to Dragonslayer. WRL#53788.

CHAPTER 6

Voices and Visions

Many people who read *Lost & Found Lovers* encouraged me to include a section on spirituality if I ever wrote a second book about rekindled romances. Percentages and significance levels gleaned from surveys, they wrote, cannot fully explain their feelings, the mysteries of these reunions. My most recent survey of 1300 lost love participants (2005) in fact revealed that the number one reason why people contacted their lost loves when they did was because they had vivid dreams about their old flames, which they took as a sign that they should find their lost loves.

Not all of these men and women observe traditional religious practices, but they believe with all their hearts that they are soul mates—that their initial meetings and their reconnections were preordained and "meant to be."

Some people quoted in this chapter have always had spirituality in their lives, and finding their lost loves was connected to issues of their religion and their faith. For other couples, their intense faith that "God put us together" took them by surprise.

Some of the tales do contain improbable and unexplainable events. Perfectly normal people—I have met many of them in person—who are not prone to hallucinations, occult practices, or even superstitions, firmly believe that they were directed back to their first loves by an incomprehensible force. The power of their spiritual feelings cannot be denied.

Last night I was flipping through television channels and found a story about your research. I was intrigued that your project had been taking place concurrently with a series of events that have so revolutionized what I previously believed about life, love, and the nature of time as we experience it. I don't think your statistical observations nullify the miraculous content. At various times over the last two years, I have felt like Richard Dreyfuss with his model of the mountain in *Close Encounters*.

I have been interviewed by the press from time to time over the past few years, and recently there was some front-page coverage of my political work. I expected telephone calls about the article, so I stayed in my office late that day to receive them. So who called? My first love, whom I had not seen or talked to in over thirty years, and who had been living in the same city as me for over twenty years, unbeknownst to either of us until that newspaper article. Incredibly, her first words were, "Do you remember me?" I closed my office door and cried with a primal spontaneity unknown to me since my childhood.

Did I remember her? Did I remember our first meeting at a teen dance in an old house at the lake when I was fourteen and she was thirteen? What she wore, where we each stood, the lights of the power plant across the lake? The sounds of the ducks and the wavelets against the pier where we held each other, and the smell of perfume and chewing gum? She was the template for all that followed. Do I remember? Oh, just to the extent of all the joys and hurts of my life exploding in me all at once!

I had recently become a widower after my wife succumbed to a long illness. Helene had just remarried, only seven months before she found me. We did commence an affair, though we wrestled against it. When she found that she couldn't leave her new husband, I saw a counselor for the first time in my life.

I pulled a lot of things up, reordered many of my concepts. I have no sensation this time that there is closure between us; in fact, I remain sure that it is a new beginning. The mutual emotional ties are strong and complex, the shared vivid memories of our past are pregnant with the sensation of meaning, and there remains a belief that somehow it is possible to go back and redo the past.

You mentioned in *Lost & Found Lovers* your reflections on time. I am sure that many of us who have had these rekindled experiences feel that if anything can bend the arrow of time to symmetry, it is this. These rekindlings bring to mind the lately popularized formalism of quantum physics, the possibility of many worlds simultaneously existing.

And I succumb to the Jungian archetype of The Ring: I gave Helene a ring when we were kids. I had sold my telescope to get the money for it, and searched diligently for a ring with two pearls. I couldn't find the ring I wanted, so I had to settle for one with a single pearl. She returned it when we broke up. Later, I sadly sold it to a pawnbroker. It was my boyhood tragedy.

When we reunited, Helene wanted a ring like I had given her. But she remembered vividly actually receiving the two pearl ring that I had actually intended to present. She even brought me a catalogue picture, which I was chilled to recognize as just what I had looked for all those years ago. I know that I never told her that I failed to find what I really wanted to give her. This time, of course, I did. I am fully aware of the frailties of memory, but this makes no sense at all.

I intend to keep testing the limits of time and realities to see how rigid they really are. But I can say this now with certainty: never have I felt so close to other worlds as when involved in a rekindled relationship. While I fully endorse psychological analysis, I am not persuaded that "formative years" concepts represent the totality of what becomes activated.

It's hard to lose someone twice, to take that second hurt that revives the first (and all the hurts and rejections in between). But I wouldn't have wanted to miss it all, nor to avoid the changes it brought about in me. It has been a renewal, and now I know that where there is a second chance there must be a third, and so on.

Now I know that life is not a game of Dungeons and Dragons, with one false step and you are damned forever. No. What Heaven must be is another chance.

I recently discovered your web site and your research project. My boyfriend and I have a rekindled romance that has an almost divine intervention aspect.

We met in 1992 in a chance meeting in Washington DC. He and I were both in high school at the time, I was only 15, he was almost 17. We were performing in a mass choir of students near the Washington Memorial. We saw each other and spoke, but I thought he wasn't interested in a tall and overly developed girl that every other guy back home laughed at. And through a series of embarrassing and interesting events, I realized he was and I gave him the number where I was staying. We ended up not seeing each other for the rest of the trip, but we spoke on the phone. He lived in the Midwest and I was living in Florida, so of course at the end of the weekend, we parted ways.

I thought he was the most gorgeous and interesting guy I had ever met. He was unlike anyone I had ever known. But I thought I hadn't made a real impression on him. Boy, was I wrong! I discovered later that he was smitten with me from the moment he laid eyes on me, and after talking to me and getting to know me over a period of a few months, he had fallen desperately in love with me.

We talked and wrote religiously and made plans to visit. But I ended up breaking it off because of family pressure and pressure from school. I wondered what happened to him, though, over the next five years, and tried to recreate what we had with every man I dated, which spelled disaster for those relationships. No one could compete with him.

So, I began to search for him online. I even called a search service. Nothing worked. I thought it was over, and I would never hear or see from him again. Until Sept. 17, 1999.

The night before, I was a refugee, along with millions of others, from Hurricane Floyd in the biggest peace time evacuation in history. That night I prayed to God to help me find him, just to see if he was all right and to make amends because I had hurt him so badly. The next day we were allowed back into town and that night, I sat down at my computer to check my email. I logged onto AOL and checked my mail, and then I went to the Member Directory to see who was online. A little voice told me to put his first and last name in. I did, and then distracted, I took my eyes off the screen. When I looked up again, there was his name and profile before me! I instantly knew that it was him, and I wrote him a long rambling email that I am sure made absolutely no sense whatsoever!

Then that same little voice told me to call Directory Assistance for his number—something I had done dozens of times before, but it had proved useless. This time, like magic, it worked and then I had his number before me. With shaking hands, I called the number and he answered (normally at that time, he is at work, I later found out). I immediately recognized his voice. I explained who I was and he said that of course he remembered me and was still a little hurt about what had happened between us. I explained why it happened, that I had found no one like him. I confessed that I had never forgotten him and that I had tried to make every man into him. I discovered with that phone call that I was still in love with him.

We talked each day for months and this past December, we met in Las Vegas and had the best time of our lives. We realized with that trip that we are soul mates and have a deep mysterious connection as well as an unconditional love. He is planning to move to Florida to be near me, and we are talking about marriage. I know in my heart that God brought us together and that he is the best thing that has ever happened to me!

In the late Seventies, my first girlfriend and I decided to end our romance of approximately five years. We were then in our early twenties. We both came from large families, and Alice wanted to get married right away, start a family, and put me through school. I wanted to get my education first, and to be established in a career before accepting the responsibility of being a husband and father. Because of that difference between us, we decided to go our separate ways. We remained friends, however, and wrote or called each other for some time after our separation.

Within a short period of time, Alice had found someone else, and she wrote to inform me that she was engaged. I congratulated her but inside I was very hurt. By the time her plans to marry had ended (almost as quickly as they had started) and she wanted to "get together and talk," I had met a woman whom I would eventually marry. Because I felt that there was no future with Alice, I married within a few months; I really didn't know her that well before we married, and the marriage was never happy.

In 1993, I purchased a CD of one of my favorite country music artists; I bought it for one particular song. For some reason, this song had such an impact on my feelings that it soon became my favorite. The lyrics had some type of meaning and purpose to me that I couldn't really interpret at that time.

Now here's the really bizarre part: the next month, I was awakened from a sound sleep at six in the morning by a "Voice" that was as clear to me as if someone was standing next to me. The "Voice" essentially told me to get up and make coffee, and then go and read the obituary notices in the newspaper. I was startled, and I jumped out of bed to see who had awakened me. At that point, I was fully awake and, when I didn't see anyone in the room except my wife, I concluded that I had been dreaming.

In any case, I did get up and make a pot of fresh coffee. By the time I had poured my first cup, I had gone into the front yard to pick up our two newspapers, a community paper and a regional paper. On that morning, I did scan the names in the Obituaries list of the local paper. I didn't recognize any of the names. At that point, I decided not to mention the "Voice" to my wife and to forget about it myself.

I began getting ready to go to my office. I was standing in front of the bathroom mirror preparing to shave when the phone rang. My wife answered the phone and informed me that my mother wanted to speak to me. Mom asked, "Are you aware that Alice's dad died? His obituary is in today's paper."

A sudden chill ran from the top of my head to the tips of my toes. It was almost electric. I jumped up and got the regional paper which I had not read earlier. Sure enough, there was his obituary with a photograph. I also saw Alice's married name and where she was living.

I decided to attend his funeral; my wife had no objections. It was there that I again saw Alice, the lady I had cared for so much, so many years ago. I also saw her family and our mutual friends whom I had not seen in almost twenty years. I sat in the back of the church and cried like a baby. I remembered all the happy times, the dreams and the goals Alice and I had once shared. I missed all that, and longed for what could have been.

Alice's husband had not accompanied her to the funeral, opting to stay home and run the business. And all I could think of was how miserable I was in my marriage.

Alice and I kept in constant, long distant contact daily for the next few weeks. When both of our spouses found out about our platonic reunion, they suspected that Alice and I had been intimate. We were quickly served with divorce papers! Alice had an amicable divorce, but mine was very bitter.

Within two months, Alice moved back to Omaha. That was four years ago, and we have been together ever since. We are married. We are very happy in our reunion, and our children even get along well and enjoy being together.

As it turned out, we had a number of extraordinary events that have continued to occur in bringing us together. The timing of finding information about your study in a magazine also fits the "spiritual" events and situations we have been experiencing.

And although I haven't heard any more "Voices," I am now acutely aware of events that happen to me, and I look and listen for their meanings. God bless!

My first love and I met and became engaged in 1960 when we were 18. I was just starting a college nursing program and he was in the Army. During our engagement, my father was pressuring me to end the romance; he felt that my fiancé didn't have enough education. Meanwhile, the young man was pressuring me to run off and get married when I only had six more months to complete my nursing program, and I knew I *had* to finish school. I was very angry at my fiancé for his lack of consideration of my needs. So I broke off the engagement.

Four years later I met another young man and I married him. The only thoughts I ever had of my lost love were filled with anger. Then comes the weird part.

One night in 1992 I was at work, sitting at my desk, trying to catch up on some paperwork. All of a sudden I felt that my first love was right next to me— not standing next to me, but just over my left shoulder. I felt overwhelming love and peace and warmth coming from him and surrounding me. My immediate reaction was, "What the hell was that all about?!" It just annoyed me no end because I was still very angry with him, even 30 years after I broke our engagement.

As time went by, I would occasionally feel him near me and feel the warmth coming from him, but never with the intensity of that first time. And also as time went by, I really had to concentrate to stay angry! I finally decided that what I needed to do was start praying for him and his family. The more I prayed, the less anger I felt.

Then I heard about a site on the Internet called Switchboard that contains millions of telephone numbers for residences and businesses. I asked a friend of mine with Internet access to look for him, and she found him immediately, living in Rhode Island. So 34 years after we had last seen each other, I wrote him a letter. He wrote back that he was married, and he had 3 children and a grandchild, but that he had never stopped loving me.

He came to visit me this past summer, and now we write and talk on the phone. He has taught me so much about love and forgiveness, and about being alive.

I told him about the time when I was at work and felt him next to me. He said he had heart surgery at that time and the operation went on a lot longer than the doctor thought it would. He said he went down to no pulse and very little respiration while on the operating table—the doctor thought she'd lost him. So it was a near-death experience.

My lost love added, "So then I really found you first!" I told him that was true, and that I would never have looked for him except that he found me first.

I was 14 and Chris was 18 years old when we met. I was being raised in a very strict household. We got engaged when I was 16; Chris was in the service by then, hoping to make that his career. I had just found out that I was pregnant, and I was worried that my dad would send me to a reform school or have Chris arrested for statutory rape, so I had our family doctor do an illegal abortion and covered up the facts from my parents to protect us all. I wrote and told Chris that we were through, that I didn't want to be married to an Army career man—but I never told him that I had been pregnant and had terminated the pregnancy.

I graduated from high school two years later and married a man I knew my parents would not like. My husband knew that I still loved Chris and always would. I kept in touch with Chris's parents, but they would not give me any information about him; they knew we still loved each other and would break up our respective marriages to get together again.

After 7 years of marriage I divorced. My parents told me that I should not try to contact Chris, that I should not be selfish and hurt his children. So I remarried, this time for almost 20 years. But I never felt like a complete person; I always felt that part of me was missing as long as Chris was missing.

Two years after my second divorce, I had a dream that something was wrong

with Chris's dad. I also had dreams that Chris was very sick and dying. I[...]
to pray that he would not die, to have God send him a message that I[...]
him and still loved him very much. After a month or so, I felt at ease ag[...]
he was okay.

After these dreams, I called his parents' home; his mom had pas[...]
The grandson answered the phone and told me that his grandpa ha[...]
had operations in both of his eyes. He asked if I wanted to speak to h[...]
said to myself, this is my chance to talk to Chris, so I said yes and he [...]
phone.

I said, "Hi, how are you? Do you know who this is?" He said t[...] course
he knew. I said I had one question to ask him: "How do you feel about me?" He
replied, "I still have strong feelings for you… no… I mean I still love you." With
that, I told him I still loved him too, and that began our renewed relationship.

From that point, we talked almost every day clear across the country and
wrote letters. We sent tapes of music, cards of love, and gifts to each other. We
caught up on past times.

Our ESP was perfect. I broke my toe one morning and the phone rang five
minutes later—he wanted to know how badly I hurt my foot.

After six months, he came to visit me after thirty years apart. I nearly passed
out from the sheer pleasure of seeing him. I told him everything about the past,
about the abortion, and we cried and cried together. He said he had been trying
to get me pregnant so we could elope. If I had known that, things would have
been altogether different.

After we had talked for several hours, he said, "You were the lady by my hospital bed when I was unconscious for a month!" He did not know at the time
that it had been me, because the last time he had seen me I weighed 95 lbs…
and the lady by his bed was a lot heavier. I had gained almost 80 lbs. at that time
but had lost it before we met again. He said the lady told him that he could not
die because she needed him, so I knew that part of my message got through to
him.

Well, we got an apartment and lived together for awhile, then married and
moved to Arizona because of his health. It has been 6 years since his death. We
had ten of the happiest years of our lives together.

Ted and I went together in high school in Ohio and planned to elope before I
left for college. But Ted's basketball coach talked him out of it.

We both went off to college in Michigan, and we dated on and off. After
graduation, I went out to Washington on an adventure and stayed. I married

there, and meanwhile Ted married, too. We had no contact for 19 years.

In 1980 and 1981, I had several dreams about Ted, in which he was in emotional turmoil and I couldn't connect with him (the turmoil turned out to be true).

A few years later, Ted began dreaming about *me* almost nightly. He decided to write to me about it, but he didn't know my address. He only knew that I was in Washington. So he gave the letter to his friend who was going to the Grand Canyon—he figured that Arizona was closer to Washington than Michigan!

His friend left the letter under a rock there, said a prayer, and went home. During that same week, I was backpacking in the Sierras and found myself thinking constantly about Ted. So we believe that I "got" the letter, or at least the message!

A year later when I was visiting friends in Michigan, I felt compelled, *guided*, to call Ted. We went to dinner, then lunch the following day. That was enough. We realized that we still loved each other and wanted to spend the rest of our lives together. It took me just four months to move back to Michigan, and we were soon married. That was seven years ago, and we are living "happily ever after!"

Carl and I fell in love when I was in high school. I was 17. He was 18. I got pregnant the first time we made love. I felt so guilty, so responsible. You see, I had been raped by a neighbor's son two months before I met Carl. The son jumped me while I wasn't looking; I fought back, but he was too strong for me. I didn't tell anyone for years, but instead I buried the trauma, blaming myself because he said I was so beautiful that "he couldn't help himself."

What I didn't realize until years later, is that the rape had made me lose trust in all men, even Carl, who I knew loved me. When I realized that I was pregnant, I panicked. This was another trauma, one I couldn't handle so soon after the rape. Carl offered to marry me, but I wasn't ready for that. I wasn't thinking too clearly. I was just a scared, hurt child. So I had an abortion and felt so horrible about it that I pushed Carl away. I felt I'd broken his heart by not marrying him or having his baby. I knew I had broken mine. So, the relationship fizzled from all my guilt and pain and eventually ended when I was 18.

I didn't see Carl for over 20 years. I went to college, got married, and had two children. I thought I was happy. But that all changed when I was preparing my 7 year old daughter to make her first confession. I felt like such a fraud. I was teaching my daughter not to yell at her sister, and I hadn't confessed my own sins in over two decades. The pain and guilt of the rape and pregnancy that I had buried all those years ago resurfaced. I felt I owed Carl an explanation of why I was so panic stricken when I got pregnant. He had no idea about the rape, the reason why I refused to marry him. He deserved to hear the truth, and I needed for him to forgive me for what I had done.

I easily found his work email address by typing his name into an Internet search engine. I emailed him. His email response was very friendly, telling me that he was married with two children and lived a few hours from me. A week later, I called and asked to meet him, saying that I needed to talk about something in our past and to apologize. He was reluctant to meet me, but eventually told me that "Mary Ann, if it helps you out, I will help you get through this."

Several weeks later, we met for lunch. My feelings were so tremendous, so overwhelming, that I couldn't look at him for ten minutes. I talked for an hour, told him how guilty I felt for breaking his heart, that I should have married him and not aborted, and that the reason I could not deal with the pregnancy back then was because I had been raped.

After I got it all out, and he forgave me, I was finally calm. I thought that my "mid life crisis" was over. Until he said, "I certainly hope that you're happily married." It was at that instant I realized that I wasn't happily married AND that I hadn't dealt with my feelings for Carl.

For months Carl and I emailed every day, talked on the phone a lot and continued to meet for lunches. We fell in love again. We just didn't know what to DO with our love. We were both married, but neither one of us was happy in our marriage. I offered to have an affair, but he refused, saying that he wanted so much more. But I didn't think I could leave my husband and break up our family. He was torn, too. It was agony.

The first time we hugged and kissed was when we decided to meet in private 4 months after reconnecting, with the agreement that we would not have sex. That's the day Carl's wife found out. She caught him in a lie that day, and he couldn't deny it. A couple weeks later, my husband figured it out, knew my feelings for him had changed, then gone away. I didn't deny it either, and told my husband I loved Carl and couldn't give him up. Carl's wife didn't want to separate, and neither did my husband. Carl and I both agreed to attend marriage counseling with our spouses and try to decide what to do for the future. Our future.

We were in limbo for months, until Carl made a conscious choice to stay in his marriage because of his small children. I believe and was told by him that if it weren't for the children, that all of this would have been a no brainer. All other possible obstacles could have and would have been overcome (such as financial issues, getting divorced). We would have been together and we would have been married.

I respect him for his decision. It was the only decision he could have made in the end, the only one that morally made sense to us. But it wasn't easy. Timing is everything, and with such small children, this wasn't our time. I will be forever grateful for the second chance, and forever heartbroken that the timing wasn't quite right.

When we reunited the MOST important thing for me was for him to know that I didn't reject HIM back then (it was the situation) and for me to explain what happened and to get his forgiveness. This was much more about getting over our abortion, than the rape. I didn't know how I felt about him until I saw him face to face. The miracle was that he DID completely forgive me, and he had also carried the pain of that abortion for 15 years, until he went to confession 10 years ago (we're both Catholic). He helped me to find the courage to go to a Catholic retreat for women who have had abortions called "Rachel's Vineyard". God forgave me, then Carl forgave me, and this past summer I forgave myself. I needed ALL three to get over this event. Gratefully, I received what I needed from him. I knew I would. What I didn't expect from all this was that he told me that he had loved me, and I believed him.

He is such a honorable man, and he loves his children SO much that he cannot leave them. He told me he would die for his kids, take a bullet for them. This was his bullet, giving me up.

Summer, 1996: There is a school reunion planned! I went to a small boarding school on the East Coast for my last year of high school. The school closed the year after I graduated. Now, twenty-two years later, a reunion will be held on the former school grounds. I am going for one reason only—to see my closest friend from that year, so long ago. Our friendship was a close and spiritual love, never sexual. We lost contact when I went away to college.

The Phone Call: The reunion coordinator gave me John's number. I called immediately, "Hi, this is Connie." Shocked, he replied, "Connie, my God! What the hell have you been doing for 22 years?" We talk and I let him know that he is the reason I am going to the reunion, and that he must go, too. "Yes, I'll be there, " he commits. The next day he calls to tell me how glad he was to hear from me after all the years and how much he is looking forward to seeing me in two weeks.

The Dream: Over the last couple weeks, we have spoken on the phone, getting reacquainted. I tell him about "The Dream." The dream is essential to this whole story. I had a surreal dream within the year following high school, and I always considered it significant. In my dream, there is a platform crowded with people. My father sits in a King Arthur style chair presiding over everyone. He sends me on a errand, and I go begrudgingly, muttering and moaning. I am about a block away when I hear a huge explosion. When I turn back to look, I see that the platform has blown up, and everyone is dead. Everything is destroyed; it's an atomic war and civilization as we know it is reduced to scattered rubble.

Over the next several days, I wander dazed. There are a few survivors and we are all afraid of one another because many people are infected with a rabies type disease. Their eyes are wild, and they froth at the mouth and attack. I hide when I see them. Then a rabid fox is coming after me, and I run for my life; I am so scared! I see a cemetery in front of me; there is no place to hide and I know that means the end, my death.

I look up and see John; I run into his arms and wrap myself around him. He holds me, stroking my hair and rocking me in a circular motion. I hear his revelation that we are all one, in harmony with the universe. "John," I cry with tears streaming down my cheek, "I'm so happy to see you; it's been so long and I missed you so much."

My fear is gone as I am embraced by total and complete love and by peace. The sun is setting over the cemetery; I have never beheld such a glorious sunset. I know that it is my time to go, but I am no longer afraid, I am no longer alone; my soul mate is with me. I know that everything is going to be all right.

The moral of the dream is that when everything else in the world falls apart, only the essence of love endures; John symbolizes that ultimate love.

As I tell him about the dream, he listens on the other end of the phone, leans his head against a window pane and looks out the back window of his home. He is moved and says, "Connie, I love you." "I love you, too," I reply, pure, simple and plain. Afterwards I wonder what exactly we both meant by that.

The Reunion Event: While walking on the school grounds, I gaze at the house where I lived. It's a beautiful, old private estate that was once the boarding school. I go behind the house and continue down the path leading to the former classrooms. I see him. "John!" I call. He looks up. "Connie!" Under the shade of a maple tree, we hug each other long and hard. Electricity shoots through me. I don't want to let go. After packing 22 years of missing one another into one hug, we spend the day getting to know each other all over again. Walking and holding hands, we talk about our lives, relationships, thoughts and feelings. Savoring our day together, we make a pact never to lose contact with each other again.

Post-Reunion and Being Real: I am back at work. I spoke to John yesterday. I want our friendship to be right; I want to be totally straight with him from the start, to be honest and show him my scars, to take a chance that he will like me as I really am.

First Kiss: John is passing through town on business, and I meet him at the airport. He takes my chin in his hand, lifts my head and kisses me. My body melts into his and the passion begins. I lose myself to lost love found.

In our hotel room later, the contact between us is intense. Looking straight into my eyes, he says, "You are it. You are the one for me." We drink wine and feed each other bad room service food.

He shows me a card I sent him for Valentine's Day the year after my graduation. It reads, "My sweet John; There are so many things I could say to tell you about how I feel on this occasion, but I won't because I think we both already know. So instead I'll just say thank you for your friendship. I love you." John exclaims, "I never knew you felt that way until I got the card. Neither of us ever told one another how we felt during high school. I was crazy about you, but I was afraid to tell you. You were a missed opportunity. I promised myself that if I ever got another chance, I would never lose you again. Now I feel as if I've been struck by lightening. If anything ever happens to me, know that I love you; you mean more than anything else."

Winter, 1998: So how do I feel about John a year and a half after that reunion that brought us back together? Kissing and embracing in the waves of the beach still feels incredibly romantic. On the other hand, when I watch John brush his teeth, I can't help but think how adorable he looks. We are confidantes, lovers, best friends, and soul mates. We believe this to be our destiny and our blessing.

After reading your book, I felt like we weren't alone in our wild, deep, crazy, soul mate, twin soul feelings for each other that are still there after 35 years being apart. Our romance had lasted 3 wonderful years but ended when I thought there was no future for us together. I never told my first love why I left him, and he was heartbroken. My heart was broken too.

I eventually moved to a different town, and married on the rebound. Now married unhappily for 25 years, my first love has located me. His search for me began when he had some dreams about me and a strong desire prompted his search for over a year; he wanted to know how I was, wanted some closure, and hoped to begin again if I were unattached. Even though he married 23 years ago and is still married, his love for me never waned.

I had never really thought about him during those years except once when I saw a man whom I thought might be him, but I wasn't sure what he would look like after that passage of time. There was a deep movement within me when I saw that person. Something I can only explain as a moving of my soul.

I also had another soul-moving experience when I was visiting an out of town friend and saw people hiking on a mountain. My soul was moved and I had no clue why. This happened before he found me. I also lost 100 lb. and grew my hair long before he found me.

He found me by locating my grown child; it was my birthday, and he remembered the date. She took his telephone number and promised to give it to me. My daughter said, "That man must really care about you to remember your birthday after all those years." That was the year my husband forgot my birthday.

I waited two weeks before I called him, but there was something moving inside me again. I discovered that for 25 years we had lived in the same city, and our paths must have crossed many times. I now truly believe that he was the man I saw that day in the shopping center.

I felt very comfortable talking to him, but I wondered why he was making contact with me, and I proceeded with caution. We also had access to email and we used that to fill in all the pieces of the years and to resolve our breakup. I am so glad he was able to get closure to that heartbreaking experience; and I was able to tell him about my own heartbreak, which he never knew about.

After three months we decided to meet each other in person. It was truly innocent. We met at a small cafe after telling our spouses openly what we were doing. Neither of us was seeking an affair. We wanted to talk about the past and to be friends in the present. We exchanged pictures before we met. What an experience—to meet someone we hadn't seen in 35 years left our minds reeling. At the end of the meeting, he asked if he could give me a friendship kiss goodbye. Without even thinking twice, I said yes. It was truly a friendship kiss, but from that moment my life was changed. The doors were slowly unlocking that I had thought were closed forever.

We talked by phone and by email, and periodically we met in person. Those very innocent friendship kisses very slowly developed into something much deeper and beyond our control. Neither one of us wanted to stray beyond our marriage vows, but something was happening. His love had never stopped, and mine had been tucked away in my mind, but all was awakened by that first kiss.

About that hiking mountain that I mentioned: he and his wife live nearby and hike it often. He was telling me about their walking and hiking experiences and described this neat place, and I just knew that was the place I had seen, and yes it was. Again that soul deep feeling when I learned that.

Where are we one year later? Deeper in love than ever before, but both of us so full of guilt and conflicts from our marriages. Mine is ready to end. His marriage is a good friendship with his wife and he is torn between his soul mate love for me and his commitment to his marriage.

There is a magic between us that neither of us has had in our marriages. The years melt away. We have learned to be completely open in our communication, and although our love continues to deepen and grow, no promises can be made at this time. We live with patience, hope, and faith. We have our memory box and our dream box. Hopefully our destiny will lead us to be together for the rest of our years.

What we are doing is not just a fling, an affair to be taken lightly to fill some need in our marriages. We do not want to hurt our spouses. We just never thought it would come to this.

I know now that soul mate love is what you dream about and read about; it can come true if you follow your heart. He is my twin heart, my soul mate for all eternity. We believe in the phrase, "You complete me."

I was 17 and my lost love was 16 when we first started going out. We only dated for six months, but still, he is the love of my life and I was his first love. Our romance was very intense and that frightened him; he didn't want us to be sexual partners, because he was focused on becoming a minister and wouldn't let anything stand in his way. He thought we were becoming too serious, so he ended our relationship. It sounds so stupid now: we were about to have sex so we broke up, even though we were deeply in love. There was never a fight, never a cross word. The minister thing got in the way then, and still does today!

Both sets of parents really liked the other. We were so perfect together. So sad! I don't think I ever really got over him. We each went on to college, and married others. I did find marital happiness, but he is unhappily married. I became a teacher, and he became the minister that he had always wanted to be. He is now prominent and well-known nationally and internationally.

I went to his 20th school reunion specifically to find him. I had to know if the chemistry between us still existed. It did!! I found out then that we still loved each other. But his sense of morals, integrity, and sense of responsibility keeps us apart today, just as it did when we were young. If he were in any other profession, things would probably be different. As it is, we are caught in between. Neither of us can let go! And I love my husband very much as well—I can't imagine life without either one of them.

Right now I keep in touch with my lost love by phone, letters, and email. I think of him constantly; he is part of my heart and soul. When we do meet, we hug but we are not sexual and don't even kiss. Our bond is spiritual, very telepathic with each other; we can tune into each other's thoughts ("T mail"?).

I realize now that, years ago, I would not have made a good minister's wife. Later on in my life I did find a deep spirituality for myself, and now I could BE a minister.

Adultery doesn't even enter into this incredible love. I feel we have traveled through time, space, and many lifetimes together. We are both healers, both hear the word of God, both have had dramatic angel experiences. The melding of these two souls has nothing to do with this earthly plane. It is a holy union. His focus and commitment to his calling and his family keeps this from developing further right now. I don't know what our futures will bring, but I do know our bond will never die. This is a love for all eternity!

While I was visiting Hong Kong, staying at the Peninsula Hotel in October of 1953, a scruffy Indian psychic kept bugging me: "Ma'am, I must talk to you about your life….blah, blah." After four days of his seeking me out every time I arrived in the palm-potted lobby, I consented to talk to him.

Somehow he knew I was living on an island. He said there would be a plane crash on December 21 and that I would lose many friends in that crash. He said that I would meet the best friend I would ever have on December 24 and that his initials were TR. I dismissed these predictions as garbage and returned to Guam.

On the eve of December 20, I was sitting with the pilot and crew of a B-50 bomber which was to return to the United States the next day. The pilot, Capt. Tom Ryan, was very nervous that night and said he did not want to pilot the plane the next day. He had been in World War II on bombers, and said he'd never had such a weird feeling about flying before.

The next morning at 6:30 a.m., I was awakened by an explosion. That plane and its crew, with a substitute pilot, had crashed. I lost many friends. It was ghastly. As a Red Cross worker I had to go out to the site. Grim, grim.

On December 23, the man who would later be my lost love arrived with his squadron to take the place of the squadron which returned to the states. I met him on December 24 at the Officers Club, and his initials are TR.

The gal who vacationed with me in Hong Kong, who knew the story about the Indian's predictions, reminded me what he had said. I had sorta forgotten. We were both amazed. How on earth could that Indian have known what was going to happen to me and have been so precise that he even got my lost love's initials correct?

TR was 38 then, a Strategic Air Command officer, and I was 23, a Red Cross worker. We met in 1953 at an air base at which we were both stationed during the Korean War and we immediately "clicked." The first thing he said to me, as he approached me in the Officers Club, was, "You need me to take care of you." I did not turn down his offer, and we became best friends for life. Soul mates, perhaps?

Our relationship created such turmoil for me (due to his being married!) that I deep-sixed (threw overboard) a thick packet of his letters when I was returning to the United States by freighter in 1955. Little did I know that such a ridiculous gesture could not deep-six my feelings for him. What I would give to have those letters back! The only memory-evoking items I still possess are a few wonderful photos and an old striped towel we sat on at the beach.

The relationship was doomed from the start, due to his being married with three sons and fact neither of us was comfortable with the idea of divorce under those circumstances. However, the deep feelings remained, and we met several times overseas and in the United States before I broke away from him in 1957.

Six years later, I married a great guy, to whom I am still married, and we have two grown children, a son and a daughter. But I had never forgotten this fellow and it bothered me that I did not know whether he was dead or alive.

So one day in 1999, when I was fooling around on the Internet, I typed his name into Google. A picture of him popped up with his B-17 crew after they had arrived in England in 1942. Well, I almost fainted when I saw his picture. The photo belonged to a wonderful web site developed and managed for his squadron. I contacted the webmaster, who had my friend's phone number; when I called him, needless to say he almost died. He said, "I was just thinking about you last week… the good times we had. Must have been ESP." He was 84 by this time.

We talked for hours at a time on the phone over a couple of weeks and then, since I was away from home doing some research for a book I had written, and the Labor Day Weekend was coming up and I couldn't work, I called him and asked if he would be free on the weekend, and he said, "Come on out." So I did. Talk about butterflies in the stomach! I was so nervous throughout the cross-country flight, wondering what on earth he would be like and if I were making a mistake.

It didn't take long for the fears to dissipate. Upon arrival at the gate, there he was, just like 42 years ago… tall, handsome, perhaps even better looking at 84. We clicked just like the first time, maybe even a stronger click, very magnetic. So I had really opened a Pandora's Box.

What I didn't know until I returned home was that a recently widowed woman (20 years younger than he) had fallen in love with him. That resulted in a major problem. She would rifle through his papers and read the letters I wrote to him and then show them to her friends and to his grown, married children.

Horrible! In the long run, however, she became the best thing an 89-year old man could hope for: a real companion and caretaker with whom he has much in common. She and I are now civil with one another, and I get along with the grown children; but, I do not see any of them. He and I just talk by phone, and I spoil him with letters, jokes, cards and gifts from time to time (I always felt guilty about breaking away, I guess.) I would love nothing more than to just give him a big hug.

My husband gave his OK for my original trip to visit with him and has been great about our chatting. I guess he trusts me completely and he really should. But sometimes I'm glad he can't read my mind, since the mind is not good at censoring out memories that could hurt others.

My lost love is very cautious about contacting me; he's very old-fashioned and doesn't think it's proper. And he's probably 100 percent correct. He calls rarely, so I do most of the calling, which is also rare. When he does call me, he occasionally chats with my husband.

Looking up old flames is a double-edged sword: wonderful and dangerous. If one decides to make the move, one had better be ready for a lot more than one expects—in my case, after a 42 year separation! What I learned, however, is so very important. I learned that the heart has its own agenda and one's feelings never really go away. They are tucked away, deep down in some corner, hidden until one makes the move. I was amazed that I reacted as I did to this guy 42 years later, absolutely amazed, and that I continue to have strong feelings about him. Always will, I guess.

Your rekindled romance research is important. You are dealing with a slice of life that no one has dealt with before, and it is a very beautiful slice of life, neglected for too long. I wonder if, at the beginning of your project, you realized what an enormous contribution you would be making to people, like myself, who worried through the years about their lost loves and then, after taking the plunge, wondered if their reactions were crazy, whether anyone else in the world ever had the same very strong reactions? The stories in *Lost & Found Lovers*, identical to mine, provided the closure I sought but never could find. Thank you.

In the American Indian culture, the Medicine Wheel is a part of spirituality and in helping people understand how life works. The belief is that everything strives to be round. Everything works to find its way back to its beginning. How many of us grow up and as adults, find that the things that give us the most pleasure are the things we learned to do as children?

It's this way I feel my destined mate will be found. My first love was Charles; we grew up next door to one another, went to school together, matured together. I feel that I will eventually find my way back to him, and he to me.

I located him several years ago, and we wrote letters back and forth for over two years before we lost touch again. I know that someday we will be together because that's how it's supposed to be—going back to the very beginning, following the Great Mystery, the Medicine Wheel, back to where we started.

CHAPTER 7

Overcoming Obstacles

Happy reunions have been hard won indeed for some first loves. Some of the men and women had been addicted to alcohol or other drugs during the initial romances. They later found recovery and became successful partners the second time around—much to their former sweethearts' relief and delight. Of course, not all of them stopped drinking and, in those cases, the reunions did not succeed. For some lost loves, the problem was that their parents had been alcoholics, and a family lifestyle of dysfunction ruined their teen romances.

Other sweethearts had to overcome different kinds of obstacles, such as illnesses and lifelong physical challenges, or disabilities that were acquired later on.

Yet whatever the hardships, whatever the roadblocks, these couples believed in each other and in their love and often emerged victorious.

We met on a sidewalk in Berkeley in 1967. Michael was eighteen, and I was sixteen. We fell in love instantly. My parents objected to our resolve to marry— and not just because we were too young. Michael was a high school dropout, drug addicted and unemployed, homeless and without a car, and certainly without prospects. My dad called him a "bum" and said Michael was "stupid." (Actually he was "stoned" all the time, but I didn't think pointing that out would help our cause.)

We continued to meet secretly after my parents told me never to see him again. He even went to my prom as my date, without stopping first at my house to escort me. We were so innocent, just holding hands and gently kissing for most of our teenage romance. We were not even timidly intimate until I was in college. But my parents filled my mind with doubts about the likelihood of Michael pulling himself together. And they threatened to stop supporting me if I didn't stop seeing him altogether. Michael refused to kick his drug addiction and go back to school, so our teenage romance came to an end.

Twenty-six years after our breakup, Michael got my phone number from Directory Assistance and left a message on my answering machine. He made his call from the other side of the country, in Gainesville, Florida! Our true love was instantly reignited. He told me that he was motivated to call me when he did because he was only six weeks away from being a college graduate and therefore "worthy of me." He had been off alcohol and all other drugs, he told me, for over ten years. And he had a respectable career. There were many phone calls after that, and also letters with photos enclosed, and cassette tapes of our voices or our favorite songs.

We re-met for the first time when I attended Michael's graduation ceremony in May. The next day, while Michael was driving us to his graduation party, he foretold that I "would move to Florida and marry" him. I agreed and added, "I guess this means we're engaged!" So fewer than 48 hours after I had arrived in Florida, Michael's graduation party turned into our engagement party, as he announced our upcoming marriage to his family.

After eight days, I returned home, but only to prepare for my move to Florida. My coworkers threw me a bridal shower/farewell party. In June, Michael and I went to the Chapel of Love in Las Vegas. We returned to Berkeley so I could move out, and my family surprised us with a lovely wedding reception, even though we hadn't invited anyone to our wedding! Two days later, we drove across the country to Florida.

We remain happily married, teenagers in love, at 54 and 53.

Ted and I were almost married September 9, 1972. I was just starting what would become a 20 year problem with alcohol, and I was a mess. I didn't want to bring him down with me, so I called off the wedding only two weeks before the ceremony was to take place.

We went on to marry others and have children. I divorced twice; his wife died of cancer. My brother and Ted continued to correspond for 25 years.

When I stopped drinking, I started thinking about him. I still loved him and couldn't get him out of my mind. I talked my brother into giving me his address.

We began dating a few months after his wife passed away, and one year later we married. We are so incredibly happy that we still can't believe this second chance is real. We talk about it all the time. After a rocky 25 years, we deserve these blessings.

Our wedding invitations read, "Jessica & Ted, after postponing their wedding September 9, 1972, have reset the date to July 29, 1996. You are invited to share their joy."

This weekend, I ran across an article in *Parade* regarding your lost love research. I felt compelled to visit your web site and learn more. May I add my story?

I met my husband while we both attended college at Michigan State University. I was instantly smitten, but very cautious, since he'd had far more dating experience than I. We dated off and on for over two years, but I was a year ahead of him and I graduated and moved to the West Coast (my decision to move was made during one of our "off" times). Neither of us was ready for marriage at that time, even though we both wanted to be together. Our romance was unable to handle the strain of the long distance, and we broke up in 1981.

That same year, I foolishly became engaged on the rebound from him. When his mother broke the news to him, he was heartbroken (although at that time, I was unaware of this). The next year his mother told me that he was about to be a father and that he had eloped! I was crushed. It made no sense to me that I should feel so deeply about it, but tears streamed down my face uncontrollably. To add insult to injury, unbeknownst to him, I had ended my engagement at approximately the same time that he learned that his "girlfriend" of six weeks was pregnant. Except for the pregnancy, he would never have married. It would be many years before I learned of these details and circumstances that led to his marriage.

In 1984, while visiting my family, I literally bumped into him on the street—wedding band, baby seat and all!!!! Ugh… talk about a knife in the chest. I moved on with my life, recognizing the end of what had always been the most significant love relationship in my life. I had always compared everyone to him and no one measured up, so I settled for less—for a while.

In 1989, I received a call from my mother. She wanted me to hear a message left on her answering machine. It was him!!! After 5 years of no contact whatsoever, he tracked my mother to her new home and asked her to have me call him. I thought it was interesting that he left what appeared to be a work number. I called out of curiosity.

He said that he'd had a dream that I was ill and had died without ever telling me how much he'd loved me. He apologized for past pain and assured me he wasn't calling to try to cheat on his wife. He explained that while he was terribly unhappy in his relationship, he did not believe in divorce and he hoped to grow to love his wife some day. He only wanted me to know that he'd cared for me more than he'd demonstrated, and that he was grateful for the role I'd played in his life. I thanked him and assured him that I was healthy and doing well. I felt that his call was God's way of testing me. He was the third of three former boyfriends to contact me in a three month period. So I was determined to be steadfast and not get entangled in any emotional dramas.

Over the next three weeks, we spoke fairly regularly, discussing the past, clearing up misunderstandings, and creating new ones. He was genuinely unhappy in his marriage. But I had no sympathy for him; I felt sorry for his wife for having married someone who didn't love her. I had no idea that he was a victim of spousal abuse.

Finally, I told him that I could not continue to speak with him because it stirred up feelings I thought I had long ago put to rest. Moreover, I explained, I would not be part of a clandestine friendship that his wife could not know about or feel comfortable with. I asked him not to contact me anymore and tearfully said goodbye. He agreed to my request, but asked me to write to his mother once a year and let her know that I was alive and well. She and I had been extremely close when I was in college, but once I learned that he was married, I felt that I should not interfere with her ability to develop a relationship with her daughter-in-law. It had been difficult to end that relationship, but I thought it was best. I agreed to contact his mother during the December holidays… but I never did.

Occasionally I would receive email messages from him, but I would delete them. He called once, and sent a card on my birthday.

Almost one year after his initial call, I became very ill with a debilitating neurological disorder. Six months later, I received an email from him, listing his new address and phone number. He'd left his wife. Nonetheless, I erased the message; I was focused on my physical healing. At that time, I was limited in my ability to walk; I was using an electric scooter to get around.

In December 1991, I returned to Michigan to visit my family. This was my first trip since getting sick. Something (I don't know what) possessed me to contact his mother. The conversation went like this:

"Hi Charlotte. This is Anne."
"Are you married??!!"
"No, why do you ask?"
"Because I haven't heard from you."

[I explained my illness]
"Do you have his number?"
"No."
"Do you want it?"
"I'm not sure… "
"Can I give him yours?"

She explained that he'd filed for divorce and he'd asked her for my number. I agreed, and just 10 minutes later, he phoned. We arranged to meet for brunch the following day.

We talked for several hours. It wasn't about love or getting back together; we just talked as friends. Afterwards, we went to a movie. While sitting in the theater, his leg rested against mine, and I found myself praying that he would NOT move it. It felt so natural to be so close to him.

The next evening he came over to visit. (I was ill and could not leave my parents' house). He said, "I need to tell you something that's going to shock you." He showed me the scar on his arm that forced him to file for divorce. His wife had bitten him hard enough to leave a full set of upper and lower teeth marks. All along my sympathies had rested with his wife, but I never knew or thought about the pain that he endured being married to someone he didn't love and who didn't love him either.

We spent the remainder of that week together. And at my mother's urging, he took me to the airport. When I boarded the plane to return to my home on the West Coast, a woman sat next to me and said, "That man you were with in the waiting area is still there. I think he's waiting to see your plane leave." More tears; it seemed like I was always leaving him. He told me he cried all the way home, too.

We maintained a long distance relationship for six months, and then I returned to Michigan for many reasons (he, among them). He researched everything he could about my illness and promised that he would never leave me again. We had real challenges during the first 24 months, but each new challenge brought us closer together. His mother repeatedly and proudly takes all of the credit for bringing us together again. I have a great relationship with his children; they were very excited about our wedding two years ago.

I have weaned myself off of all medication. I left the scooter in San Diego, and now I'm back to work and feeling well more often than not. My family calls him Dr. Feel Good—as if his love healed me. Well, perhaps it did. Every time we bump into classmates, they are amazed and pleasantly surprised that we are together again.

I would never have imagined that we'd be where we are today. I am grateful for the many challenges we have faced individually and together. We are stronger, better people as a result and therefore, I think, better able to love and support one another through the hard times—and truly appreciate the good.

I am a 37 year old woman, divorced, 3 kids, and waiting to start my new life with my first love. Our story starts 23 years ago when I was 14. I went to live with my aunt in Hawaii for the summer when I was 14. Well, there I was, a young girl in a strange town and in a new setting.

One day while sitting in a restaurant, a tall and handsome young man introduced himself to me. He was also 14, but he seemed so mature for his age. He had soulful brown eyes and a dazzling smile. He asked me out for a date—my very first date! He took me to a private stream surrounded by tropical flowers, very romantic, and he brought a picnic lunch he made himself. Right then and there we fell in love. Unfortunately the summer was too short and I needed to return home to Idaho. Was this puppy love or the real thing???

We kept in touch as young kids. Then I returned to the islands in my senior year of high school, to party with friends, and there was the love of my life. Simply magical! We made love for the first time—we were falling in love again. Then I had to return to Idaho to go to college; he was crushed.

I moved on. What happened next is just so typical of life. He found out I got married, and then knew he had lost me forever. Years went by without any contact, but we always wondered about each other. We wondered what it would have been like if we had stayed together.

One day out of the blue I got an email from him. He found me on Reunion.com; he knew the high school I graduated from and I had listed my email address on my Reunion.com profile. My heart skipped one hundred beats! He wondered how my life was and if I remembered him. Are you kidding? He was my first love! We agreed to meet in Boise on his next trip to the mainland.

The years had changed us, but he still had those soulful eyes, and when he touched my arm, it was electric. At 33 he had never married, but I had a husband and three kids already. I knew I still loved Ron but I just didn't know if I should even let him know. We kept in touch by email over the next year.

Then I received an email from Ron's sister. He had suffered a major stroke! He would not be able to communicate for some time. I had an overwhelming feeling of helplessness. I wrote him a letter telling him that I still loved him, but I just didn't know if that was good enough. I wanted so badly to be near him, but I had my family to care for.

And then I found a lump in my breast. The tests confirmed it was breast cancer. My world was falling apart! How could 2 people so young have such awful health problems? His recovery continued and my chemo and radiation treatments began. And we couldn't be there to support each other!

When I found out about Ron's stroke, I didn't know at that time if he still loved me as I loved him. It was hard to hide my feelings for him—really hard! I wrote to him constantly during those months of hell. Then I had my own worries to think about. Breast cancer is a bitch. I had to rely on my family and friends to get me through surgery to remove the cancerous lump, 4 rounds of chemotherapy, and 6 grueling weeks of radiation. Lost all my hair and felt like a shell of a person.

Then I received an email from Ron telling me he was okay and to be strong—and I knew then that I had way too much to live for. My marriage had been falling apart for the past 5 years, and all this stress was made it worse. My kids gave me strength to survive, and the hope that Ron still loved me drove me from one treatment to the next.

After we both spent a year recovering from our health problems, he came to visit me, just to make sure I was okay. He had limited use of his right arm, and I had hair that was just starting to grow back., but even so, when Ron got off that plane and our eyes met, I knew. I love this man! And then he told me everything, everything I had wanted to hear. He said that even through his deep depression, and learning to walk and talk again, he constantly thought of me… to someday come back to me. He said that the only cards and letters he read were from me. I couldn't believe that what we were going through was real!

And it was magical all over again. We could not deny that the original love we felt for each other had never died. Today we are planning our life together. He is moving to be with me and my children in 6 months, after my divorce is final. He is my first love, my last love. I truly believe in soul mates now.

For my mom's 40th birthday party, I decided to find her first love, of 20 years ago. I hope I did the right thing. She has fallen madly in love with this man, but the problem is that he is a recovering alcoholic. It's a long distance relationship. My dilemma is how to counsel her—should she give up her security at her age to go to this man who has nothing but love to give her?

She is obsessed with this man and has been all of her life. She is the happiest I have ever seen her; in fact, this is the first time since her mother died, 15 years ago, that she has come out of her depression and started to enjoy life. But what if this love affair ruins her life worse than ever?

I only want my mom to be truly happy for once in her life. Is this possible with this man? I'm feeling guilty for finding him. What if this destroys her? Everybody tried to tell me not to look for him.

I asked God a year ago to give my mom some happiness. She raised five children and worked hard. She is the most compassionate woman you will ever meet. I feel like this man loves her, too. As a matter of fact, when he saw her for the first time, he held her and said he finally felt like he was home. What more could be said in his favor? He is very attentive to her and treats her like a lady. Well, maybe I should leave them alone in their love.

A little over a year ago, my life came full circle. It was Christmas, and as usual all 4 children, 10 grandchildren and 1 great-grandchild got together at Grandma's house in Texas for our annual reunion. It is always a busy time of catching up on births, deaths, marriages and divorces. Whenever the marriage/divorce subject comes up, I am usually the subject of conversation, and this year was no different; I announced the demise of my third marriage. I'm the youngest of the children and this year I'll be 58.

My brother and I were talking in the kitchen when out of the blue my mother said, "Oh, by the way, guess who called the other day?" We looked at her and I said, "I give up. Who?" She said, "Dennis." I almost fell out of my chair. Then she continued with, "He calls every year just to ask about you." I was shocked and confused, and wondered why he has been calling and why my mother had never mentioned his calls before now. I asked why she hadn't told me he had been calling, and she said, "He's probably happily married and I didn't want you screwing it up." I couldn't get any information out of her other than that she thought he lived in Ohio and she thought he was a physician.

As soon as I got back home, I went to the library to research my first love's name in the physician reference books. I found nothing. I enlisted the help of a librarian who became interested in my quest when I told her I was looking for my first love, with whom I hadn't been in contact for about 40 years. I searched through phone books throughout Ohio, with no luck. As I was leaving, the librarian asked if I had searched for the name in the computer; I had not. She typed in my true love's name and there he was… with his address and phone number.

All sorts of things went through my head; what would I do with it? First, I looked up on a map where he lived and realized I had a business meeting scheduled in two weeks only an hour away from where he lived. I took a deep breath and dialed his number as soon as I got home. I left a message on the answering machine, "If this is Dennis from Texas, this is Sandy Wilson; please call me at my home number." A few days later, I received a call from Dennis. After we talk-ed a short time, I asked him if he would be interested in meeting me for lunch on one of the days I would be in Ohio. He said that would be nice.

The day of the lunch date, I was to meet him in the lobby of my hotel, next to the piano. One of the things I remembered fondly about Dennis was his pia-no playing, and his wonderful hands. It's amazing how first love impressions stay with you throughout your life—I have since been attracted to men's hands. We had a lot of things to discuss, catching up on 40 years. Mostly it was small talk about our families, spouses and children, and professions. When Dennis broke up with me I was only 18, and had not yet graduated from high school.

My first date with Dennis was when I was 15; he was 19 and a freshman in college. It was a blind date. I lied about my age on the first date because I thought if he knew I had just turned 15, he wouldn't have gone out with me. By the time he learned I was 15, we were dating steady and it didn't seem to mat-ter.

We had gone together for 3 years and had gotten engaged. Dennis was in college and I was living at home in our home town in Texas. We were insepara-ble. The love we had for each other was more real than either of us understood. We were passionately overwhelmed with each other and Dennis was my first sex-ual partner.

During those 3 years of dating, Dennis was often jealous, but it was un-founded; I was never unfaithful to him and all I thought about was graduating from high school and marrying Dennis, traveling with him while he was in mil-itary service, being his wife and the mother of his children. Unfortunately, we had very limited communication skills and for reasons only known to Dennis at that time, he broke up with me.

I remember making a life decision that day, while walking to the door of my house from the car, after we said goodbye: I decided that no one would ever hurt me like that again; I would not get close nor would I let anyone see that vulner-able part of me. I was devastated and cried for days. I didn't understand why I was dumped, so I assumed that he had been dating college girls and found some-one smarter, prettier, richer, more worldly and experienced, and probably older and more sophisticated, but he didn't want to tell me.

Dennis called me a few months later and asked to see me. I was still hurt and wanted to show him that I was all those things he left me for, so after we met, I asked him to drop me off at a Go-Go Club where I was singing with a dance band, and his imagination could go wild; I wanted to hurt him back. I never saw him again—until a year ago, for the three hour lunch.

Soon after Dennis dropped me off at the Go-Go Club, I was coerced into becoming a call girl. It fit into the decision I had made when Dennis left me: no one would ever leave me again, I would become more worldly and sophisticated, I would be in control, and no one would be seeing the real me—even down to assuming another name and identity. I could guarantee that I would not be emotionally hurt by love. Needless to say, that life can be crippling on a young soul, especially one who had such limited experience, like me. I was fortunate to escape that life with most of my self intact. I was careful not to become like what I saw, and though I lived in it, I learned how to survive with limited drug use and self destructive behavior. Through the grace of God, I emerged, cynical and untrusting but still sane and beautiful at the age of 22.

Dennis had heard from his father during those few years that I had gone into "the life," and though he tried to forget that he knew, he began "looking for love in all the wrong places" by frequenting prostitutes. In a strange way we were punishing each other by hurting ourselves.

He married a college girl shortly after he left me, earned an M.D., had 2 daughters and a son, and until last year, led a very comfortable, stable, predictable life—passionless, but safe. I have been married and divorced three times. I have an uncanny sense for picking narcissistic, pathological liars who charm their way past my good sense. After many self-actualization courses—Primal Therapy, E.S.T., T.M., several therapists and marriage counselors (as well as antidepressant drug therapy)—I came to "relationship burnout." That's how I felt at the time I met Dennis for lunch.

I had no idea what feelings would be stirred by having lunch with Dennis. We hardly touched each other, but he seemed to make love to me with his eyes. The meeting was so compelling to me that for the next three days of business meetings, I could hardly think of anything else. I began writing down my feelings—feelings that had been buried away for 40 years. It was like uncovering a time capsule and taking each object out, dusting it off and lifting it up to the sun to watch it glimmer and glisten. It was exciting and scary, safe and intimate, confusing, sincere, fearful, emotional and uncontrolled. I wrote Dennis a letter from my hotel room before leaving, explaining how I felt, never imagining that he felt the same way. I was putting myself on the line, I had decided to be open and honest once again with the only man I had ever really loved, I would take the chance because at middle age, I knew what I had to lose. This time if I lost, I would have given it my best shot.

Although our lives had gone in separate directions, we were somehow always connected. I have tried to explain it with karma and destiny. None of it makes much sense; it's love in its purest form. I believe it will survive and it will grow.

Since we have reunited we have written volumes of letters; that was in the beginning, but letters became too slow for us, so we switched to email. We share our thoughts and feelings electronically on a daily basis. We talk on the phone for hours each week, and when possible we plan short trips to be together.

Dennis still has trouble dealing with the circumstances of my past, while I struggle daily to deal with the circumstances of his present—he is married. This life is full of pain one day and unparalleled joy the next. I don't know where we are going. But as long as we are alive, the heart has the chance to win.

Several years ago, your book, *Lost & Found Lovers,* was given to me. My wife had deserted me when she reconnected with her first love, whom she hadn't seen for 27 years. After eight months of insane devastation, and after reading your book, I called you at your university office, although you may have forgotten me by now. I was failing to make sense of what had happened to me, and I thought you could help me understand my wife's crazy behavior, and counsel me as to how I could get her back. But what I heard instead was your explanation that the situation would probably never "make sense" in terms of traditional logic. Thank you for helping me through that difficult time.

We had several phone conversations, and finally you asked if there was someone in my past whom I would want to contact. At the time, no one came to mind. But after several months, a memory emerged…

My first meeting with my lost love, Cindy, was at age 5 or 6. The images of that first meeting are still crystal clear. She was playing in her front yard, in South Carolina, on a seasonably warm summer afternoon. It was clear, bright, mid afternoon, and I was walking back to my house with my older sister (Cindy lived about 1/2 mile from my house in the "projects," and I wasn't allowed to go that far alone) as we returned from the fairgrounds. I was anticipating the arrival of the fair, a real big deal in our small town of less than 12,000. That was July of 1955. Cindy lived in a house on a corner lot, about half an acre, with her father's paint and body shop on the back opposite corner.

The sun highlighted her golden blonde hair, and when she turned, her blue eyes sparkled and her smile beamed. Cindy has always been petite, she's an even 5' tall. At 6 years old she was skinny, like a kid, and the most beautiful girl in the world.

The feeling I had when I saw her was instant, intense, and permanent. She doesn't remember anything about it. It wasn't significant to her. But when I first saw her, the overwhelming feeling of wanting to be with her struck me. Her image stayed with me from that day.

My family of origin was very dysfunctional: an alcoholic father and a Bible-thumping mother, both from rigid, semiliterate, fundamentalist families. They came from the backwoods—Deep South farmers with extremely limited social skills, rigid fundamentalists, and a long history of "poverty conscience" as the norm. My father put a gun to his head on Good Friday of 1980, and my mother hasn't let go of it yet.

I was the fifth of nine children. I'm the first to get a college degree (at age 40), to sober up, and to retire from a job with a pension. Without reservations, I can say that I'm the most functional person in the family.

Cindy, on the other hand, came from a nurturing family. Her parents were, and still are, religious, but tolerant. Her father owned his own business in the late 1940s, and it's still in operation. Neither parent is addicted, both parents are supportive of their children and extended family.

During the school years, we went to different schools most of the time. My family moved out of her district, but we only had one high school. Over 12-13 years, I saw her at school, in town (we lived in a very small town of about 12,000 people), and at occasional social functions. I made excuses to be where she was and sometimes talk to her, but I always felt ill at ease and awkward. Overall, I probably talked to her less than 30 minutes, tops. Whenever I saw her, my mind went screwy, my voice tightened, and I built a fantasy of who she was. In one of the most awkward moments of my very clumsy youth, I asked her out, but she declined. And at age 15, I went to her house, stood in her front yard and told her that I loved her. Being a healthy girl, and a Southern Lady, she responded that I couldn't possibly love her, because I didn't know her. She was right, but so was I. The vocabulary to explain the depth of my convictions wasn't, and still isn't, available to me

After that, we saw each other occasionally, but not in social situations. When I graduated from high school, I joined the Marines and went to Viet Nam. I spent a year and half in Viet Nam, as an artillery man, and had many lessons presented for my education. Though I had it relatively easy, a few near-death experiences got my attention, and gave me cause to question some of my core values.

Cindy went to school in Raleigh, North Carolina, and then worked in a hospital. She dated the cousin of my best childhood friend, and eventually married him.

I did my time in the Corps, and returned to continue dating a girl I'd dated prior to going in. After accepting that I was not suited to factory work and I was not educated enough to do anything else, I went back in the Corps. While on this tour, at age 24, I married the girl I'd been dating, even though I had been warned that she was bisexual. The bisexuality wasn't the divorce focus; it was the secrets that killed the relationship. After approximately one week, I remember rolling over in bed, noting the clock reading 3:19 am, and thinking, "What have I done?"

I completed my second tour in peace time and got out. I enrolled in a community college, majoring in business administration. Over the year and a half in school, I refined my drinking traits, maintained a position on the Dean's list, and wondered what was happening to my marriage. The marriage lasted less than a year and we separated.

After receiving my second DUI, I enlisted in the Navy, because they offered me electronics, and as an active duty member, I could afford to hire a lawyer to keep me out of jail. I also knew electronics could be useful as a career.

My first tour of duty was aboard an aircraft carrier, and it was on a med cruise. I worked on getting off sea duty, and went into a specialty that didn't go to sea. I was sent to an isolated base in Florida, where I learned about electronics, and got my third DUI. I also had an accident that left me with permanent physical damage to my spine and right shoulder. During my 9 years in Florida, there were many girls, some relationships, a fourth DUI—and then an introduction to AA and Twelve Step spirituality that didn't have the religious baggage I had been assaulted with during my formative years.

Cindy, meanwhile, got a job with county government, married, had two kids, added onto her house and built a social network of functional friends and relatives.

In 1986, I married a woman I'd met in California a year earlier, while going to an electronics school in San Diego. Approximately one week later, I rolled over in bed and looked at the clock… 3:18 am… and wondered what had I done, again.

A few months after our marriage, I changed careers, from electronics to Addiction Counseling. There was an extremely demanding school in San Diego, which I barely completed. In this career, continuing formal education was required. The courses available emphasized functional life skills, and I determined that I needed more help than most. When I compared my upbringing to a list of 20 traits of a functional family, my family had none of them. We came entirely from the dysfunctional list. The introduction to spirituality in AA, along with the realization of my level of dysfunctional upbringing, gave me the idea that I needed to learn new coping skills.

My second wife probably had a borderline personality disorder. She sometimes went from feeling fantastic to feeling like hell in less than 3 minutes. I remember sitting with her watching TV, and listening to her talk about how much she liked our house, our friends, and how she appreciated our life in general. I got up to go to the bathroom, and when I came back into the living room, I knew something had changed. She looked like she had just learned her mother died. Complete personality change. We went to marriage counseling, and over the next 11 months, went through 5 different therapists, and she got into arguments with all of them.

We were on vacation in Yellowstone National Park, when she asked me what I wanted out of that marriage, and I answered honestly, "What I want out of this marriage, is out of this marriage". I told her that I didn't want to fix it, I was tired of trying to make it work, felt like it was a waste of time and effort. She agreed, and we decided to get a divorce.

Eventually, I took a job in Alaska and met my third wife. The marriage only lasted 3 years, but was still the longest monogamous relationship I'd ever been in. With her, there was a deeper level of love than with any previous partner. When she left me in 1998 to reunite with her first love, I was devastated. In the first month, I lost almost 35 pounds. It took almost 4 months to get more than 4 hours sleep in one stretch. My therapist put me on a verbal contract because I got closer to suicide than ever before. The thought of returning to alcohol or other drugs was transitory; that kind of relief wasn't an option. Somewhere, deep down, the conviction that "this too shall pass" asserted itself. I suffered through the worst emotional pain of my life, possibly because I knew that the only way through it was through it. Coping by denial was not an option, and I had learned that finding someone else to make the pain go away didn't actually work, and it hurt another person. That was the point in my life where I accepted responsibility for being an adult.

I couldn't talk to my ex-wife without tearing up, couldn't talk about her without choking up, and I was an addiction therapist. I owned my pain, but saw myself as unsuitable to practice therapy while my life was so painful. I retired from the clinic in 1999.

While I was in therapy and trying, awkwardly, to resolve my grief and anger, I was still talking to my ex-wife. She gave me your book, *Lost & Found Lovers*, to help me understand the dynamics of her rekindled romance and accept the end of our marriage. I read the book, and the idea to question the validity came to me. I contacted you, and you listened. You gave me no encouragement that my ex-wife would get tired of her lost love and return to me, because there was no evidence to suggest that my ex was any different from the people in your research project who were happily reunited with lost loves. There was no support for false hope.

In one of the last discussions we had, you asked me if there was anyone in my past that I could reconnect with. I said, no. The only people who came to mind were people who I had been left behind for good reasons. But, within a few weeks, the memory surfaced about my attempt, 35 years before, to tell Cindy about my feelings for her. And suddenly I also recalled the 1998 news from my childhood best friend that Cindy had been widowed; her husband had committed suicide. I had been married at the time I received that news, so I had stuffed away the memories and thoughts of Cindy.

Also around that time, a lady was transferred into the office area next to mine, and I ran into her in the hall—she looked very much like Cindy. In fact, within the week, I met several people who reminded me of Cindy, and so I began to search for her. Our first contact in 27 years was that January.

When she answered the phone, I attempted to tell her who I was, and to explain the purpose of my call, including the idea of meeting. She was nice, noncommittal, and wondered who the hell I was (though she was a Southern Lady and would never say something like that). I called her several times in the next few weeks, and we talked about many things. During the course of our conversations, she agreed to meet me, and go out to dinner. She decided that even though I seemed unusual, I was not insane.

I flew to North Carolina, and met her for the first time in May of 1999. I looked at her and saw that little girl from the most fantastic summer afternoon of my childhood. At fifty, on our first date, I saw that same beauty, the golden hair, the blue eyes that remind me of perfectly cut blue diamonds, and once again felt the tightening of my chest, the welling up of gratitude, and the eagerness for what comes next.

After our first date, she kissed me goodnight, and I lost several seconds. My brain fused, and the feelings of a teenager took over my 50 year old body. Over the next year and a half, I took many flights from Alaska, and spent hundreds of hours on the phone with her; we agreed to a plan where I would come to North Carolina for 2 months, and then decide if we had a foundation for a long term relationship. In early November of 2000, I drove from Alaska, and stayed in North Carolina until Christmas. We saw each other almost every night.

I sat down with her and told her about my past failures, my infidelities, my shortcomings, my legal record (DUI's), my finances, goals and accomplishments. I was also willing to tell her any details of anything, no matter what. If she asked how many times, what position, how intense the orgasms, ANYTHING, I'd answer to the best of my ability. I had never before had the willingness to do that in any relationship; there was always my belief that secrets needed to be protected. With Cindy, I wanted to begin the most functional relationship of my life.

Cindy shows very healthy traits, in letting go and accepting situations, and she is very patient with me. She is preparing to retire from the county government job after 30 years, she owns her home, and is supporting a daughter in college; her son has his degree and is a manager at a department store.

But she has had her share of life's traumas. In 1997, Cindy's husband of 23 years killed himself with a hunting rifle. His family had a history of suicide, and he had been clinically depressed for 10 years. She found the body and handled everything. She sought counseling and has been actively involved in resolution since.

When we met again as adults, she was still resistant to the idea that I loved her before I knew her; but I am no longer hindered by the dysfunctional social ineptness. She believed that I was living in a fantasy world, and she was simply on a pedestal. Cindy wants to live a real life, with real problems, real experiences, and real love. We agree on this. But she has learned that sometimes we know things without knowing how we know. Maybe my love for her was borne of a child's innocence, and the openness to receive blessings, without conditions.

She has been supportive and very patient, and I've never felt so loved and honored. Some of the wonderful things I've learned in the last few years, she has always known. The joy of sitting on the couch, reading and massaging her feet make my heart sing, and she feels my adoration when I stroke her hand. I love how she makes me feel.

Love is growing between us now, from our shared experiences, our communication, and her patience. A couple of months ago, I asked if she was going to marry me, and she said "eventually," then added, "probably sooner than you think," and my soul lit up.

I have heaven on earth. I've tried to imagine how my world could be better, and can't. The last three years have been the best of my life, and every day I feel a tremendous gratitude for our relationship.

Thanks again, Dr. Kalish, and may you be blessed.

It's 7:30 am on Valentine's Day and I happened to see your segment on *Montel.* You mentioned that out of all the people you researched, very few couples broke up for the same reason the second time as the first. Well, if you had interviewed me, I would have added one more to that list.

Let's go back to 1980, when I was nineteen, and a girl named Melanie came into my life; she was eighteen. She had been my sister's best friend since they were in kindergarten, like a second sister to me, but I never noticed her with any interest because she was just a little brat.

When I was nineteen, I suddenly noticed that she was a beautiful young woman, and she suddenly noticed me, too. We went through a teenage courtship, started dating, and fell madly in love. I had had one or two girlfriends before that, but no one ever made me feel like that before. I knew that nineteen was young to think about marriage, but I knew I would marry her someday; I felt like I could carry the world on my shoulders for her.

For almost two years we were together; then I started to find little notes that her coworker was writing to her, and they kept meeting for drinks. We broke up over this, and my heart was truly broken. I cried for years deep inside myself. In fact, I still cry from this old wound. To top off my pain, she married that coworker after three months of dating him.

After a few years, the pain faded a little and I was able to start new romances. You might think it was no big deal to lose a first real girlfriend; I was still young, but I was truly devastated.

When I was twenty-six, I was playing in a rock band in a nightclub and who do you think walked in? By that time, I had a nice girlfriend, the place was packed, the band was cooking, the crowd was dancing. And from the stage I saw her and my mind froze. She was with a girlfriend, no sign of her husband, 300 people in front of me, and it was time for my guitar solo. I couldn't think and I couldn't move my fingers—at least that's what it felt like in my mind. Actually I was playing perfectly fine, though sweating bullets. We ended the set. I knew I MUST talk to her, but what should I say? Somehow I managed to chit chat with some ridiculous non relevant sentences. Before she left, she said she wanted to keep in touch. Okay, I thought, but what about hubby? She told me she divorced him; he was an abusive, cheating alcoholic (oh, like I felt really surprised and sorry).

A few months went by before I finally got a call from her. My own relationship had ended, so we decided to meet with some friends of hers, just go together as friends. Okay by me. But before you know it, we were dating and all my old feelings came rushing back, and this time she acknowledged that she loved me, too! (Ohmygod! I am now the happiest man in the world; who would believe this? Thank the Lord!!! YES!!!!) She said she wanted to get married, and I always knew that's what I wanted; so I bought a ring and went to a beautiful park in upstate New York, got down on bended knee, and asked her to marry me. She said yes!

Right before Christmas we went to Quebec City for a romantic getaway. It was a Victorian Christmas there, beautiful, snowing, picture perfect like a story from a romance novel. In the snow at the gazebo in the middle of town, with carolers all around, I got down on my bended knee and asked again, and again she said yes.

This was really my dream come true. We went home to tell our families this time. My parents were ecstatic, and they started the wedding plans immediately. Her parents were subdued and cautious; although they liked me very much, they were not sure about their daughter (now I know why).

The following year we had the greatest wedding, honeymoon, and the next two years were great!! I was happy, and she appeared to be. But then something took a wrong turn. She started working with a new group of people and going to happy hours after work; then weekend parties where I wasn't invited even when the party was at our house. The happy hours turned into 6 happy hours, then 4 am happy hours, then every night was a meeting and stop for drinks. Then co-worker George was her new drinking buddy.

Soon she didn't want to be married anymore. Well, I wanted to kick George's butt, even though I'm not a violent man. I blamed him, although it was not his fault at all. I would have tried anything to keep our marriage together, but once alcohol was involved, there was no hope.

So we were divorced after only two and a half years of marriage. It's now four years later and I feel the pain in my heart as if it were yesterday. I have been in counseling, I don't drink or use drugs, I exercise and meditate, but nothing seems to dull that pain. Like a lower back pain, it is always there, some days more than others.

So that's my story on Valentine's Day. Thanks for letting me vent.

Ralph and I have known of each other since the 8th grade, but I really didn't have my eye on him until our senior year in high school. He was popular, good looking, a super jock and all the rest. I asked HIM to the Sadie Hawkins dance. He was going out with another gal at the time and broke up with her in order to join me (he has told me all of this just recently, of course!).

We went together for a year. He recalls us leaving school every lunch hour to make love in the nearby woods… which we did almost daily. We went to the Senior Prom together, and worked on Homecoming skits together and all the rest.

But it was a tough year for both of us. His abusive father died right before we began to date. And my parents "kicked me out" while I was still in high school and only 17 years of age. I was forced to get a job, a car, an apartment and learn to live on my own while still attending classes. He would spend the night at my house quite often; we still recall his mother bursting into my bedroom back then, screaming at us, that because I had my own place I was "too old for Ralph," and she said that she prayed for us to break up.

Maybe that worked, because I broke up with Ralph in order to date my future husband. I invited Ralph to the wedding; he recalls being sad to read a huge banner in front of the band that read, "One sweet dream came true today," from the Beatles. I lost track of him after that, which in retrospect was good… as he turned into a raging alcoholic. (He is clean and sober now for 9 years.)

Perhaps our romance kept his demons at bay for a year or so, but he began to drink heavily right after I left him. He moved to Alaska to be a beer delivery salesman, of all things, and lived there for 10 years. He was ultimately fired because of his heavy drinking. I didn't know how bad things got for him in our absence from each other.

My marriage ended, and I went on to several other long relationships. I saw him once, a few years ago, back in West Virginia where we grew up. He took me to his car to kiss me; he was obviously drunk. I thought that was a one night thing; I had no idea the problems he had with drinking. He threw up in the car, and it was such a mess.

Well, 7 years ago, I started receiving checks in the mail from him. First came $20, and not knowing why, I mailed it back to him. The check was replaced with $50. I mailed that back as well. That was replaced with a check for $100 and a note that said, "If you don't cash this, the checks will get larger and larger." I wrote him back and asked him why he was mailing me money. He said he was in A.A. and he was on the step to "make amends." I told him he had no reason to make amends to me. He wrote back and told me it was a symbol... because the night we met (that night he was so drunk) was the last night he drank... seeing me inspired him to get straight... and I had to cash the check for his recovery. I did cash that check, and he sent me several more. I continued to cash them.... .I liked the idea that I had inspired him to stop drinking.

I saw him for the second time in all of these years at our 20th high school reunion. I was in the bar ordering a drink, and he was fairly newly sober. We were pleased to see each other, but I felt self-conscious about drinking in front of him, and he kept staring at my martini. We were both involved with other people anyway. But we got on so well that night, that I swear, if it weren't for the drinking, we might have gotten back together then. But we said goodbye that night, and didn't see one another again for five MORE years.

I didn't hear from him again for some time. But I knew he'd begun a career at Motorola (where he still works to this day) and lived in New York, about an hour and 20 minutes from where I relocated.

I heard from him again one other time. He wrote a letter asking my views on marriage and children. When we were kids, we both spoke about the fact that we never wanted to get married or have children. I went on to get married, but had been divorced for years, something he knew. Out of the blue came this letter from Ralph, and he recently told me that I responded in great detail (something I'd forgotten), taking the subject from a variety of different perspectives; from society's views, religious, legal, etc. He said my response was at least 6 pages. He has told me since that the reason he wrote to me was that he had gotten engaged at the time to a gal who wanted a big family, the white picket fence, and the rest.

He recalled fondly that I never was interested in the traditional family, and only succumbed, so to speak, when I was young and desperate for help. I think

I married in great part to enable me to go to college. I wanted to be a painter. I earned my degree in Art History.

Ralph received my letter, and I've since learned that it inspired him to break off his engagement. Not only did he not want the children and the traditional roles, but reading my letter, he told me, also made him realize that she was not his soul mate. He told me that somewhere in the back of his mind, he always thought that I was, but that it was unlikely that we'd ever find our way back to one another.

So our 25th high school reunion was planned for this past August. I was on the planning committee with three others, and as the confirmed list grew and grew, I kept asking if Ralph had been contacted and if he would be coming. They all teased me about it endlessly, joking that I was hoping to rekindle the romance. In truth, in the back of my mind, I was. I had just broken up with a boyfriend and it had been a rough break up. I'd only been single for a couple of months, but in truth, I had never forgotten Ralph.

Eventually, the head of the reunion committee, Paul, found Ralph. He was still working for Motorola and had become quite a financial success. But Paul warned me sadly that "a woman" answered the phone" when he called. "He has a girlfriend," Paul teased me. I said, "Oh? How serious?"

"They've been living together for 8 years. They met in recovery; she's clean and sober, too. They sound pretty tight." Well, I'm not one to break up happy homes, but I was certainly disappointed.

The night of the reunion came, and I was taking tickets at the door when he came in. He looked unbelievable. A sober life had done him well, and he was fit—even buffed. He had a better body than in high school, all his hair… he looked gorgeous! I also heard he was rich. Now, I have never cared much about that, but hey, it's not the worst thing either. And the way he looked at me when he came through that door made my heart skip a beat.

Early in the evening, he and I and another classmate were talking, and the subject of his girlfriend came up. I said, "too bad," when they brought her up; and our mutual friend, shocked, said, "Marge, that's not nice!" I laughed it off, said it was "too bad for me," but walked away embarrassed. Ralph has told me since that my comment didn't even register. He had come to that reunion to FIND ME. His girlfriend and he had been in a bad place for 2 year… their sex life had ceased completely, and he even told her that he wanted to date again. The night of the reunion, he told her that he had a girlfriend in high school whom he'd never forgotten and was hoping to reconnect. Apparently she had cried, and he walked out of the house in a fight.

It was almost the end of the evening when he asked me for my phone number and we went outside to talk. I laughed and said, "Are you asking me to get back together with you, 26 years later?" He said he was.

I brought up the girlfriend, and he said he "needed to extricate himself" from the situation, explaining it had been terrible for years. I told him I wouldn't see him behind her back... that I wouldn't be the "other woman." He said he would never expect me to be. But that it couldn't happen overnight. I feared a situation where I would be hanging onto a man in another relationship indefinitely... as we all hear, married men SAY they'll leave their wives but never do. I had to force myself to trust him. He said, "I've never forgotten you... I have always believed you may be my soul mate. I can honestly say I want to spend the rest of my life with you." I told him he didn't even know me anymore... he said he did.

We had our first date a few days after the reunion. When he came to my house, I had our prom picture on the table. He laughed and stared at it, his remark was "this is better than a drink," which was really his way of opening the subject on drinking anyway. He has become an important figure in the AA movement... he's a sponsor and a speaker, etc. I told him that I DO drink and asked if that would be a problem. He said it wouldn't at all anymore... not from his perspective... but he worried that it would bother me if we could never share a bottle of wine together. I told him I couldn't care less.

We talked about his girlfriend and he reiterated that she knew he was seeing me that evening, that it was hard, but she'd been told. When I was as sure as I could be that he was on the up and up, we found ourselves in bed almost immediately. It's not my style, but as soon as he kissed me, it was like an electric current running between us. He said the same thing. It felt like our heads were going to blow off, the chemistry was so intense.

He spent the night with me. When he came home the next day, the girlfriend understood. She found an apartment and moved out two weeks later.

He's everything I've ever dreamed of. He's kind, considerate, fascinating. He's BRILLIANT. He's gorgeous. He's RICH, and although I don't care, it's been fun to be treated for once. Our sex life is the best I've had my entire life. I wake up every morning thanking the universe for giving me such a wonderful gift in the second half of my life.

Within a very short time, I'll give up my home of 20 years and move in with him. Yesterday he called me and asked me where I might want to live in 25 years. I asked him, "Do you think we'll be together in 25 years?" and he said, "I've finally reconnected with my soul mate, and I'm never going to let you go."

Recently, he picked me up on his motorcycle, and we drove to the woods where we used to make love in high school... and then we went up to the high school itself. We were walking around, talking about memories, and then we went out to the football field where he once was the football star, and I was the "mascot" dancing around in a cougar outfit.

I looked over at him and saw a tear dangling from his nose… .and turned around and he collapsed on top of my shoulders and began to sob. I'd never seen him cry before and I was shocked. He sobbed like men rarely do.

He was talking about how he used to make football his "real life," because his real life, with his abusive father and all, was so terrible that he had to pretend that his real life was his dream life. And then he cried about the days we would sit on those very bleachers together… .and how for 26 years he wished we were together again.

And now we are.

In the spring of 1946, three year old Anne moved with her family to Pittsburgh, Pennsylvania, just four houses down from my family; I was five, and we two became immediate friends. I was Anne's protector and hero. I walked her to school when she started first grade; I taught her to ride her bike with no hands. Our parents also became close friends, so the two families took summer vacations together and spent Christmas Eves attending candlelight services at the same church. Life was exciting, joyous, fun.

In August of 1957, at the age of sixteen, my life took a new course. While doing a back dive in a pool, I hit the diving board and dislocated my neck, leaving me paralyzed from the chest down. My family built a house across town that was wheelchair accessible, and Anne and I went our separate ways.

We each graduated from college, married, and devoted our energies to our individual families. But again life for each of us took unexpected courses. Anne divorced after 20 years of marriage, and I lost my wife after her long struggle with breast cancer. By 1996, my son was in college, I had been teaching high school English for 29 years, and I was looking for a new challenge. Anne's children were also launched, living in Europe. Her work in Denver with the managed care industry required a great deal of travel, which she enjoyed, but it also left her quite alone.

I learned over the Internet about research being conducted on spinal chord injuries at a rehabilitation hospital in Denver, and I went there for an evaluation. I hadn't spoken to Anne in more than 30 years, but I knew her sister lived in Denver so I gave her a call when I arrived. She told me that Anne also lived in town, and she suggested that we all get together.

As soon as Anne and I saw each other, our hearts were singing. All of the excitement and joy they we had experienced together as children transformed itself into a mature form; we were in love. We saw each other once more before I returned to Pennsylvania and Anne left for Europe to spend the Christmas holiday season with her children. But now even a continent couldn't separate us. Thirty-seven email messages and 20 phone calls later, Anne couldn't stand the separation any more; she changed her plans and made reservations to fly to Pennsylvania for the last week of her vacation.

The change meant taking a train from Florence to Frankfurt and flying from there. While she was changing trains in Milan, she was robbed of all her money and her passport. The conductor said she would have to get off the train in the middle of the night when they entered Switzerland and advised her not to board. Anne could only think about being with me; she took the risk. She managed to cross two borders and enter the United States without a passport. After 48 hours, my arms were around her.

For the next eight months, we did everything together. I accompanied her on business trips, spent my winter vacation in Denver with Anne, and her work provided many opportunities to spend time with me in Pennsylvania. Soon I retired from teaching, put my house up for sale, packed up my car and drove west. Anne found a beautiful wheelchair accessible apartment for both of us in Denver.

Today we are living our lives together, again with joy, enthusiasm, and excitement! This Christmas, for the first time in over thirty years, our two families will celebrate together. And of course now we have our children, too. What a miracle!

We met at the Perkins School for the Blind in Massachusetts. I have limited vision; Anjali has very little vision. I didn't really pay attention to Anjali until several months before I graduated. I was nineteen at that time, and Anjali was almost 4 years younger. Sometimes I would stay at Perkins for the weekend to see Anjali; I lived close by, maybe ten minutes away. Anjali lived at the school, because her closest relatives were far away, in New Jersey. We would go for ice cream, or to the mall now and then with friends.

One day I went to the Watertown Mall and bought a friendship ring for Anjali. We even told some friends we were engaged. We both went to the senior prom, but we didn't go together; I don't know why it happened that way. My friend asked her before I did, and she accepted, so I went with another very good friend. You would think that after I gave her the ring, she'd go with me, but she accepted his offer.

In 1982, her financial scholarship, provided by the school, ran out and was not extended, so she had to go back to India; she finished high school there. That year I graduated from Perkins, and we lost touch.

My life has not been limited. I went on to attend college in California, and I even had a wonderful experience swimming with dolphins in Florida, down at the Keys. I've always loved dolphins. I wound up taking the trip down there by myself. I stayed in a little "mom and pop" inn, and they were really kind to me, drove me around.

Meanwhile Anjali went on with her education and earned a Masters degree in medical and psychiatric social work. She worked at a hospital in Orissa, India, where her parents are administrators; she opened a wing at the hospital for psychiatric patients.

I never forgot about Anjali. When I tried to write to her, all I had was that old address. And for 14 years I kept trying to get in touch with her through letters, hoping that if she didn't get my mail, somebody who knew her would. But she never answered. It went that way until 1996, when someone (I think it was a postal worker who took pity on me after all those letters) sent a little note back to me, saying that she had moved and giving me the updated information. So I wrote again, and this time she received it. But she didn't answer until she got my second letter.

We wrote back and forth from April until September; then I wrote, "After fourteen years, I know I love you." Her cousin was a little suspicious and told her, "How can he say that? He hasn't seen you in fourteen years." But she was in my heart all those years. You never let the memory die and always have that glimmer of hope.

We started talking on the phone—you should have seen my telephone bills! I was planning to go to India to see her in the winter of 1998, but Anjali said, "Why can't you come sooner?" She wanted to know what my intentions were. I thought it would take me that long to save the money. But then I realized I had a gift that my brother left me (he died), so I went with that.

I left for a six week trip to India on December 28 and got there on December 30. It's a long flight! And there was a long layover, seven hours. I had an engagement ring in my pocket, and I clutched it tight through the whole trip. I was even worried that my pants would rip all of a sudden and the ring would fall out.

Her brother met me at the Delhi airport, and I spent the next day with him. Then I had to take another plane to her aunt's house; I stayed there for four days. Anjali and her parents were there, too. They drove us to Anjali's house, a twelve hour car trip.

When I saw her silhouette, she was just as I remembered. On New Year's Day, 1997, I took her out into the hallway of her aunt's house and handed her a box. She asked, "What's this?" I said, "It's a ring." She asked, "What for?" Then

I asked her to marry me. She said yes, but she said she'd better talk to her parents.

So we called them into the hallway. They saw the ring and loved it. But I had only been there for one day and they wanted us to wait and get to know each other again. They were also a little worried that my physical disabilities were worse than they are (along with limited vision, I have mild ataxia, a balance problem). In spite of their hesitation, we got engaged January 28. They are happy for us now.

In India, getting engaged is a big thing. There were 80 to 100 guests at our engagement party, held on the grounds of the hospital complex. We still had to wait ten months after that before we could get married. We were separated again, until Anjali could get all the necessary papers to come to the United States.

We got married in Massachusetts in June, 1998. Also in June, we attended a reunion of my class at Perkins, and it was fun to go back there together.

Anjali is waiting for her immigration permit to come through, so she can work. But it's hard to find something in her field. Marriage is always a challenge, and it's especially difficult coming from different cultures. We aren't sorry that we got married, though. It just felt right. That's what love is—it never dies.

CHAPTER 8

Divorced and Found

Some reunited lost loves had been married before—to each other. The first time around, they were young and unable to effectively communicate to resolve problems; they had difficulty coping with the demands of marriage and the pressures of the outside world. These situational problems clouded their love, and they parted. Although they eventually married new partners, they never forgot each other.

Some former husbands and wives longed for each other but did not reunite. Other couples, when their second marriages failed, returned to each other.

My research findings indicate that even people who return to ex-spouses can have successful reunions. Here are some stories from these divorced and reconnected couples.

Eleanor and I were married in 1950 after a relatively brief courtship. She was 21 and I was 23. Our marriage was a happy one in the early years, especially for the two years when our daughter was born and I was on active duty in the US Navy. We were out of the pressure that she had been feeling in my hometown, and that strengthened the marriage. When we returned to my hometown environment with all of my family and friends, the relationship weakened and we drew apart. I actually felt so unhappy that I thought maybe we would be better off separated. However, when Eleanor actually asked me for a divorce in 1958, I was stunned, and I felt very guilty.

She and our daughter left our home to return to her hometown, leaving me deeply distressed. I realized that I didn't want to lose them and sought help from our pastor; he referred me to a pastor/counselor in a nearby town. For the next year I worked with this counselor to sort out my feelings. All the while I was trying to get Eleanor into counseling and into a reconciliation. Finally, I felt the prospect of an actual divorce might somehow lead to a reconciliation, so I agreed to proceed. The divorce became final in 1960.

During the next several years, I tried to renew the relationship while I continued with counseling. It was a time of real soul searching for me. My thoughts of suicide at my lowest point reawakened my faith in God, in Jesus, and in the church. This, I feel, was the good that came out of our divorce.

Four years later I met the woman who would become my second wife. We enjoyed a marriage full of love and deepening religious faith. We had four wonderful children. In 1992 we were told that she had ovarian cancer, and within a year she died. Her faith through her ordeal was beautiful and deepened my love for her.

It is a bit difficult to explain, but I began to think of Eleanor, even though we had only seen each other twice in the 33 years we were apart. Our daughter had kept us informed of each other's lives, though. I tried to date several women during this period, but found it very unsatisfying. One evening in 1994, when I knew Eleanor would be at our daughter's house for her birthday, I called to talk to my daughter but also asked to say hi to Eleanor.

The following June, I was participating in a sailing regatta near her hometown, and I called to ask if she and her husband would have dinner with me at the lake the next day, after the races. When I came off the lake, Eleanor was waiting on the shore. It was good to see her and we talked so much we hardly ate anything.

When I got back home several days later, I found a letter from Eleanor in which she poured out her feelings for me and related the unhappiness of her current marriage. I truly felt that within me there must have been a spark of love for Eleanor that had never gone out through all the years. In a number of long telephone calls, our love blossomed. She arranged to divorce her husband and we married shortly after the divorce in 1997.

We have now been married for 2 years and worked our way through some rough spots. We are now 66 and 68 respectively. We enjoy sailing, golf, and work together. We worship together in the home and at our church. I think we most enjoy laughter and wonderful sex beyond our wildest fantasies. I feel this is God's way of answering my prayers of many years ago to reunite us.

My father was stationed in Japan when I fell in love at 16 with a handsome officer in the Maritime Self-Defense Force (navy). It was love at first sight for both of us, and we spent the next few years fighting everyone's objections to be together, especially his parents. When we married, I was only 20. We were so in love with each other that we just had to spend our lives together, so we married.

My family returned to the States soon after, and life away from my family and the stress from having to conform to a different society, and having to be bothered by the disapproval of the other officers' wives all the time, made it too difficult for me to bear.

I left Japan and returned to the United States in 1990. When I left, he had no idea that I wasn't coming back. For 2 years, he kept pleading with me to return, but often I would just hang up when I knew it was him. I guess I was really afraid that if I spoke to him longer, my resolve would break down and I would return to him. He once said that he would come to get me, and I willfully told him that I would not change my mind even if he did. However, I knew that I would not be able to say "no" if he came here, but he did not come to get me like I secretly wished he would.

I finally divorced him in 1992, in Japan. It was ironic that when we met for the divorce after two years of not having seen each other, we were holding hands and spending time as if we had never been apart. There were lots of tears after signing the papers and again at the airport as I was leaving. We both thought that we would not have these feelings for each other since we had known all along that we were going to get a divorce.

We were still very much in love, but staying together, especially when he was in the military, would have been too difficult for me again. He called me a week after my return to the United States and said that he was still missing me and that if he still felt this way after a few years, he would not care what anyone said and would come to get me.

I heard from him again after six months, when he called to say that he was going to remarry. He needed to remarry because divorce was taboo in his conservative naval unit, and apparently there were no divorced personnel still active in the forces. He had trained for a lifelong career in the service, so the only option he had was to remarry and get his life "back to normal" again, so that our divorce would not have an adverse effect on his chances for promotion later. Further, his father was dying, and his last wishes were for my ex-husband to have a stable family life. So my ex-husband hastily made the decision to marry after three months of meeting her (his father died a few weeks later).

I was devastated and had to struggle very hard with the urge to go back to him. However, I was also painfully aware that even if I really did return to him, there was no way his family and friends would accept me again. I dreamed that I flew there to stop the wedding, but I did not make the trip after all, and I did not hear from him again.

More than 7 years have gone by since our divorce. I went on with my life, not knowing where he was or what he was doing. I have met other men throughout the years, but these relationships did not touch me enough to want to settle down with them. However, the strangest thing started happening the last couple of years: I began to dream about him and our life together. It was really weird, because I honestly thought I did not regret my choice and was very happy with my life. As I have matured over the years, I have come to realize how much pain I had caused him. If someone had hurt me the way I had hurt him, I don't think I could ever forgive that person. I felt I needed to talk to him and say that I was sorry; so I began my attempts to track him down.

Last November we spoke for the first time in 7 years. I knew it would not be right to contact him now that he has his own family, but I wanted to know that he was happy with his life. We spent almost 3 hours on the phone catching up. We found out that although we hadn't been in touch, we had been missing each other and having dreams of each other. We both had been wanting to contact each other, but did not, because each thought that the other party would not want to be reminded of the past. There had even been several times when he had called me, he said, but he always hung up when he heard my voice or when my phone started ringing. I remember those times and could not figure out who was calling me.

He remembered every detail of how we met, the places we used to go to, and even the orange coat I used to wear when we were married. There seems to be some kind of connection, because those times when he dreamt about bad things happening to me, or when he started to call me but did not complete the call, were difficult times in my life. I dreamt certain things about him, too, that I didn't know about, but after our conversation, I realized they were true.

We could not believe that time and distance had not taken away our feelings for each other, even though we had not been in touch all this time. He now has one son who is five and another son who is three. We both know that the fact that we still having these feelings for each other is not fair to his wife; he says that he really feels sorry that when he is with her, I am always in a corner of his heart. I asked him if he is happy and he said no, but that he was simply living out life.

Can you imagine that he says he sees my resemblance in his daughter's face and remembers me again when she puts on his parka that is the same color as the coat I used to wear? He recalls certain things we did together or places we went together in the past when he goes there now with his family. After I left him, he told me that he lived in a house without unpacking while he waited for me to return… for 2 years.

We finally met up, for the first time in 5 years, last month. When we saw each other, we exclaimed spontaneously that we each looked the same as the time we last saw each other. We both felt as if the years had melted away and we hadn't been apart at all. We spent a day together and everything felt exactly the same like the time we were married and so much in love. I thought that he would not be comfortable walking with me in public, but he actually asked for my hand and held it the way he always used to do when we went out. I did not sleep very well that night, because while he was holding me snugly in his arms with my head on his chest as he slept, I kept looking at him. I wanted to save every single moment I had with him and remember him properly.

I asked him how he was able to "move on" and decide to remarry. He said that he does love his wife, but that love is different from what he and I had (have?), because he loves her as part of his family. He said that he has never been able to forget me, but he buries those emotions and memories and keeps busy with life. He thinks it will be the same for me when I remarry. When he's with his family, he has to be responsible to them, but when he's alone, especially when he's out at sea, his mind is free to wander and then he can think of me.

He feels duty and obligation towards his family, especially since his kids are so young. He feels pain, being stuck in the present situation, not able to turn either way. When he asked what I would do in his shoes, I told him I would do the same and would stay with the family. Perhaps someday, when his kids are grown up, he will be free to come to me. He realizes that it is not fair to ask me to wait that long for him, so he wants me to find a nice guy, marry and have kids. He has asked me whether I thought I would still love him the same after I remarry someday. I believe that my feelings will not change and he thinks this, too.

We agreed that we would now keep in touch mostly by phone. He cannot travel as he wishes due to his military status, but we could meet up if I travel to Japan. It is ironic that I am now the third party, considering how I was his first wife. I never imagined I would be in this painful situation.

I was very sad the day I left and was crying on the limousine bus on the way to the airport; but hearing him tell me something just before I boarded the plane changed my mood entirely. I could feel that he was trying his best not to express his emotions, but he did tell me that he loves me "a lot, so much." Although we realize that there is nothing we can do at this moment, just knowing that he loves me and has always loved me this much warms my heart. It is that thought that gives me strength to go on.

Before reading your book, I thought that the possibility of us coming together again in 10 or 20 years' time. when his kids are grown up, was just wishful thinking. I told my closest friends that it would take a miracle for that to happen. But now, after reading about your research, I see that it might not be impossible after all.

It is one month since our reunion. I have been on an emotional roller coaster, trying to deal with the feelings he awakened. I recognize that I have to let go of him to do what he has to do, just as I have to get on with my life—for now at least—but I cannot handle the total silence from him.

We met when I was only thirteen and got married when we were still teenagers. Looking back, I can see that we were just too young. We divorced, even though we never really stopped loving each other. We just didn't know how to work out our differences.

Twenty-six years later, his mother brought us back together. Once we reunited, I understood why I was never happy with anyone else. My emotional attachment to my first love, my first husband, had merely been buried so that I could go on with my life and make the best of what life offered.

Both of us found new spouses, but we were again divorced when we saw each other again. We had been in bad second marriages, thinking that was as good as we each were going to get. But within minutes of meeting at his mother's house, we realized how much we still loved each other.

We remarried nine months later, on the twenty-eighth anniversary of our divorce. I tell people we "had" to get married, because the monthly phone bills were about $600; it was cheaper to get married than stay single. Our remarriage to each other has had some perks—when we mixed our furniture, everything matched into its original set!

Sure, there have been minor adjustments in living together again. Some are issues that were insurmountable when we were married before, but they're nothing we can't live with easily now. And we are far more ready to accommodate to each other now, in our maturity. For instance, over the years he has learned to pick up and clean up after himself (thank goodness!), and I've learned to cook and to allow him some space of his own.

We like each other and we are best friends, along with the deep love we never lost for each other. There's no doubt that we will be together for the rest of our lives.

Shelby and I knew each other in junior high, in the early 1940's, and all through high school in Washington, but we didn't date then. He went in the Navy after graduation, and I dated others for a couple years.

One day I was on a double date with friends and we went to the local ice rink to watch the skaters. I noticed a handsome man who looked familiar in the center of the rink doing figure 8's. I waited at the rail until he came over and asked if he wasn't Shelby, and he said yes, that he'd just returned home from his duty with the Navy and would call me when he purchased a car.

In the meantime, while waiting for his call, I continued to date, and one of the men, George, owned a used car lot. I'd been dating George while waiting for Shelby's call. Shelby didn't know I'd been specifically dating George.

Three months later, Shelby called to announce he'd bought his used car, and would it be okay if he came over to show me. I literally broke a date and waited for him to come out with his "new used" car. I saw the car driving up the driveway… and felt sick because it looked like the car George owned. A closer look told me that it was Shelby driving the car he purchased from George. He was so excited about his "new car" that I couldn't tell him I'd ridden in it and driven it all over! But I managed to share the enthusiasm with him, and he literally knew nothing—zip—about it for months afterward. To this day, we laugh about it. So anyway, that was the start.

Once I started to date Shelby, we dated exclusively. Months later, on July 17, 1948, we were married in a local church that was filled to capacity. The local newspaper wrote that it was one of the prettiest weddings of the season.

Nearly 3 years later, our daughter was born. I was a stay-at-home mom for the most part, participating in community affairs and working part time for local dentists and physicians. Shelby was with the telephone company.

We had an active social life, and we were invited to house parties every weekend, where liquor was always served. At first I did not enjoy alcohol. I was a teetotaler, but I began to have a beer now and then, just so I wouldn't be called a party pooper. But over the years, about 13 years into our marriage, I acquired a taste for it. Shelby and I put a bar in our home. I started to drink heavily.

But did I think I had a problem? Of course not. Even when my hands trembled each morning, alcohol was not my problem. And when my at-home liquor consumption went from $21 to $128 a month, I still did not have a drinking problem. Shelby knew that if he didn't go to the store to get me the booze, I would drive drunk, so he went—so often that he made friends with the liquor store clerk. She became his shoulder to cry on. But no one could tell me I had a drinking problem.

In truth, of course, I was slipping deeper and deeper into alcoholism. Eventually, Shelby couldn't handle it anymore. He said he didn't know what to do for me, and he saw everything he had worked for going down the drain, so he left me. I hold no grudges. If he hadn't left me at that time, I probably wouldn't be here today.

At first, after he left, I continued drinking. But after I got four DUIs in one year, I was sentenced to jail, with two weeks to get my affairs in order. That's when my friends told me about a hospital in Seattle that treats addictions. I was admitted to treatment in lieu of the jail sentence, and I haven't had a drink since then, 1970. Not one slip.

Shelby stayed in our hometown in Washington, and married the clerk he met at the local liquor store where I'd send him to buy my beverages! He continued his work with the telephone company. During his marriage to the liquor store clerk, he spent his free time alone, going to Reno or hunting or fishing. They did nothing together. He didn't want to go through another divorce, so he simply made the best of it. Sadly, our daughter wasn't able to have much contact with her dad in those years, because "the clerk" was extremely jealous and insecure.

When his wife got Alzheimer's, he couldn't leave her, so he stayed until she died, all the time caring for her at home with the help of a nurse-aid 40 hours a week. He retired in 1993, after 43 years with the phone company.

As for me, I stayed in the family home until 1979, working for the Washington Department of Labor and Industries (workers' compensation). I kept busy, but I never once dated. No one could hold a candle to Shelby, so dating was never even a consideration. Through sobriety and celibacy, I prayed daily for him to return to me.

I moved to California in 1979 to be near our daughter, Carol. I worked for the County of San Diego, workers' compensation, until my retirement in 1993. I kept busy, invested in real estate and stocks, and pursued my hobby, photography. And every day, I still prayed that Shelby would return to me.

I was on a trip to our hometown, to see my family in Washington, when Carol called me from California; she said that she'd given her dad a wallet for his birthday but he didn't like it; she asked if I would accept it from him, if he came over to my sister's house, so I could bring it back to Carol to exchange it. I had not seen him in 30 years! My heart was all aflutter—I told Carol I didn't look too good, but she just told me to fix my hair and put on some lipstick... I did. When he came, I was like a kid again.

I shared with him that there were two things I said to people during our years apart: 1) that he left me when I needed him, and 2) that he left and saved my life. I've been told that I had been near death, and if he had stayed and enabled my addiction, I would indeed be dead.

I returned to California, and he called to confirm how sick "the clerk" was. And we exchanged feelings for each other. He called a few days later to tell me she was dying, the next day to tell me she had died, and on the third day he called to invite me to come see him. I got on the next flight. And although he felt guilty for not being around for the last 30 years, we picked up right where we left off, as if there had been no separation at all. It just shows that prayers are answered.

Our daughter has never taken sides, and she told me that I was ill and to forget about it; she understands that I didn't know what I was doing during my "dark years," and she was so moved and happy to see us get back together. She gave us a beautiful welcome home surprise after our trip from Washington, when we'd gone back to settle his affairs prior to his move to California. She'd come into our home (she has a key) and cooked a beautiful dinner, set a festive table, put up balloons, candles, a Welcome sign… the whole nine yards for us!

And that brings us to our remarriage, in February, 2002, with our daughter and grandson as our attendants. Tears ran down her cheeks at our wedding. I wore the same wedding gown I'd worn some 54 years ago, with no alterations, and it was the wedding photographer who suggested we share our amazing story; it was in the newspapers and on local television.

It truly is like we've never ever been apart (except we are a little slower in activities due to so many birthdays—I've had 75, and he's had 76. We spend a lot of time with our daughter and her family, I am active in a homeowner's association, we enjoy the casinos (our daughter was planned, but no luck, so we went to Reno in 1950 and she was conceived). We go to horse races during the season, and take advantage of all the other things there are to do in San Diego. We share a lot of history, obviously, and there's never a need for disagreements; we simply know each other too well.

He'd left me in 1969 in sheer desperation, I received treatment in 1970, and he reentered my life in 2002. That makes 33 years apart. Our story is about determination (to not drink), patience (a 33 year wait), true love (no one could ever hold a candle to mine), prayers being answered (I honestly prayed for his return daily), and I suppose I could add self-respect (because there was NO WAY I'd ever think about a drink following treatment).

He knows I've waited 33 years for him to return—just like I waited for "my husband" when I got married. Guess I'm not too trendy to be a virgin when I married and all those years of celibacy during the second wait for him, but I really see nothing wrong with that.

My heart still flutters when he enters the room!

I bought a copy of your wonderful book for my first wife, after buying myself a copy and finding it so true to life. I gave her a copy for her birthday. We had just begun speaking again after 7 years. We are both 33 and were divorced after a rocky three year marriage. No kids. Since last year, we have emailed regularly and spoken on the phone some. We've made a couple of short day trips. I am married with a young daughter, and my former wife is living with the man she left me for.

Anyway, one evening three years ago, I called her and she said I could stop by that night; her significant other was out of town. I had visited at night a few times before (I'm a cop and it's easy to just stop by while on patrol). The other night I was working plain clothes and went off duty at 9:00 pm. So I stopped and bought us a bottle of wine. Not trying to be romantic; I just thought a glass would be nice. Really.

The wine and the talking led to hand holding and then a kiss and then passionate kisses, then admissions of still loving each other by both of us. We both cried and held each other and kissed some more. After a while I left and went home to my wife and little girl. But I haven't been able to think about anything but her since that night. I have always loved her, even after we divorced, but she had not shown any romantic feelings for me since we separated, until that night. We both had betrayed the other and hurt each other so bad that I guess it took that long to forgive each other.

Nancy, I guess I'm writing just to say that you are on the right track with your research. People who have never been reunited with a true love lost cannot appreciate the intensity of the feelings and the overwhelming emotions when it finally happens. I knew in my heart, even before I read your book, that first loves are the best loves. I knew that if we reunited, we would make it the second time, because it is true love. Also I want to say thank you for giving me the courage, through your writing, to try to repair some of the damage and to try to have some kind of relationship with my true love. I'm a good father and would never break up my family for my own feelings outside my marriage. I will remain here for my daughter. Don't get me wrong, I love my wife. She is a good wife and a great mother. But that first love… ..Nancy, you understand, don't you?

The attraction some people have for each other and the deep feelings true lovers share are too strong to resist. I imagined that eventually we would wind up in bed together, my first wife and I, and so we did. I just wasn't strong enough not to. And I hate it. I want to be a better husband and father than that. But I just don't know. I'm in a hell of a situation. I have a dream come true in that my long lost true love finally told me that she loves me. I have dreamed of hearing those words from her. Now that I hear them, I can't have her without losing my daughter. I couldn't stand to not have my little girl in my house every day I'm there.

We live only miles apart and work in the same small town. We see each other only when her significant other goes out of town on business. Usually that is only two or three times a year. I go to her house where we sit on the couch and drink our favorite wine, watch music videos, hold each other, and I'll rub her feet while we talk. Just good quality time that we steal when we can. On a few occasions (three to be exact) we have crossed the line and made love. Those few hours we occasionally have together make me so happy and fulfilled. I yearn for more, but I remember how it was when I didn't see or talk to her for over seven years and then I am thankful for the few hours now.

The last time we were together we both shed tears again and told each other how much we love each other even though our lives are so separate. The only reason we aren't together is because of circumstances. We don't want to devastate our partners who sincerely love us. We love our partners, we have discussed that. It is just a different kind of love. Also, on my account because of my daughter. I would rather live without my love than tear my child's family apart. I couldn't live with the guilt of doing that.

So, my first wife, my soul mate, and I talk on the phone a few times a week and look forward to the next time we can steal a few hours to be together. We don't know what the future holds for us. But we do know that we love each other and never again will we lose that. Even if we aren't together in our daily lives.

We met at a high school dance in 1954. He was an eighteen year old "college man" and I was a sixteen-year-old high school sophomore. I thought he was the most gorgeous thing I'd ever seen: tall, dark, a musician in a local jazz band. We started dating, and my parents loved him.

Three months later, my dad was being transferred by his company; we simply could not bear the thought of being apart. We pestered my parents to let us get married, and they agreed. But it only lasted a year, and then we went our separate ways.

In 1991, my father died. My ex-husband was throwing away some junk mail. Before he tossed away a hometown newsletter that he received every month, he flipped open the first page. There was my dad's name in an obituary.

He called my mother, and she gave him my work number. When he called, the first thing I said to him was how sorry I was for our breakup. We were both divorced from second marriages at that point, and single again. He was coincidentally going to be in Mississippi on business, and he made plans to visit me at that time.

The weekend before we were to meet, he went to his parents' house to visit. He hadn't yet told them that he found me. When he walked in the door, his mother pulled out a box she had saved for more than thirty years. It contained the only remaining set of our wedding pictures. She asked if he'd like to take them home. Needless to say, he was stunned. Then he told his parents that he was going to bring *me* home.

We were remarried in November, 1992—thirty-seven years after our first wedding. He is my miracle. I thought I'd never see him again. We are very much in love, and I thank God for him. I have a little needlepoint pillow on our bed that says, "Real love stories never have endings." How true.

After my mother passed away, it was my task to dispose of her belongings. Among her receipts were several hundred dollars worth of savings bonds in my former husband's name. Over the years, I had thought about him and fantasized about seeing him again. This gave me a reason to contact him.

I only had the address for his parents, so I sent the bonds in care of them, with a quick note explaining the circumstances of finding the bonds. Within three weeks, I received a reply from him, requesting information on the son I had borne with him. I wrote back with two letters—one about our son and the other about me (to be opened only if he were interested). He was.

The letters escalated into phone calls. It was obvious that we both still had strong feelings for each other. After a year, we decided to meet to determine if our relationship only existed on paper. The meeting was instantly sexual!

We love each other deeply. The son we share approves of our renewed romance. I can't imagine that we won't have a future together.

I would like to relate to you the miracle involving my mother and father. The story begins in Yugoslavia where, after World War II, Mom and Dad were first loves and were married. I came on the scene a few years later. It was a very hard marriage. Dad would drink and beat up my mother. Mom eventually divorced him and went (by herself) to America.

In the United States, she connected with her godfather and established a steady job. She saved enough money after a year to ask the Yugoslavian government to release me to her. The Yugoslavian government at first would not let me leave the country because Dad was still there. But one spring day in 1957, I waved goodbye to Dad at the train station and came to America.

Mom took care of me in Illinois until I was of age. I went away to college, and while there I received a call from Australia. It was Dad. He had worked his way eastward and settled in Australia, where he had remarried (and divorced) and had three daughters and another son. In this brief exchange, Dad told me that he had wanted to establish a relationship with Mom, to make amends, but that she had snubbed him. That ended any possibility of healing old wounds, let alone any possibility of reuniting.

Time passed. About a year ago, I was out dancing and met someone from Australia. One thing in conversation led to another, and I told her I had family there. When I told where Dad was, she said her family lived in near proximity. She promised that she would find Dad when she got back to Australia.

Around Christmas time, her family wrote to me to say they had found Dad and that Dad was anxious to establish ties again. A couple weeks later, I received a flurry of calls from Dad, who wished to reestablish ties with me and Mom. I discussed this with Mom, who lived near me. She responded that if Dad would call, she would tell him to drop dead. I told her that was not a good way to start off a conversation, and that she needed to bring an end to the bitterness she had toward Dad (for her own sake), and that Dad needed to bring his guilt feelings to an end as well. A week or so passed; then Mom told me she would give Dad another chance.

So, Dad came from Australia in March to see Mom and me. After over forty years, it appears that they are reunited. Mom is 66 years old, and Dad is 73.

My name is Alex and my lost love is Susan. We played little league baseball on the same team, grew up living in the same rural area, went to church and school together. We began going steady in high school, went to the prom together, and eventually married when we graduated. She was 17 and I was 18 when we married.

In my youthful foolishness I was unfaithful in our second year of marriage and caused her a great deal of pain. She forgave me; then I did it again. This time she didn't forgive me. She divorced me and found a much older lover who was mature and somewhat wealthy. They moved in together at his house and she wouldn't answer my calls or letters. I sent flowers for years to her at work. I begged and I cried and I waited. Eventually I resigned myself to the fact that she was gone and I had to move on.

I began dating and found a girl who looked like her, had mannerisms like her, reminded me of her. I married this girl and tried my best to be happy. We had a son and a daughter together, and it was a good life. But she wasn't Susan. I thought every day about how much I loved Susan, and about how I needed to have her forgiveness for the hurt I caused her.

Ten years to the day of our divorce, I sent her a seven page letter, through her mother, who has always been there for me; I told her how sorry I still was that I had betrayed her, and I told her that I continued to love her, even though we both had moved on. I told her how I dreamed about her almost every night, and I told her how bad my heart hurt every day for the last ten years.

So much had changed in that decade. She became a nurse and I am an elected official in state government. We both still lived a few miles apart and worked within seeing distance of each other everyday. During that ten year period we hadn't spoken but two or three times. Once was when I was injured slightly and went to the emergency room, she was my nurse. She treated me as if I were just another patient. That hurt worse than the injury.

She called me the week after she received my letter and told me that she forgave me. She said that we had both made mistakes in our youth that hurt each other and that she had often thought of me also. She had been the strong one who kept the wall up between us and it took ten years to tear it down. I found your book *Lost & Found Lovers* online and ordered a copy for each of us.

We began emailing almost daily; and we have been having lunch in nearby cities a couple of times a month. We even made a day trip to Cape Cod, where we held hands and walked and talked. There has been no sex. I am still married and probably will stay that way, to keep my children in a stable environment and so I can be with them. But I have rekindled a fire in my heart and in Susan's that smoldered for ten years. I am more happy just getting an email from her or having lunch with her than I have been in ten years of marriage with my wife. My wife loves me deeply and I should love her like I love Susan. But I don't, and I know that I never will.

Who knows what the future holds? Maybe Susan and I will one day be together again as man and wife. But even if we don't remarry, nothing will ever take away the love we have found again in each other. I realized by reading your book that I am not alone in the way I have felt for so long. Thanks, Dr. Kalish. Susan and I are a storybook romance. God bless you, and us.

Jim and I were first loves, and we married at twenty and nineteen, respectively, in 1961. Within the next six years, we had four children (one set of twins), we were transferred around the Northeast several times, and we didn't have much money. Lots of stressors! We divorced in our early thirties.

We each remarried. Over the years, we saw each other at events concerning the children. Jim contributed generously with child support, college tuitions, weddings. All that time, I didn't see Jim in a romantic light, or didn't let myself, but I always looked forward to seeing him.

As time went by, my second marriage became a horror, and Jim's marriage also crumbled. Our twin daughters were getting married, one in June of 1992, and one in October, 1992. No double wedding for them! Jim and I were thrown together on a number of occasions to discuss plans for the weddings, much to our increasing delight!

During one lunch to discuss wedding details, I asked him for a $500 loan—he was always very generous and kind—so that I could join a Catholic singles group. He thought about it a few minutes, then smiled and said, "No. You don't want to do that." That was so uncharacteristic of him—that's when I knew.

By the time the second daughter's wedding rolled around, we were back together again, but not very many people knew. We wanted the focus to be appropriately on the bride, not on us. At the wedding, Jim asked me to dance. The song that was coincidentally playing was, "Can I Have This Dance for the Rest of My Life." Although the guests could have regarded our dance as an innocent, conciliatory gesture between the two parents of the bride, our loving feelings for each other were evident. Suddenly everyone cleared off the dance floor for us and started cheering and clapping!

The rest is history, as they say. We bought a house near the beach and soon remarried. Our kids are thrilled, our parents are thrilled, our friends are thrilled, but none as thrilled as Jim and me. He is handsome, sweet, generous, loving, and fun.

We have a wonderful, active life and are enjoying ourselves, our kids, and our grandchildren. And we are only 52 and 53! We couldn't be happier.

My ex-husband and I originally met in the California Conservation Corps in 1983. I was attracted to him the moment I saw him, and little did I know he fell for me at first sight, too. We went through the whole year of the Corps as friends, and then we got together romantically. He had a very bad temper and was hard to deal with, but I loved him anyway. We moved in together, married, and I soon got pregnant. Our marriage broke up two weeks before our son was born.

I didn't contact him for a year. When I did, I hoped that he had changed in that time apart. We remarried, and it happened all over again, with his temper getting the best of our love. I guess he needed a louder wake-up call before he would change.

We divorced a second time, and from what he later told me, that just about ruined his life. I didn't know that he loved me so much but just didn't know how to express himself.

He had my name tattooed on his forearm and wouldn't remove it for anyone. He told me later that it was all he had to remind him of me. Meanwhile, I kept everything of his to remind me of him—pictures, knick knacks, and the wedding ring that I still wear. The feelings we had for each other were still strong and I could never forget about him.

Then last December, I located him so he could meet his twelve year old son and get to know him. Our boy was nearly a teenager and needed a father. He started talking on the phone nightly to our son, but little did I know that he longed to talk to me, too. When we did begin to talk, I learned that through all those years apart he had made several attempts to find me but to no avail. We began talking every night, and when I took our twelve year old son down to Southern California to meet him, all the feelings I had for him came flooding back like a rushing river in flood season.

We have both matured since our last meeting twelve years earlier, and we are sorry we missed out on the young years, but he is now the man I wanted then. Our love for each other is so strong that we are in a permanent daze all the time. It hurt so much to be away from each other that he moved here from Los Angeles to be near us.

We are now very happy, but even so, we are taking it easy this time so that we can get to know each other again. I am still as infatuated with him as I always was, and he with me. I hope it works this time!

A few months later, when two reporters called me for interviews about rekindled romances, each asked me for names of some couples to interview, too. I thought of the woman above, and sent her an email to ask if she'd be willing to participate in a story for a California newspaper, or to be filmed for a local television broadcast. Here is her reply:

Thank you so much for thinking of us for the newspaper article, but we have a slight problem! It's my grandmother, the matriarch of my family, the one who sits in the LayZBoy and rules the roost. She is the one who helped me pay for both of the divorces from Michael, and she hates him. I can understand—when you have to help someone out of a bad situation, you really don't want to see them get into the same mess again.

She hates him with such fury that if she even knew we were on speaking terms (let alone back together) she would have the granddaddy of all fits! No one likes to see an 87 year old woman scream and yell and jump up and down. At best she'd put off the jumping for fear of hip displacement, but she can sure yell! So we want to skip the newspaper thing for now, until we can slowly bring things together for Grandma, or she may have a stroke. She is the only barrier that keeps it all hush hush.

The television thing is all right, since we don't know of many people who watch that channel; chances are good that no one would see it to tell her. And she is slowly losing her sight, so if she were surfing the stations she would never recognize us for that fleeting moment she grazed over that station.

I love Michael with all my heart, and our son really needs his father now. We are determined to make our reunion work, and I won't let Grandma wreck it. We will ease Grandma into the idea slowly so as not to shock her into a stroke! If you have any good ideas on how to break this to Grandma, let me know!

Just a few days later, she wrote to me again:

I finally did what I thought I could never do. It took a lot of guts and nerve—in fact it made me physically ill—but I finally told Grandma about Michael. I kind of left out that we wanted to get back together; I made it seem like he wanted to be here for his son. She seemed okay with that, but made it clear that I wasn't to get involved with him romantically! I hope she doesn't watch Channel 6! I think in time it will all work out.

A year passed, and they married, happily, for the third time. But a year after that, she contacted me to say that his temper was worse than ever, and they had again divorced. Grandma was right.

CHAPTER 9

Married ... With Ticking Time Bomb

In my media interviews, I warn against contacts between lost loves if either person is married, because my research has uncovered so many unintended rekindled romance affairs. From 1994 to 1997 when *Lost & Found Lovers* was published, 30% of my survey participants said they began their reunions while they were married. Since then, the invention of the World Wide Web, Internet search engines to find people, and web sites that put classmates and old friends back in contact have made lost love reconnections easier and more impulsive; the extramarital rate reported by participants in my 2004-2005 survey (most of whom reconnected online) has more than doubled, to 62%.

Many of the lost love affair partners in my original population left their marriages to be with each other. The stories of happily married reunited couples, who left spouses to be together, appear throughout this book, not just in this chapter.

However, my 2004-2005 survey data indicate that it has become increasingly uncommon for lost love affair partners to leave their marriages. With Internet and email reconnections, more lost love affairs begin without intent; the lost loves only wanted to catch up on old times: out of curiosity, to find closure, to form a friendship, or because they had vivid dreams of the long-lost love that triggered an obsession. Although the former sweethearts exert an addiction-like pull on each other, most of the recent extramarital reunions are ending in excruciatingly painful breakups when one or both of the lost loves recommit to their families.

Each time I discuss this subject in interviews, married men and women write to express regrets that they did not find me before they met with their first loves. People in good marriages are just as vulnerable to intense reactions to old flames as people in conflicted marriages. This is not about the spouse. The lost love was a ticking time bomb that existed, unnoticed, within the marriage from the beginning.

My research participants wrote that they never cheated, would never cheat, with anyone except this particular lost love. Many of them labeled themselves as "religious" (including a few who are clergy men and women) and said they felt consumed by guilt, yet they could not let go of their lost loves again. They tried to stay in both the marriage and the reunion for as long as they could tolerate it, which in my professional opinion is the most painful option. By putting off the inevitable choice, the loss of one or the other will only become more devastating.

Lost love affairs have shattered families, and these stories need to be told, too. Some of the stories in this chapter were written by jilted spouses. Lost love affair partners often forget that the decision to leave a marriage or to stay is not theirs alone: reunions are discovered by the spouses, who then initiate divorces or take the slow, painful path to saving the marriages.

The lost loves, who only intended to talk or write casually, were shocked when overwhelming, passionate feelings sprang to life, and they did not know how to handle them. Rekindled romance is a different kind of romance. It is a love that was interrupted.

⁂ ⁂ ⁂

So, it's been 3 years since I first wrote to my lost lover in early 2000. We met that summer after being apart almost 30 years. Then, after several months of intense longing, we got deeply involved in a long distance affair for about 9 months. I actually went to counseling to stop this from happening, but it didn't work. My lost love and I are like longtime friends who never left each other. Now I see why we liked each other in grade school and then dated and corresponded from a distance through high school.

And even more amazing is that we've had such different lives. I doubt that our profiles or life histories would match us up. We are so different but are also the same inside. She is my best buddy. I know that we could do anything together today and so does she.

So what happened? Well, after about 9 months both of us knew that she was not going to leave her marriage. For her sake, my sake, and her family's sake, I did not want to carry on with the affair. It was too stressful for both us. She felt the same stress but wanted to carry on with both situations anyway. I could not do that, so we agreed to create distance physically. For a while, she continued to call me; now we just do an occasional email for birthdays and other special days.

So what else happened? I walked into the life of a woman unhappy with her marriage but bound by her commitments—her kids, and caring for her aged parents in their hometown. She has been very conflicted about her marriage, but she wanted to prove it could work. He was a verbally abusive alcoholic who quit drinking a few years ago. And believe it or not, when she married him, he looked a lot like me. I just learned all of this, 30 years later. She's a talented, tough, and capable woman but she's also so stuck. She feels that she's got too many things to take care of and I can certainly understand that, even though I wish it were otherwise. And, she admits to being scared.

I've been trying to get on with my life for almost 2 years. I could pick up where I left off, but all the indications are that is not going to happen.

Would I do it again? Yes! Actually I had very little choice in the matter. She's too deeply a part of me. It was good for me to know that I could feel deep love for someone after so many years, as I've not been successful in relationships as an adult. It was actually a very validating experience personally. I'm a better, more solid, and in-depth person because of this relationship, even in its messiness, hurt, and longing.

But I'm also glad that we got as far as we did without making too big a mess of things. In fact, I found that amazing! Either her husband is pretty stupid, or doesn't care, or she's really slick. I could not figure it out.

My therapist showed me a picture of a young man gazing at an old violin, and asked me, "What do you see, Jeff?":

> Anticipation in my gaze,
> Of music I would play.
> If I could touch that violin,
> And hold it close today.
>
> Once the bow within my hands,
> Pulled gently to and fro,
> Found deep within the violin,
> Sweet notes it did not know.

Your symphony was brought to life,
When resting in my arms.
The worn and tattered violin,
Released its joyful charms.

I know each string, each curve of wood,
Can play each note so bold.
The violin my hands caressed
'Twas home when in my hold.

Its owner never showed respect,
Acknowledged not its worth.
With honored touch and praise it found
In my hands a rebirth.

The violin in sadness stored
Beside the owner's bed,
Discarded and left out of tune,
Its spirit nearly dead.

The violin four years I played,
Its owner never knew.
My gentle touch and patient hand,
Found notes so pure and true.

The music from that violin,
The notes which once had died,
Now played glorious melodies,
When held by me with pride.

A steady pressure on the bow,
When sliding 'cross the strings.
The violin once at my side,
In my lost heart still sings.

Oft' I'd caress the polished wood,
Deep rubbing brought a shine.
Its music found a sweet release
Within these hands of mine.

When in my arms, the violin
One with me became,
With my soft touch we'd soon be lost
In passion's hottest flame.

The violin, a work of art,
I wished it mine to keep.
Its beauty filled my heart with joy,
And ears with music sweet.

The violin is silenced now,
Has spurned my graceful touch,
My eyes no longer gaze upon
That which I loved so much.

We met when I was fifteen and he was seventeen. I had just moved with my family from San Francisco to a very small town in Southern California. My years growing up were spent being very socially involved with school, sports, and outside activities, so when I met Kevin in this small town, he was far from the "lettermen jacket" boys who had always attracted me. His jeans, T-shirt, hat, and greasy hands (he was a mechanic) were not what I pictured for myself. Yet he was my first true love; he gave me a promise ring.

I got pregnant at sixteen and, deciding I was too young for motherhood, had an abortion. After that, our relationship was very volatile. I was busy experimenting with my sexuality, and Kevin was doing everything he could to hold onto our love. I always felt I could get him back whenever I wanted, and I usually did. With both of us causing each other so much heartache, he decided to move out of state. We kept in touch with calls and letters.

While Kevin was gone I began a romance with a wonderful man, and we married. Fifteen years went by; I had three children. But Kevin was never fully out of my mind. I had very clear and vivid dreams of us seeing each other innocently, as friends. After each time, I would spend the following several days trying to forget each dream. Through mutual friends, I learned that he had also married, had a child, and lived about 250 miles from me.

A year ago, I attended a meeting very close to the town where Kevin and I had spent our time together, but nowhere near where either of us currently lives. I was in a store, and Kevin walked in; I had not seen his face in well over twelve years. He walked up to me and said hello, and my heart stopped when I realized who he was. We spoke, and I thought my chest would explode from pounding so hard. We stumbled through some "how are things" small talk, then said good-bye. But the minute he walked out the door, I began to think of all the things I wanted to tell him and should have asked him. I thought if I did, I could finally get him off my mind for good.

I thought of him obsessively all afternoon, then called him at the friend's house where he told me he was staying that weekend. We talked for over two hours, and carefully but truthfully shared our feelings—how we often thought of each other, had dreams, tried to figure out what went wrong. It was so strange, because it was as if we both knew exactly how the other felt, and it was so won-derful to hear him tell me he had never stopped loving me.

I will never forget the next time we met, purposefully, and held each other. How clearly I knew his smell. I didn't realize until that moment what I had been missing. It was the most incredible relief to share how we felt, but at the same time it is as much a burden, given that we are both married. We try to talk at least once a week, and manage to see each other every month or two.

We are having a hard time coming to terms with leaving our spouses but desperately want to be together. Up until the time of our reunion, we had both been faithful to our spouses of 15 and 17 years. The guilt has been horrible, but at the same time it feels so right when we are together.

Last February, I received a letter from my first love. He was writing to apologize for his behavior when we broke up in 1954. We had steady dated for almost a year when I was sixteen and he was seventeen.

He married young, and that marriage was shattered after he had two affairs and his wife had one. He married a woman from one of those affairs, and that also ended in divorce. At the time he contacted me, my own marriage was very rocky, with my husband having had an affair years before. Over the years we had grown steadily apart, but remained together because it was easy and comfort-able.

All through the years, I kept pictures of my first love and looked at them periodically with thoughts of "what if." Little did I know that he, too, had kept the photos and looked at them with the same thoughts. I even shared the story of my beautiful first love experience with my daughters as they grew up, tell-ing them that I could only hope their first love experiences would produce such wonderful memories.

As I read that first email from Bruce in February, my hands shook and the tears started and my heart was beating faster. I was having all those feelings I had felt so many years ago. I wrote a very noncommittal letter back to him, talking about my family. But still, the correspondence began in earnest after many months of writing. We knew we had to see each other. We had to know if the feelings were real or some sort of fantasy that we wanted to believe was real.

We met for a weekend, and the magic was still there. Those days were better than anything we could have ever imagined. Then came the difficult part—what do we do now? He placed no ultimatums on me, just said he would wait forever, until I could decide what to do with my marriage. And this "I'll never get married again" guy was talking about marriage and commitment.

I returned home, having made no firm decision on when I would leave my husband, only sure that I would do so. Ironically, the movie *The Bridges of Madison County* was showing on the plane on my return flight.

We continued to write and exchange email daily. One day my husband returned home from work several hours early and found some very explicit email on the computer. We had been busted! Now came the big decision about what to do.

I decided to move to Chicago and live with Bruce. I filed for divorce and it will be final in two months. I left behind a career, my home, my 2 grown children, and five grandchildren.

We are now enjoying each minute to the max. After having been separated almost forty years, we're as in love today as we were then, perhaps even more.

I had been happily married for 47 years before his first love showed up and interrupted our life together. We have four grown children, and several grandchildren. I was 20 when I met him; he was my coworker at the time, and he was 24. Over the years, we had to move numerous times for his career advancement. Each time, I gave up a job and many friends to move my family all over the country for this man, whom I dearly love still.

His former girlfriend had kept in touch over the years through Christmas cards and a few phone calls. Three years ago, her husband had a fatal stroke while they were traveling; she called my husband from the airport as soon as she landed with his ashes. She was announcing her availability, as far as I am concerned.

Within a few weeks, my husband launched into a long distance romance. She is in her seventies and lonely, and has given my husband a $250,000 line of credit to jump-start our family's failing business. I didn't find out about that until recently. I was extremely angry—about the deceit involved in not consulting with me first, as well as about the source of the money—and immediately filed for a divorce.

The legal process takes several months in our state, and it was a painful period for me. Meanwhile, he just ran to be with her in Alabama, happy as a lark. Two days before the decree was final, I called him to say that I was having a really hard time accepting the finality of our marriage. He answered, "You know I'll be back, don't you?" The divorce went through.

He claims he really loves me, but is not IN love with me. He is still in Alabama, but says that by Christmas he will make a final decision. I think he is having second thoughts about abandoning his family. In the meantime, I sit alone, thinking how this first love has made my life HELL!!

After a fairly happy (as far as I knew) marriage of 25 years, my best friend, favorite companion, and only lover—now my ex-husband—kissed me goodbye, went on a business trip, and came home six days later, telling me he didn't want to be married anymore.

I begged, pleaded, suggested talking to our priest (we were practicing Catholics) or a marriage counselor, but he said he had changed and I hadn't, and he wanted out. We had never had a major quarrel in all those years, and never discussed our previous sexual relationships because I hadn't had any, and he told me 26 years ago his were none of my business.

Apparently my ex-husband had left an old girlfriend pregnant when he left for Viet Nam; she was able to marry someone else quickly and blame the pregnancy on her husband. This woman's husband died in May 1997, and she looked up mine that June. I will swear that my ex-husband never knew he had another child until he was informed of this when the woman looked him up.

Two weeks after reconnecting with her, he moved her back to his hometown in Minnesota, and they moved in together one month after he dumped me. He became a Born Again Christian, and they married two days after our divorce was final. Yes, I was crushed and devastated; but that is not even the worst part.

Our 22 year old daughter was pushed from his life by his first love and the newly-found daughter. He let our child be replaced by one he never watched grow up, probably because he felt guilty about the whole situation. I've read all the divorce books that warn not to make the adult child choose between the parents, and I didn't. I kept saying to her that, no matter what this man has done to me, he was a good husband for 25 years, so forgive him for wanting more than me. My darling daughter tried and tried, but he continued to push her away. She was canceled out of her trip to see him last Christmas because the new wife felt "uncomfortable" when my daughter was around.

She is excluded from her father's new life in no uncertain terms. She has to leave messages for him on his work phone, because he won't give her his home phone number or address, because she "might be a pest" to the new wife.

This child, even though she is a credentialed teacher, is still my baby, my only child, and my heart is aching for her. I have wonderful friends, a satisfying career, enough money to do what I want—I am okay. If another man ever looks at me, I'll probably be completely recovered. But my baby!

I lost my dad about the same age, to cancer, so I know what losing a father feels like, but my father never had an unkind word for me, so I can't imagine that extra pain she carries. My daughter played soccer for her dad, learned to do auto mechanics (well!) from him, and they went camping together. He was far and away her favorite parent. He never had to discipline her for missing a curfew or not doing her homework, and I never minded being second because they had such a wonderful, close relationship.

At first, before I realized that he had found his first love, I tried to reason that the changes in him were due to our aging, or his dead-end career, or medical problems. Wrong! I have often searched for some explanations to make sense of the end of this marriage, and your explanations in *Dear Abby* were as good as any.

But there is no way to rationalize or justify this treatment of a wonderful daughter. My daughter and I are truly friends after all these years of being mother and daughter. I wish she could have her father back, but right now that doesn't seem possible.

My husband passed away a year ago. We were married in 1943 and had three sons. I am now 78 years old, and I have tried to repress the knowledge of what went on for 42 years between my husband and his lost love.

She was his old girlfriend, his first. She married only briefly, in 1941, and came back into his life in 1955. Their affair went on until he became bedridden in 1997 and was no longer able to contact her.

It was like a light bulb went on suddenly in my mind; I can see clearly now so many things that I didn't fully understand at the time they were happening. He took so many business trips to her hometown; she often showed up in our city unexpectedly. There were inadequately explained receipts, lots of little things that a wife might rather not confront. I finally caught on when she came to our home to visit for a week; the last night she was here, I realized that he was sneaking out of bed to go to her. Even on his death bed, he talked about her.

This affair has disturbed me terribly since his death; it's on my mind morning to night. It interferes with my grieving for him. I've lost a lot of weight to the point that one of my daughters thinks I am trying to kill myself. I will seek a therapist.

He stayed with me for over fifty years, but I don't think he was happy. He had promised her that he would leave me, but I don't think he could stand the thought of another divorce. He had been married before.

I have tried to confront this woman, to talk to her on the telephone and tell her how betrayed I have felt, but she denies the affair and hangs up on me. I thought if I could talk to her honestly, maybe hear an apology from her, that I might be able to heal. I feel so stuck, trying to sort the reality from the false memories of my marriage.

I was 15 and he was 18 in 1966. We grew up in Tennessee; we rode the school bus together, and went on some Sunday night drives and "parked" under the trees. The pull of a girl closer to his age, and the Viet Nam war, separated us. We never really said goodbye.

We each married and divorced, then remarried. We are both in long term marriages now, though they are not very successful. In the fall of 1993, he started looking for me. I was more than ready to be found.

The power of what happened between us is indescribable. I never dreamed that a love could be so complete, so passionate, so sexually fulfilling. I have teenage children, so we have another couple of years of living in our old lives before we can make changes and start our new lives. Meanwhile, we talk daily and could have made a down payment on a house with the money we spent on long distance calls. We see each other about once every two months.

It is nearly like we were born together; we are alike in ways that generate chills when I think about them. This relationship has answered so many questions for me which I could never figure out. I have been in love with him all my life. I was consciously in love with him until I was 19, then I let it slip down deep inside. I tried to love others but never succeeded.

I am fortunate to have a psychologist who is wise enough to encourage me to truly feel during this process of renewal. It has been five years since we found each other. I look forward to the changes that will allow us to grow old together. I can't imagine a more glorious way to grow old than with this man.

Thank you for writing to *Dear Abby* to warn other married lost and found lovers of the possible pitfalls. Your call for caution is right. Even so, I have never been happier.

Lost love is called that because it's lost, part of the past—gone, even if not forgotten. If found and rekindled, it might lead to happiness, but it also might hold potential peril that ends in nothing but pain for all concerned. I've experienced that pain, as my wife of 11 years embarked on a reunion—unwittingly and, as I understand it, innocently. I found out in one of the cruelest ways imaginable.

I'm 57, she's 55, and this is a second marriage for both of us, one that was strong, affectionate and loving. Many people pointed to our union as an ideal marriage, a perfect match of two soul mates who adored each other. We even have given numerous talks about marriage and male-female communication. My two children and her two children are adults, although mine still were in high school when we married. After mine graduated, we moved halfway across the country to be close to her children. I was willing to do that because I loved her and I knew that would make her happy, which I had made my main goal in life.

I'm the type of man who finds it easier to do things to show my love rather than speak the words as often as I should. The benefits to her have been more gifts than I can afford and pretty nice digs, as well as my tendency to wait on her hand and foot. The disadvantage is that she apparently needed more words and touching than I had been giving her. Even so, our sex life was nothing short of astounding, one that left us both more than satisfied. That wasn't so in my first marriage, during which I often prayed that somehow God would make it so my wife couldn't keep her hands off of me. He did, but delayed it till the second marriage; that used to be a great joke for us.

A year ago, my wife's interest in sex took a major dive, to the extent that I even asked whether there was another man. She assured me that there wasn't, that it was just menopause. But an affair had started.

The previous fall, she had gone to a high school reunion and ran into her first love. They were happy to see each other, she told me, but that's all; she even introduced herself by saying that she was in a good, happy second marriage.

She and this lost love had moved to different towns when they were dating years ago; they kept dating for awhile but then drifted apart, and she married her first husband. As I understand it, she rarely, if ever, thought of her first love until the recent high school reunion stirred her emotions; I noticed that she was morose for days. I found out later that she even asked her sister: "Why do I keep thinking that I could have had a wonderful life with him?" Her sister's answer was brilliant in its bluntness: "Because you could have had a wonderful life with him."

Despite that obvious first danger signal, she decided that she would like to have "closure" with him, so they began communicating. She swears to this day that she did not go looking for romantic involvement, and I have to believe her. I don't know a lot of the details about their closure discussions, other than the fact that they created an opening instead of a closing. She has told me that, at one point, she told him they needed to be careful not to dishonor their spouses. Danger Signal No. 2: things were getting hot, and they knew it. But they ended up dishonoring us anyway.

His wife found out fairly quickly, so they concocted a charade of exchanging emails, saying they were breaking up, but they brazenly continued to communicate, meet and be sexually involved. They switched much of their communication to text messaging. I pay the bills in our household; she started paying the cell phone bills online so I would not see the phone tracks. Stupid me—I thought it was odd, but the real reason didn't occur to me until after I found out about the affair.

Their meetings during the nine month affair weren't often, because of a 1,500 mile distance, and I trusted my wife enough that I didn't question why she was traveling so often to "get together with old girlfriends from high school." (Ironically, my stepdaughter and I used to joke that she actually was linking up with an old boyfriend, ha-ha.)

Our sexual encounters went from few to nil, and I challenged that, again raising the possibility—not believing for an instant that it could be true—of another man. She said no; I trusted her, as frustrated as I was. One night I told her that I was angrier at her about the lack of sex than I had ever been with anybody, about anything. I should have known when that didn't seem to worry her (she's normally sensitive to a fault and a people pleaser who doesn't like anyone to be angry with her) that something was amiss. But I trusted that she never would be unfaithful to me, even if she wasn't being sexual with me. This was a woman who had saved herself for her first marriage; a good, Christian woman; a grandmother, my best friend; my soul mate; my mentor in so many ways. An affair? Totally unthinkable, hardly speakable.

The bubble burst in a merciless way one Friday afternoon. It was 1:25 p.m. Oct. 7, 2005, to be precise—a moment that is frozen in my time memory bank, joining other indelible recollections such as where I was and what I was doing when Kennedy was shot and what I was doing on Sept. 11, 2001. I was bringing groceries into the house after shopping for vittles to feed relatives who would be visiting for a week. I heard my wife, upstairs in our bedroom, talking to somebody on the phone. I surmised it was a friend. I listened for a moment and, when it sounded like a discussion of a marriage issue, I returned to bringing in groceries, because one friend in particular had been going through a rough marital patch, and I assumed this was another chapter in that story.

My third trip in with groceries, I froze in my tracks when I heard her say, "But your children will be accepting and happy when we're together and they see how happy I make you." I realized, with a knife to my heart, that she was talking to a man she had chosen to replace me. She was plotting to leave me, after telling me for months that there wasn't another man.

Fighting tears and the urge to vomit all over the groceries, I continued to listen, clinging to the hope that somehow I had totally misheard, or misunderstood, what she had said. Then the talk turned to their wonderful sex life. Without going into details, I'll note one sentence that stabbed me in the heart: "The reason everything is so wonderful when our clothes are off," my wife told the Other Man, her lost love, "is because of the things we do when our clothes are on." She used to feel that way about me.

The conversation went on for several minutes—she still didn't realize I was in the house listening—before the call ended with words of love, affection, missing each other and longing to be together. "Nobody has ever made me feel as alive as you do," she said. The knife in my heart twisted violently at those sentiments, so similar to what she used to say to me. She even called him by the same pet name she called me from Day 1 when we discovered we were in love, and she made several other endearing comments that used to be reserved only for me.

(As odd as this may sound, one of my first thoughts was: "What becomes of me and the grandkids?" They are my step-grandchildren, but I love them dearly, as my own. Indeed, several times when she went off to meet her lover, I was home taking care of the grandkids myself. Losing them would kill me.)

I confronted her and she obviously was dismayed that I had found out about the adultery and the deception. To her credit, she felt badly about what I had heard. After all, it was tantamount to walking in and finding them entangled in a sexually climactic embrace.

It's an understatement to say that it was a rough night of tears and vomiting on my part (I lost 10 pounds in the next seven days; not that that was a bad thing, other than having buy all new pants). And I was stunned, at one point when she said, "Do you think there's any chance for US to stay together?" My response was that the phone conversation made it fairly obvious that she had no interest in that. I basically threw in the towel.

I was equally stunned the next day when she said, "You just don't GET it, do you?" I allowed as how I did but countered that it was a damn cruel thing to do, chucking me without giving me a chance to try to meet the needs of whatever he was doing. I also resented the fact that I had spent more than a decade treating her like a queen and he waltzed into her life and won her heart without having to pay any dues whatsoever. It was especially hurtful when she said, "If it makes any difference, he is a good, Christian man." Well, hell no, that didn't make any difference because the good Christian man had committed adultery with my wife and she with him. They cheated and lied for damn near a year (God only knows whether it still would be going on if I hadn't stumbled across it). Was the message that he was a good Christian man, but I wasn't?

Problem was, I still did love her. After a couple of days of being resigned to my fate, all the while putting on a smiley face for company, I announced to her that I had decided to fight for her. Jesus had forgiven her, obviously, and I proclaimed that so would I. (I'll be honest, I'm still not forgiving toward him. This is one Christian man saying in an un-Christian fashion: I hate his guts, and I always will. If that puts me in hell, so be it; he has put me THROUGH hell.) I have found that forgiving my wife is possible, but forgetting takes a gargantuan effort that I may never succeed in.

She explained the "Lost Love Phenomenon," that reconnecting with lost lovers can lead to an uncontrollable urge, akin to a chemical reaction in the brain, to make it a total reconnect, as if the person is powerless to do anything else. All I can say to that, because it sounds like so much New Age, do-it-if-it-feels-good poppycock, is that I know that something very, very strong had to have been at work here. You see, despite my wife's nine months of lying and cheating and making up stories and hiding phone bills and flying off to be sexual with another man, I still have to say that she is the most honest, moral person I know (well, except for this rather sizable blip). Something does exist that made her abandon all of her values and virtues to disrespect someone she used to tell: "I love you more than you know." She swears to this day that the affair had nothing to do with me, that I actually was a good husband with a few flaws like anybody, but rather, that it was all about the Lost Lovers Phenom.

Perhaps the hardest part was that, even though she wondered whether there was a chance to get back on track with me, she stubbornly continued to communicate with him. How intransigently? Daily; perhaps more than once a day. She brazenly called him several times when I was in the house. Although she thought I was out of earshot, I heard a couple of conversations in which she told him how much she loved him and how badly she missed him. One day, when she was having heart palpitations for some reason, I heard her tell him on the phone that they were palpitations of love for him. When I mentioned it, she accused me of eavesdropping. Well, duh, it's my house, too. I told her it actually was an incredibly romantic thing to say, but her timing sucked and I wished she had said it to me rather than the man who had turned her head and her heart from me.

So, the situation I put myself in was going along with her communication with him—he who had gotten a free ride into her heart and who had to meet no tests for her love and loyalty—while I was jumping through hoops like mad to try to get her back. We each spoke with Dr. Nancy Kalish, separately, whom my wife had pronounced as the guru; I think my wife assumed that Dr. Kalish would straighten me out and tell me I had to put up with whatever. I felt that my wife was being cruel in making me wait while she decided whether to throw me under the bus (I don't think she realizes to this day how cruel, demeaning and heartbreaking the process she put me through was). But Dr. Kalish agreed with me that I was being treated shabbily. She listened understandingly when I said I felt I should just walk, but she observed, "Of course, the problem is that you still love her."

Ah, and there's the rub: What's a guy to do when he loves somebody who has pulled his heart out of his chest and tossed it into the blender?

My wife proclaims that she loves me, only in a different way. Something about mature love vs. passionate love. So I guess I am supposed to be satisfied with the old-fart love, of sitting on the porch, holding hands in the swing in the golden years, while he gets the unbridled love of sexual excitement and undying devotion. Because, you see, even though she told me, after four months of jumping through hoops, that she had decided to stay with me, she still said she always will have a special love for him. I try to put the best spin on it, that she loves me enough to stay. But when I'm alone in the can, trying to read the sports section, I can't help but feel like chopped liver, that she'd rather be with him, and that it's just more convenient and less painful to more people to stay with me.

That raises this point: Anyone selfish enough (sorry, but injured parties can't be blamed for being inflammatory and saying it's selfish; it's part of the "phenomenon") should realize that more than three people are involved. There are children who will be shattered, grandchildren who will be confused, and friends who may make uncomfortable alliances. Even if a lousy marriage is involved (and ours wasn't a lousy one) the whole phenomenon can lead to a nuclear bomb. I suspect that, if our children found out, for instance, it would leave them reeling in confusion, anger and hurt.

My wife and I are trying to work things through. We always have and still have a strong bond of love and respect for each other, as astounding as that may seem, considering the circumstances. I feel sorry for her because I know that she is telling the truth when she expresses profound regret for all the hurt she has caused. (I know it's not popular to be a "victim" these days, but I have to say, as the "victim," that she has NO idea how much she has hurt me, and I can't imagine her ever experiencing the same hurt in her life.) I know she's hurt, and I know he fills a need I can't (or, possibly, she won't let me, out of devotion to him). And that is devastating to me.

Nearly as devastating is how I found out. She has told me she wanted to tell me but couldn't find the words. The question is: Would honesty have served me better? It's hard to tell and impossible to know, but I think it's fairly obvious that the way I discovered it has left me scarred and impedes our progress to this day.

All we can do is try to recover. Some people are recovering alcoholics; others are recovering Catholics; and we're recovering from Lost Lovering. My wife does say she's staying with me, but we both know that things will never EVER be the same, and that's a tragedy because we had something that we both said and many others agreed was an incredibly special and loving relationship. I had hoped to live long and lovingly with her. Sadly, I still hope to live lovingly with her, but there have been days when I wasn't too concerned about how long I might live. And that's the horrible, depressing, dastardly short of it: I'd say that any person reading, seeing and hearing about how much happiness the phenomenon of reconnecting with a lost love can be should check the ring finger: If they are married, or you are, DON'T DO IT. At the least, it's the death of a relationship; at worst, you can become suicidal (my wife has said more than once that she's been tempted to put a gun to her head; fortunately, we don't have guns).

As I said, forgiving is much easier than forgetting. There are nights when I'm in bed with her, listening to her gentle breathing (and, OK, an occasional snort), when I feel like the loneliest man in the world. Even though I'm blessed to be snoring next to the love of my life, I can't help but wonder whether she's dreaming of him.

We're trying to move on, together, but the big stumbling block is that she is on record as saying she'll always love him. And I'm on record as hating his guts. Not much in common there for rebuilding a marriage.

John and I were first loves; I was 14 and he was 16. We dated steady for six months, and then I broke up with him to date others. We grew apart and went our separate ways.

Over the years, I thought about him from time to time. I had been married for 30 years when I decided to contact John's mom. I wanted to find out where he was, what he was doing, and if he was happy. My husband approved of my doing this.

John's mother was willing to give him a letter I wrote, and he soon called me. I enjoyed the conversation immensely as we caught up on each other's lives. I thought that as long as I didn't see him, it would be acceptable for me to talk to him by phone; he called weekly after that. Soon the calls became more frequent, 4 or 5 times a week.

After a year of telephone calls—and me still not agreeing to see him face to face—he told me that one day he would just stop by and surprise me, unannounced. I thought I'd rather know and be ready to meet him, so we set a date for him to come to my house and we would go out to lunch—again with my husband's approval.

I never would have recognized him by his appearance, but everything else was the same. Our memories surfaced and we reminisced all afternoon. We had a wonderful day. At one point he stopped the car in a pretty spot and kissed me; it was just as if we were 14 and 16 again. I remembered his kisses as if it had been yesterday, and I responded.

An affair began, of course. I had a lot of guilt to overcome. I divorced my husband and married John immediately. We love each other passionately—and passion has not been part of my vocabulary for over 30 years.

My four grown children are very upset over my decision to leave their dad, and they have severed all ties with me. I begged for their forgiveness. I even tried to stop seeing John for their benefit. But the love between John and me was stronger than anything, and I decided to take my happiness and love John openly. I just couldn't see living my life to please my children; they have spouses of their own and their own lives.

I never wanted to hurt my husband, either. I have beaten myself up over what I did, and have suffered a lot for it. I was not prepared for my old feelings for John to return, but they did. I have advised others not to do what I did, unless they are ready for the consequences. Yet how can I be sorry? John and I have had the best year of our lives together, and we love each other so very much.

In August of 1997, I contacted my first boyfriend by sending a birthday greeting to him. I had been disowned from my family by my father in December of 1982, and he was the only person who knew all the people in my family, because we knew each other from high school.

It had been at least 11 years since we had really talked. He immediately empathized when I discussed my family situation with him, and he even offered to do anything he could to rectify the situation. At the same time, he apologized for the way he had treated me when we were young, and he acknowledged that I had always treated him with love and respect. It felt so good to receive support from this old friend!

There are no words to describe what happened over the course of a few weeks. Although we lived a thousand miles apart, we almost immediately connected again, via email, on many common areas of interest. Then our respective spouses discovered our correspondence. I was ordered by my husband to cease my conversations with my first love, and apparently his wife was very angry as well.

I suffered a miscarriage in July and turned again to my lost lover for support. But there was a quick end to this once very cherished reunion. He blamed me for all of his marital problems. I expect to be named in his divorce proceedings by his wife.

My marriage is troubled, and I will most likely be in therapy for at least another year, trying to resolve the problems that have arisen because of this rekindling. No, we are not in contact any more. It is my understanding that he has not lost his wife, home or children after all, as was his fear if his wife ever found out we were speaking again. I wish him well, as I would any human being, but beyond that there is nothing left.

I am the first to admit that I made a BIG mistake by contacting him. The saying, "We cannot go back and make a new start, but we can begin today to make a new ending" has become my credo. It would have been better for everyone concerned if the events had not unfolded as they did. I would advise extreme caution to any married person who is considering a reunion with a former love. Sometimes it is best not to look in the rear view mirror!

I decided to contact my first love—my only true love—because my therapist suggested it might be the only way to get over her. She and I had dated for three years, and had even been engaged, but it all ended while I was away in the Marines and she fell for the college boy who was after her. I married seven years later, but I never recovered emotionally from losing Jan.

Although I am married, I had been thinking of her approximately fifty percent of my time over the past several years. It was affecting my life in a negative manner and I needed closure to "get on with it." I was not interested in renewing the relationship, just in trying to get over it. My therapist told me that, by contacting her, I would see that she was happy with her life, that she had probably changed considerably and we would have nothing in common, and that she had more or less forgotten all about me. That's not what I found at all.

I am still not sure what happened or why. Did she really miss me as much as I had missed her all those years? She seemed to be really scared of her husband, who hit her now and then. If she went anywhere during the day, she had to call him first and tell him where she was going. She said that everything had to be "just right" for him, or he would fly into a rage. She had lived that way for 35 years, and was too afraid to leave him.

We used a beeper to communicate. We had beeper codes all worked out: for example, one meant "I Love You," another meant "Call Me," another meant "Cancel Plans; I'm Stuck in the House." Sometimes we used phone booths and quarters so nothing could be traced; the amount of money we spent on calls was astronomical.

Our sexual experiences surprised me the most. We had never been sexually active as teenagers; she wouldn't let me touch her in private places. But when we met again, she said she had become sexually addicted over the years, and this turned out to be true. We had sex during the majority of the time we were together—in her car, in the park, in various motel rooms, at her parents' house while they were gone, on the hood of my car, in the back of her husband's truck, in a Victoria's Secret dressing room, in the stairwell of a doctors' office building, on her dining room table, in her bathroom, in my bedroom, in their hallway, and even in a funeral home (don't ask). She was very passionate, and always the initiator (which I loved and was a real turn-on for me). She told me if I didn't like it, we might as well break it off right then. Sex seemed to play a major role in her life, and I think in some ways she was using me. Don't get me wrong—I loved every minute of it. Now that is one of my big problems. It was like she had injected me with a drug, gotten me hooked, and when it was over, that was the end; she left me to die from withdrawal.

We finally got caught. Her husband found out and called my wife. It was quite a battle for the next few weeks. I moved out of my house. She asked her husband to leave and he went ballistic. He lost weight, cried for hours, couldn't go to work, and got very religious all of a sudden. He told everybody at the church, and all her relatives. She called me in tears and told me, "They don't understand! I told them I love you but they won't allow me to leave him." She was too weak to go through with a divorce. She couldn't stand the pressure. She finally told me, "I can't see you anymore. Please don't try to call me. It's too dangerous. They are watching. I can't do anything." It was over.

Remember when Forrest Gump is standing at a big window staring out at the red sunset, thinking about Jenny… the lost, hopeless, hurt in his face? That's me. That's my whole life right there in that one frame.

I really don't know how I go on every day. The pain gets so overwhelming. Some days I cry at work and have to leave early. I go home and crawl into bed and pull the covers up around my head. Sometimes I just lay there until the following morning. There is a prison within me.

I happened to come across an article about your research on rekindling old flames. Last Thursday, at an office party at my law firm, I saw my high school girlfriend for the first time in ten years. She is now married and has four children. I have never married.

She is two years older than I am. Her parents couldn't stand me. Nevertheless, she was my first kiss, and we fooled around a little. I was her first love, I think.

When I saw her last week, she looked exactly as she did then, only more beautiful. We spent a lot of time talking about the "good ol' days," even though her husband wouldn't leave us alone for ten minutes.

I am seriously interested in seeing if she would have lunch with me. Quite frankly, I am interested in seeing what, if anything, could develop. I know that you advise married people against such meetings. I also saw, though, that the odds of something developing are rather good.

The jealous, controlling husband could be an invaluable asset in my pursuit. It is the laid back, trusting husbands that make these types of endeavors difficult. The more jealous he is, and acts, the more he will push her away.

Now, is such a pursuit on my part fair? Morally, no. But we live in a world where most marriages are unhappy ones, where people stay together out of fear, convenience, and the timeworn excuse of "for the children." I look at it very simply: if she is willing to cheat with me, then there is something missing from her marriage. I simply provide the opportunity, the forum in which to find that missing element, whether it be lust, romance, compassion, or simply the need to feel desired again.

If she is happy in her marriage, then the odds that she would cheat are very slim. She would make that very clear, and the pursuit would end. I think that the idea that these underlying, long-repressed feelings toward a past love create this powerful force to reconnect with that person oversimplifies the reason for cheating.

I do agree that it has a lot to do with returning to simpler times, to the days when life wasn't so complicated. Plus there is the additional element of familiarity. Nonetheless, it is a conscious choice to cheat, and that would be due to the fact that there is something missing from the marriage. I would simply provide that missing element.

Richard was my first "real" love. I was in 11th grade and he was a senior. My parents ADORED him! He was not only a gentleman (he didn't kiss me until after we'd been dating for several months), but he also became the best friend I'd ever had. He was my first date. My first kiss. And he always said that I was the first girl he'd ever really loved.

We were young, and we both had college and careers ahead of us. He received an appointment to West Point. You've no idea how hard it was to let him go. We kept in touch for almost a year… writing ten and twenty page letters, calling and talking for HOURS, and visiting during holidays. It was the hardest year I could imagine as a senior in high school.

I never once worried about us. Then, his little brother (who was a year younger than me), enrolled in my school later that year. He filled my head with wild stories about Richard's wild West Point adventures, and told me the best thing I could do for his brother was to let him go… "That's what Richard really wants, but he hasn't got the heart to tell you."

And so, I did. Later on, when his brother began to hit on me, I suddenly felt very stupid. Richard visited me at work one time shortly after that… we stood beside his car as he held me, and we trembled in the cold together. He put his ear to my lips and began saying something, but a huge truck went past us and I couldn't hear him. Before I could ask what he'd said, he kissed me on the cheek and he was gone.

My heart left with him. He was driving from my hometown in Georgia to Washington D.C., to be with his family for Christmas. I felt so stupid and lost that I quit work for the day and went home. I told my father my story, and he quickly gave me fifty bucks and the keys to his car: "I'll bet you can catch him if you get on the Interstate!" I flew like the wind, all the time praying that I WOULD catch him, but a speeding ticket put an end to my trip.

I didn't hear from him again for 20 years. He called my house after I was married and had two children, almost nine years ago. We talked for over two hours… catching up… sharing stories… it was as if a day hadn't passed between us. And yes, the ache around my heart was still there.

After the call, we started writing. He'd been divorced for several years and said he'd always kept me in the back of his mind. I told him all about my husband, and about my father's death. To my amazement, the next time I visited the place where Dad was buried, I found flowers that Richard had left.

We FINALLY met silently at an airport, a month ago. My husband and I were at the airport picking up a neighbor. Richard and I had talked a week before this, and he had mentioned that he would be passing through the airport on that day, and we LAUGHED about the possibility of us actually bumping into each other. But that was all that was said… the meeting was totally unexpected. The following poem will fill you in on the rest::

> For the first time in twenty years, our eyes locked.
> There we were on the tram, between concourses B & C
> With our spouses on our arms.
> He is The One I never forgot.
> He was my first. He knew me well.

He understood my heart. And there he was…
Two feet away.
And all we could do was stand there, speechless.
Thoughts ripping through my mind like fireflies
Memories coming at me like freight-trains.
Then he smiled that heart-piercing smile.
I instantly knew that he was remembering, too.
And then his features softened as he brushed away (a tear?).
His hand moved to the side.
We had learned sign language in school together.
"I ache," he secretly signed to me.
My heart moved and then my hand:
"I understand."
Then his: "You're beautiful."
"You're handsome. I like your hair."
"You haven't changed."
"Don't forget me."
"I never will."
The train doors opened. We all stepped out
Me and mine going left; he and his going right.
And though we parted,
We somehow left the train holding hands.

Those looks over the shoulder stick like glue. The last GLIMPSE of him I could have POSSIBLY got was a glimpse over the shoulder, and he was looking too. It was beautiful… almost creepy, but completely precious.

These first loves are such sweet desperations, aren't they? Being without them in our lives for twenty years is like being hungry… then suddenly, when we ARE with them, EVEN if it is the moment contained in an innocent glimpse… it's like we have been fed… full, satisfied, lost in the moment, not wanting to lose the satisfaction of the fill. Inevitably, the hunger soon sets in again… the face vanishes in the crowd and distance becomes the adversary again. First loves… as painful as they are exciting.

And, so many years too late, I found out during our reconnection what it was that he'd said to me that day at my work when we stood beside the car, what I couldn't hear … he said he whispered, "Please come back to me."

CHAPTER 10

Lost Again

On the spectrum of romance, there may be nothing more painful than a lost love who is found and then lost again. Of the first love participants in my 1990's survey, 72% reported that they were still together. This is certainly a high percentage, but it was no comfort whatsoever to the people in the remaining 28% of the reunions that failed.

The failure rate is higher now: my survey data from 2004 to 2005 with 1300 new participants indicates that only 50% were still together at the time of the survey.

Devastated

When people write to me with stories of failed reunions, the word that inevitably appears in their narratives is *devastated*.

The current failure rate of rekindled romances is greater than the percentage published in *Lost & Found Lovers;* this is a consequence of the sharp increase in extramarital affairs—from 30% of participants in the first survey to 62% in the new survey. One or both of the lost loves remained married and ended the rekindled romance.

Other lost love reconnections ended because the couples were mismatched during their initial, teen romances. As one participant reported, "At least now I know that our original breakup was meant to be. Nothing has changed at all."

Some rekindled romances were fairy tales come true, but they ended as nightmares. Suddenly something snapped in reunions that had been beautiful. Most often (but not always) it was the men who left. Some men gave no explanations and disappeared without a trace; it is possible that the men themselves did not fully understand why they needed to run. The discarded lost lover's inability to give meaning to the rupture intensified the relationship's loss and created overwhelming shock, grief, and humiliation. As one woman wrote, "I felt stupid for even trying the reunion. He left me years ago, and I gave him the opportunity to leave me again. How dumb is that?!" Abandoned participants reported seeking immediate psychotherapy and taking antidepressants; these recovery measures were helpful, but the healing still took, on the average, three years.

Till Death Do Us Part

One of the most heartbreaking losses of renewed love is saying goodbye for the final time. Reunited first loves are so bonded when they marry that the death of the spouse feels especially tragic to the survivor. Yet the spiritual aspects of lost love give meaning and comfort.

Too Late

For some lost loves, there can be no reunion at all. Men and women wrote about searches for former sweethearts that ended with the discovery that their lost loves had died. These people were heartbroken and stuck in a perpetual limbo, unable to heal.

When we learn that people from the past have died without our knowledge, there may be a grieving for the loss of that person, for the loss of that part of ourselves (where our lives intersected with theirs), and guilt because we did not even know they were gone: maybe we could have, should have, done more, if only we had known on time! There may be so many things that we wish we had said, but now that opportunity is lost forever.

Searchers who found that their first loves had died felt emotions that were exactly the opposite of the lost loves who happily reunited: instead of closure of past hurts and regrets, they experienced new regrets; instead of feeling young again, they suddenly felt older and more vulnerable; they did not recapture old aspects of themselves but felt a new loss of self.

I hope the stories in this chapter will bring some comfort to people who are not with their lost loves, as they see that their feelings, though terribly painful, are not unique. And I can try to reassure these men and women that time does heal broken hearts, even of the rekindled type. They may never get over their first loves completely, but as time passes, they will think about their lost-again loves less often; and they will think about them as loves from the distant past of adolescence and from the distant past of the reunion. Most of these men and women who lost their soul mates will go on to love again, but they will not believe me now. I understand.

Devastated

This a story bout a girl long time ago. This girl me, age 17. I see this boy one day, he sweet, he strong-legged, he funny, he olive-skin tan. This why I call him brown boy. Day I meet him he still the boyfriend of other girl I know. He sitting with her, arms around her, this a pretty circle but she big girl so this funny, too! I think myself, I like to be that girl. It's hot summer day, we at some lake house. These kids' parents got lake house. This another world for me. I in their world I got right grades, I classmate, but I not really in their world: good jobs, big houses, trips, clothes from stores I never go in. But they don't know none of this. Because their parents passing on little tunnel vision problem: they only see their own lives.

I never really think about brown boy after lake house time. Time pass. I get myself first real boyfriend. He nice, I like him, I start have sex, we kinda dating. I start college, he in college far away. I go one time see him, get train lotta hours then hitchhike to college town he in. Turn out he have girlfriend there who hang on him all night, I don' have one second with him. I sleep alone, they go off different room. I wanna wring this guy neck for not warnin' me that I traveling to get myself such a miserable, lonesome night. In the morning I have to pull this lil coward aside, he not gonna even say a word less I do.

Couple month later somethin' happen, friends make date happen for me and brown boy. Other guy history no time. I thrilled! Me and this boy comfortable. This good! This boy never have to woo me, he just fall in my eye. But damn, this boy go college too in far away town. First winter vacation we have lotta fun, we go to New York, we go to Broadway. We try n' get dressed up. My boy pants too short. He cranky his parents too cheap to get him new pants. I wearing my mother's skirt—I a small girl, long-time queen of hand-me-downs! But I not one bit mad, I on cloud nine. This boy make me so happy. But then college start again. We apart. I try make best of it, and college good thing for me, I like lotta new ideas, this place full ideas, so I pretty happy but sure I craving too to see this boy.

This boy drive long time see me sometime. I finally get to see this boy I "home" seeing my family. My family not like his asking for much my time. I torn. I like be with this boy—I love be with this boy—but I young and dumb. I don't know to handle it good. Ok, I say to my family.

So hard this long-distance thing, lousy. And we changing too in-between visits, we in growing years, each time gotta figure out who this boy now, who this girl now? And I complicated girl, busy mind, and family life with daddy who drink too much make stress for everybody. And boy complicated, too, he mix up in his own way, he dark inside sometime but he never talk about it. This why I call my boy melancholy. This why I write my boy like a dark lake. This why I write poem how my boy have wounded-bird in chest like me. He never understand me! I funny girl, way I talk.

This boy love me but he not so happy with me. I not interested one bit baseball, that true. I definitely not kind of girlfriend go watch boy play. I got own thing to do. This boy have a few other problem with me too: find me bit too wild, bit too independent.

Second summer I decide me and this boy gonna go somewhere nobody bother us. I gonna be better girlfriend, have lotta time for my boy. We gonna have fun. But the boy mopey, he gotta figure out what he do next, and he have no idea where I fit in and I resistin' being pin down. I active young feminist and world make me mad. This too much for my boy. I too damn serious. I walkin' out of movies when content displease me! And then come bad news. My family in state of crisis, anxiety truly rising out of control. I drained. I suddenly decide break off with this boy. This bad decision, I start think because I missing this boy too much. This not a good time make any decision but I so young, how I know that?

We break up, I sad for a long time. I start make plan go away next year few month, clear my head. I sad girl but it's true I also adventurous girl! This gonna be fun!

One day spring this boy call me, he got new car, he say we go together see place where he grow up. I go, this beautiful day. I so glad we making peace me and this boy. We making peace. Brown boy invite me home. But this not warm sex I remember, this cold, this sex between stranger. I go home.

I gonna forget this boy. I gonna forget this father drink too much. I gonna forget this brother now in rehab. I gonna forget old grandma need care at home. I gonna forget mother nervous wreck all these pressure. I leave my sisters too many problem, this not fair, but this what I do.

Couple year pass I married now. I very happy with man I with. But urge find this man come back again few years later. I write, he no answer.

Twenty years I no lay eyes on this person. Some reason I feel urge again to find this boy. I find him Internet. This boy really grown up man! My heart thumping. I so curious, how this boy grow up? Who he become? What he doin'? What he thinkin'? I surprised, this man divorce two time. Six month pass, this man never ask me one question bout my life. So okay, I say, this just guy thing that he not asking any question, I keep write this man.

After one year, I write this man, I say, I gotta go now. But I write. I tell friend, I not gonna write again. But I write again. More I write less I like myself. I feeling like crazy person. I so desperate I ask my mother, what I gonna do? This nice, this the first time I ask my mother advice in twenty years! She say, leave him alone.

Maybe this story I tell you about brown boy sound like I stop love my husband, but this never true.

So this the way the story turn out. I always know it never gonna work. Someday I gonna think of this boy and not one bone in me sad, not one bone angry. But this gonna take time. This just ongoing human-being story bout imperfect boy and imperfect girl, man and woman, try to live. I just ordinary woman crave see boy who love me and who I love long time ago and have so hard time let go again. I queen of figuring-out like I queen-of-hand-me-downs but I never gonna know why. This just the way the story go.

The man tell another story. He tell short story. Sometime I think this man smarter than me, make life less complicated. I get all mix up! He say he fear get rejected again. He also say we not compatible. He as mixed up as me. If someday my boy decide tell me lil bit more elaborate story, I gonna read it or listen careful, that sure thing.

In the meantime, this my story. I not guilty. I not innocent. He not guilty. He not innocent. This grey-zone, this just lil bit of real life and real contradiction mix up with dream.

My first love is Thomas. He is Hispanic; I am not. I met him when I was fourteen. My home life was atrocious—full of drugs, violence, and fear—but Thomas treated me like a queen. He picked me up to go to school, bought me lunch, and took me home each day. A perfect gentleman with perfect manners, handsome and smart. I fell in love as hard as any fourteen year old can.

At fifteen, I was taken from my parents and sent to live with relatives back East. Thomas and I were devastated. He gave me a custom-designed gold ring with flowers and hearts. We pledged eternal love.

I went to school back East, and Thomas went into the Army, then to Viet Nam. He was the only man in his platoon who survived (I found out later), and the trauma and guilt ate at him. My gentle man was not the same. I saw him once more to say goodbye. He said he was "going away." I went through an incredible long depression. The one truly nice thing about my life was gone, and I didn't understand why. Where was my guy who took care of me?

I married and had a son, then divorced. Thomas wrote to me and said he had kept track of me over the last five years and wanted to see me. Oh my God!!! Miracles do happen! My first love had returned and all was right. We dated and found our love once again. He told me he left me because the trauma of his losses in the war devastated him, and he had wanted to protect me.

Almost a year later, we decided to get married. His dad liked me, but his mom hated me. She wanted him to marry a Latina. I attached to her anyway—I needed a mom, and I hoped she would love me and my son. I eloped with Thomas. Mom was PISSED!!! She took me aside and told me privately that she would destroy my marriage.

I believed that Thomas loved me enough to make our marriage work. But it took less than six months for his mother to destroy it; she told him horrible lies about my past, and pressured him to leave me. I moved away, got sick, and miscarried our baby after three months. I threw out the ring he had given me when we were fourteen.

I am forty-eight now, and I still love him. I try to remember only the times in high school when I was so special to him, and so loved. His mom found him a Latina woman. They married and had children, I heard.

I met Jimmy, my first love, the summer before my senior year of high school. I grew up in a rural part of Virginia. Several of my girlfriends and I had discovered a great swimming place along the river that summer. To get to the river, we had to drive down a steep, curved, dirt road, then walk across an old, dilapidated iron-frame bridge to get to the other side of the river where everybody swam. On one particular day that summer, as we walked across the bridge, some boys who were leaving passed us. One boy looked soooooo cute! I was immediately drawn to him. He smiled at me and said hello. He asked if we came down to swim often, and I told him we did. He told me his name was Jimmy, and that he would be back another time to swim and maybe he'd see me then. He smiled and said goodbye. My girlfriends and I giggled about him talking to me and continued across the bridge.

A few minutes later, I noticed Jimmy coming down the side of the river bank. He came over to me and said he had some extra time to swim. Of course I realized he had come back to get to know me. He had a little red TR4 Triumph; I was impressed. He asked for my phone number at the end of the day.

We dated for the remainder of the summer. Without a doubt, Jimmy was the man for me. Our relationship was passionate, intense, intimate, and full of love for each other.

Fall came, and Jimmy went away to college. We dated mostly on weekends and kept telling each other how much we loved each other. We could barely stand to be apart. I was going to go away to nursing school after high school, but Jimmy couldn't handle the thought of being away from me. He surprised me with an engagement ring and proposed. Our parents were not thrilled with our news. They thought we were too young, and there was pressure from both sides to end our engagement. But we were determined to stay together. We were soul mates.

I did go to nursing school and had the worst case of homesickness! I missed Jimmy and my family. But I stayed and graduated, then went back home… to Jimmy. He was finishing college and was in ROTC. He would be sent away to pilot training, and we would be parted again. This time we made arrangements to elope. I was twenty-one and he was twenty-two. We decided not to tell our parents. But when he left, we missed each other so badly that he did tell his parents and made arrangements to fly me down to be with him. His parents were very upset! But we stuck by our vows and were very happy being together as husband and wife!

Soon the pressure from Jimmy's parents became too much for him. He decided we should get our marriage annulled and just live together. I went along with the annulment so I wouldn't lose him.

Our relationship deteriorated after the annulment. Eventually I left Jimmy and moved into a place of my own. By then I was twenty-three. I met someone and dated for awhile. When he asked me to marry him, I did, and moved away from Jimmy (who was crushed).

This marriage lasted for twelve years. I thought of Jimmy often during those years. I never had the intimate or passionate love with my second husband that I had with Jimmy. I would daydream about Jimmy and wonder what he was doing and what kind of woman he was with. There was sadness in my heart because I didn't have him in my life. I hid that sadness from my husband all those years.

I was single again at thirty-five. I had lost all contact with Jimmy and didn't know where he was. But life had to go on, and I turned my heart and mind to other matters.

A little over a year ago, I got a call from my cousin that Jimmy was looking for me. He told my cousin how much he missed me and that he would always love me until the day he dies. I was so shocked at what my cousin was telling me! I got his address from her and wrote him a letter. Then I waited.

It took a few months for him to respond. He wrote, "I have often thought of you over the years. I have loved others in different ways and different places, but it never had the intensity or passion that I remember with you." The letter also said that Jimmy was married. Months went by until one day he called and told me he had a business trip to Maryland; I agreed to meet with him.

I was curious to see how he looked after almost twenty-five years. He looked great! He gave me a big hug, and we just looked at each other for a moment.

Then we talked about many things, about our past relationship and that neither of us has ever loved others the way we loved each other. We have both cherished our memories of the love we had. Jimmy has all of my old love letters that I wrote to him while we were dating. His wife knows he has these letters and finds it strange that he won't get rid of them.

I was in my forties when we reconnected, but I felt like a teenager in love all over again. He told me how unhappy he was in his marriage, but that he intended to stay for the children. He told me why he felt we are soul mates and how he loved me all of these years. But he is married and unavailable to me.

When he kissed me goodbye, he had such a sad look on his face. I could tell he didn't want to leave me. I wished he didn't have to go, too. I drove home and cried the whole way. It took me a month to stop crying. Even now, I get tears in my eyes just thinking about being away from him.

I was so emotionally distraught, I decided to write to him and tell him it would be better for us not to have any contact with each other while he is married. He never answered that letter, and I might never hear from him again. But I know I had to do what was right by not continuing to have contact with Jimmy, because I know it would have led to an affair, and that would have left me an emotional basket case. It was hard to send that letter, but it was the right thing to do.

My heart is filled with great sadness, and it has been very difficult for me! I wish now that I had not met Jimmy again. I thought we could just meet and be friends. I was wrong. Our emotions go much deeper than either of us knew.

I have chosen to remain single these past ten years because of my love for Jimmy; but he is married and may very well remain so. I believe with all my heart that if we ever do get back together, we will be the happiest couple in the world!

I dated a boy from ages fourteen through eighteen. Soon after I went away to college, I broke up with him. He had wanted us to marry and was devastated by the breakup. I wanted to see what else life had to offer. We were both from small towns in Delaware.

Twenty years later, after we had both married, had children, and divorced, Alan contacted me. The letter was brief, but enclosed were some photos of me, taken when I was eighteen. I was terribly moved that he had kept and hidden these photos from his wife for so long.

We were both unattached at the time, and things got very hot very quickly. We got along extremely well, the sex was outstanding, our children became friends. In less than a year, we became engaged and I moved from California back to New York; both of our families were thrilled. Then two weeks later, he backed out.

He didn't want to go through with it, and he gave no explanation. I moved back to California, my tail between my legs, humiliated, devastated. The only romantic fantasy I had always hung onto had evaporated for good.

Three weeks later he called me in California. He wanted to sell his house and business and move to be with me. He said he had made a big mistake. I agreed, and told him he'd have to live with it. I could never marry him after that betrayal. We stopped communicating. He asked me to keep the ring because he wanted to marry me "someday."

Our reunion, courting, engagement, and breakup took eleven months.

Susan loves me! I know she does! She's told me so!
When we're together, she's shown that her love for me is real.
Now she's writing to say, "It won't work."
She's giving up on "PS" (Paul/Susan).
Her husband is sick. Cancer. Unchanged in 9 years.
Lifetime of heavy drinking. And heart troubles.
When is "enough" enough?
She tells me, "You're so patient, so understanding."
Yet she's ready to give up all that we've dreamed of.
I've cried. Bawled like a child. Taken down all her pictures.
Still, her nightgown and robe hang in my bedroom closet.
Her toothbrush stands in the bathroom.
I'm willing to wait still longer for the lady I love truly, deeply.
She writes, "It's time to quit fooling ourselves."
I love Susan! She loves me! Our Someday will be!
After almost 40 years of being apart, Heaven was finally ours.
I often prayed that God would guide Paul and Susan,
Help us to know and do His will.
Isn't it awful when your prayers are answered —
And it's not what you wanted?

Dr. Kalish, thank you for your recent note of comfort. It seems that the only strokes of comfort I feel right now are when I'm talking about him to friends and family. But, after a year and a half, their patience is wearing thin, and their only real concern is my "letting go," not hanging onto the memories.

What might be making matters worse is that sometimes he calls me (when he's been drinking). I don't know which would be worse—a clean break, or the hope for an occasional letter or phone call.

I can't seem to find a comfort zone for myself. I try to be nice to myself: I filled this summer with friends, travel, and fun. But I find myself thinking how much better it would be with Gary there, too. I go to the seashore and it is so romantic that I long for him. He said he spent almost thirty years thinking about me; will I spend the next thirty years yearning for him?

I even tried to emphasize only his faults in my mind, or remember someone else who might have been sexier, someone who drank less, someone who never made the driving mistakes he made, and on and on, but that "therapy" didn't work. I am hoping that time will heal this pain, if I can only drop the "what ifs!"

It doesn't take much to bring on thoughts of him: seeing a car like his, seeing a couple kissing at the airport, noticing a teenager wearing a Cal sweatshirt like his. Why did this all happen, if not for us to be together? What was the point?

This obsessive thinking has taken a toll on me. I happen to believe that stress has physical manifestations after a while. Since last winter, I have had unexplained ailments that no doctor has been able to improve. They have no explanation, but *I* know!

The "easy out," I've thought, is to transfer these feelings to another man (or maybe a dog?). When I've traveled, I've noticed my seat mates. Could I flirt? Could I be interested in meeting someone else? NOT REALLY!

Or, maybe I could try hypnosis? Change the feelings and redirect the thoughts? I need to do something. Where do I put these feelings for him? The longing? The passion? The love?

Till Death Do Us Part

Morris and I met when I had just turned seventeen and was ready to begin City College of New York. He was twenty and had just returned from the South Pacific where he had served in the Navy for two years during World War II. He had actually been my sister's beau before he went overseas. However, by the time he returned to New York, my sister had become involved with another young man.

Morris was not really dismayed. He and my sister had not actually been romantically involved. And so, when he came to our house to reactivate the friendship, my sister was not available, but I was. In no time at all, Morris and I became sweethearts.

For five years we dated. I completed my education and began teaching. Morris, an orphan who had been brought up by an older sister, attended college part-time and then worked as a counselor at a boys' home. His need to help others followed him all his life.

In spite of our great attraction for each other, I felt that we were not suited for marriage. I wanted to marry a man with a profession, a Renaissance man, the kind of man I thought my father was. Morris was not interested in scholarly pursuits. He was very artistic, creative, athletic, clever, and talented, but not a scholar. And I thought scholarship was an important attribute for my husband-to-be.

Morris finally became impatient. As an orphan from age two, he desperately wanted to marry and become a family man. I wanted to spread my wings and be a career girl. And so with much sadness on both sides, we agreed to end our romance. Six months later, I learned from my sister that Morris had married. I was devastated. I couldn't believe that the boy/man who professed to love me so much could fall in love with someone else so quickly.

The years passed. I continued to teach. Morris seemed to want to stay connected to me, but I found his wife to be a bore, and it became uncomfortable for me to be around them.

In 1974, twenty-six years after Morris and I had ended our romance, he called me and suggested lunch. I thought he wanted to talk about his children, so we made the date. I had never married. At lunch, I learned that his marriage had ended eight months before he called me. And Morris and I took off exactly where we left off—just as attracted to each other as when we were young, but older and wiser. It was amazing. It was beautiful. It was the most fulfilling relationship I had ever had. We couldn't get enough of each other, physically or emotionally.

We finally married in 1981. Sadly, it took me seven years to figure out that he was the best thing that ever happened to me. He, of course, was ready to marry me immediately, but I still had hang-ups to resolve. Thank God he was patient.

We had almost eleven years of marriage before his giant heart gave out in September, 1992. We had just returned from a two hundred seventy mile bicycle trip along the rugged and hilly Oregon coast, something he had wanted to do. As we had in our younger days, we did hiking, bicycling, laughing, hugging, kissing and this time around, actual love making, through our fifties and sixties. It was absolutely marvelous. I grew to love him completely as I felt he had always loved me—with no reservations.

I have been bereft since he died, so suddenly of a heart attack. I have many lovely memories that I wouldn't trade for the world. My only regret is that it took me so long to recognize and appreciate his true value. However, when he died, it was with the knowledge that we had a special love that is not given to everyone to experience.

My precious husband has been gone for ten years and I am still trying to deal with this loss. But as you no doubt have deduced, I love to talk about my sweetie. Writing about him is like having him in my arms.

My Dad fell in love with my lost love long before I did. In high school, friends of mine kept pointing him out to me and telling me that he was looking at me. He was the most breathtakingly beautiful guy I'd ever set eyes on. So handsome that I couldn't look at him because I'd feel my face grow red and my heart would feel as if it would jump out of my chest.

This went on the majority of the school year, until the Valentine's Day dance. I had been invited by several friends, but I turned them all down in hopes of being "available" if HE ever asked me. He never did. Little did I know that he was having the same problem I was… his friends were beside themselves trying to get the two of us together.

The night of the dance, his friends and my friends got together behind our backs. One of his friends asked me if I wanted to dance, and one of my friends asked him if HE wanted to dance. On the dance floor, our partners danced us over together and switched partners. And so we became a couple.

We dated like we'd known each other forever, but it was my FATHER who REALLY fell for my boyfriend first. The two of them fished together and hunted together, and my boyfriend was even the best man in my cousin's wedding! My entire family adopted him LONG before I realized I was falling in love with him.

He left for military school and it wasn't until then that I realized I was in love with him. Oh, we'd said we loved each other, but I didn't realize the depth of it till I was without him. He asked me to wait for him until Christmas and gave me his mother's engagement ring. We planned on getting married immediately after his college graduation. I was elated, but so sad that we had to be apart for four years.

One summer, I wrote him a letter and ended it. It was a crazy thing to do, and I'd put very little thought into it, but I broke up with him for no other reason than I was afraid to love someone as much as I did. Stupid… and a regret I'll have for the rest of my life.

Even stupider, I married the next guy who came along. It didn't last. We were married a year and a half. I was still in love with my lost love.

Ten years later, he called me out of the blue, right after my second husband

and I had our first child. We chatted like not a day had passed, and I suddenly began to feel a strange familiarity flow through me. I felt young, renewed, and full of life for the first time in AGES! I was happily married, but hearing his voice again brought back WAVES of emotions I thought were LONG gone.

We met a year later and boy, was it some reunion! I'd never felt as happy, and we were both fighting like everything to keep our feelings for each other at bay. We failed miserably while saying "good-bye." Once again, we parted. He married wife number two and we lost contact.

Another six years passed and he emailed me again out of the blue. Once again we rekindled our romance, but this time there was no denying that we were truly meant for each other. We talked of marriage and timing. We talked about our families and helped each other get through sticky times with our spouses. We encouraged each other to have good, successful marriages. He and I were the dearest and best of friends. I loved him more than anyone in my life, and shortly before September, we'd planned to decide how and when we were going to proceed with our relationship. It was going to be hard, but we knew it was something we needed to do... for us.

Circumstances changed quickly. He was in a tragic automobile wreck and was seriously injured. I confessed everything to my husband, then flew to be at his side, and on August 11th of this year, I sat with him for the last time. This was very difficult for his wife, who, like my husband, knew nothing about our reunion until that moment. He died peacefully the following Sunday.

His brother sent me a box of things that my lost love had instructed him to put together for me; one of them was his mother's engagement ring that I'd given him back 22 years earlier. I now wear it on my hand all the time and will never EVER take it off.

My husband and I are going through a rocky time right now, but we're slowly finding our way. Everything is out in the open, and I'm finding it easy to be honest with him about everything for the first time in our relationship. My husband in no way is the love of my life, but I'm hopeful that we'll grow closer over time. There isn't a day that goes by that I don't miss my first love dearly, and right now, I'm fighting rough bouts of depression. Last week, there were a few days when I just crawled back into bed after the kids left for school.

I miss him. I miss him more than I can express. To know that I may never have that feeling again... that closeness... that ability to have someone read my thoughts and know me inside and out and still LOVE me... God... I miss that so much.

Still, I have some wonderful memories of him that I will always treasure. We had some incredible times together and until I die, I will always think of him as my closest friend.

Too Late

I met him when I was only seventeen. He was from Vermont, but he was attending college in New York and living with his elderly aunt who was a friend of my mother. He was so handsome. We saw each other as often as we could, and corresponded in between, for two years.

He invited me to his graduation prom—with Skinny Ennis' orchestra, no less. He rented a tux! I was very excited—I just knew he would pop the question before he returned home to Vermont the next morning.

But it was not to be. At the last minute, the aunt had to go out of state to tend to a sick relative. My parents saw that there would be no chaperone and therefore they would not permit me to go to the prom with him. It broke my heart and I literally cried for days. I kept saying over and over to myself, "If I ever have any disappointments in my life, none will ever hit me as hard as this." I was right.

I went to college, and our correspondence faltered. I met someone and married him, even though I didn't like him; I was curious about sex. Today, it would have been an affair; back then, it was a marriage.

Some twenty-five years and five children later, the new feminist movement and counseling gave me the courage to leave my unhappy marriage. On a business trip to Boston, I obtained a rental car and drove to the small hometown of my lost love. The phone book did not reveal his name, but I had a good idea: small town newspapers know everything! So I called, and an elderly lady at the newspaper told me that she had known his family. My lost love had become a physician in a nearby town.

I got back in the rental car and drove there. Still no record of him in the phone book, so I went to this town's newspaper office. The man behind the counter answered my query with, "Yes, indeed, he was a prominent man here; he passed away just a month ago." My legs turned to jelly, and I looked for a nearby chair. I had enough presence of mind, however, to ask to see the obituary.

I read that he had been a high school biology teacher, then had gone back to school to get his medical degree. Looking down the column, I discovered that he had been divorced. The death had been sudden; no cause was listed.

All the way back to Logan Airport, after my first cry, I kept saying over and over, "It's so sad! If only I had been here a couple of months earlier… "

That was more than 25 years ago. I am now 75, but the sadness remains.

I have always thought about a young woman named Melissa. I say this in the past tense because Melissa was killed in an automobile accident at the age of 18. I loved her so much, for so many years, yet she never knew how much I thought of her and longed for her.

We met at a summer camp in 1980. It was love at first sight. My heart was so alive! I needed to know her, her name, everything about her. It felt as though a dark cloud had lifted from me and was replaced with my love for her.

Melissa lived in Rhode Island and I lived in Connecticut. I didn't care how far she lived from me. I had a job at a restaurant, and I was going to spend my money on bus fare and on her. Nothing was going to keep me from her. Nothing.

Then suddenly she stopped writing. I called her after school one day to find out what had happened. She told me she only wanted me as a friend, but that we could still talk to each other on the phone. But I wanted more. My heart cried out to her. I was losing someone who meant more to me than anything else in the world. She didn't realize how much I cared for her. A lot of people called it puppy love, but I would not have gone through three years of high school without dating anyone else, or kept thinking of only her, if it were just puppy love.

I know her parents must have somehow influenced her to change her mind about me. I still carry the guilt of what we did together sexually. Maybe her parents knew.

It's hard for me to write about this, but I want someone to know that I still have these strong feelings of loving Melissa truly, not love based on sex. I married twice and divorced twice. My feelings for my wives never approached those I had for Melissa.

Recently, I went to visit her high school; I found out that she had died soon after she graduated. I reminisced with her teachers. They all talked about her in glowing terms—she was an honor roll student, and a natural at drama, a kind and sensitive young woman. I felt so damn lucky to have been loved by her.

I've enclosed a copy of a photo of her, to show you how beautiful she was. I've had this picture on my dresser all these years.

Maybe if she had lived, she would have given me a second chance. But I'll never know. I hope others get the chance to get back together with their first loves, because I still miss mine. I will always think of her. No one could ever take her place in my heart. No one.

I have just finished reading an article about your research on lost loves, and I felt compelled to share with you a recent experience of mine, in hopes that you might be able to explain some of the things that have happened to me.

First let me tell you about myself. I am a 53 year old man, still married to the same lady I married at twenty whom I love very much. I have grown children, and four grandchildren. I am financially comfortable and satisfied with what we have been able to achieve.

In high school, I went out with a girl named Mary Ann. I loved her very much, but she moved away with her family. I asked her to marry me before she left, but she was noncommittal. After that, I managed to visit her a few times and stay at her parents' house, but I realized her dad was not really happy to see me. I asked her dad if we could marry, but never got an answer.

A year later, a friend of hers called to tell me she was getting married soon. I don't really recall having much of a reaction to this news.

I met my wife not too long after. We have had a good marriage for these thirty-three years. I love my wife very much, and my children, and they are all very supportive of me. They have known about my search from the start.

My dad died last year, and there have been other recent deaths in the family. I had an almost overpowering need to find her. I went looking, and found that she had died in 1992. It was devastating news to me.

All of those years when she was seldom more than just a random thought now and then—and then she was gone forever. I would never be able to find the answers to so many questions. She would always be the beautiful seventeen-year-old in the pictures—the always seventeen-year-old ghost that had apparently always been there just below the surface, and now I could never see her again.

I found Mary Ann's daughter and returned some things of hers, and we talked on the phone a couple times. I asked for a picture of her mother taken later in her life, so that I could age her, because I can't seem to do this in my mind. But for some reason she hasn't responded to my request, and I no longer expect her to. Yet I have this urge (or need) to know about Mary Ann and her family.

I've always been analytical and couldn't relate to emotionally based actions. Now my emotions are right at the surface and the simplest things bring tears to my eyes. I can't rationalize this. I seem to be on a nostalgia trip, and I can't stop it.

Why did I go searching when I did and not years ago, when she was still alive? Why do I have such a real sense of loss now, when she has been out of my life for nearly forty years? Did I also lose the chance to return to earlier, "perfect" times? And why has this whole thing opened up communication and improved my relationship with my wife? Was the search for a seventeen-year-old girl because of a "mid life crisis?" Am I grieving?

I need to turn this situation into a comfortable memory that I can live with. Somehow. But how?

As I was growing up, my family and friends let me know that, because I was blind, I was disqualified when it came to romance. As my friends hit adolescence and turned boy crazy overnight, I withdrew into the safety of music. I didn't even have crushes on boys; I wasn't going to put myself through the inevitable pain of rejection. Even at the age of nineteen when I met Bob, I didn't recognize my feelings for what they were. Since we met while I was assigned to a psychiatric hospital as a summer work-study student and he was a patient, I just thought I was getting overly involved in my work by trying to be his friend.

Bob had had a breakdown after the collapse of his marriage and the loss of his two little children in a custody battle. When I first met him, he was very bitter and hostile toward nearly everyone, but we quickly formed an intense bond. He told me that I helped him tremendously, and many times he thanked me.

Because of the situation, we were always under severe constraints. I was constantly afraid that I would get into trouble for spending so much time with him. I tried to be professional, but it was clear to both of us that there was more between us.

At the end of the summer, when I left the program and returned to college, I asked Bob to write to me. For several months we had an intense and important correspondence (my roommate was my reader), even though we never spoke on the phone and never made any gesture toward seeing each other. One day Bob wrote that he had just realized something for the first time—that I loved him. He didn't say how he felt about that, or what his feelings were for me, but it was a very exuberant letter.

I panicked; I did not feel ready to love anyone, and I wasn't supposed to love him, a patient in the program! It was all very distressing to me, because I knew that he had really hit on the truth. I was afraid to admit it to myself or to him. I wrote back about how of course I loved him as a friend. Our correspondence petered out very quickly after that, and I never heard from him again.

Short-lived as it was, that experience was a turning point in my life. Bob gave me a sense of confidence in myself as a woman and awakened longings in me that I had never dared to feel before. After that summer, I was determined to overcome my shyness, to learn to talk to boys no matter how often they rejected me, to become someone interesting and desirable to the male gender. Eventually everything I sought did come to me. Today I am happily married and have two wonderful grown sons. I know that I would never have dared to tackle the things I feared if Bob had not come into my life. He said that I helped him, but he helped me far more.

Ten years ago, I played my tape recorded journal from the work-study program. I was swept back to that long ago time, and I became profoundly aware of how much he had given me and how I had never thanked him. To make matters worse, I realized for the first time that I must have hurt him by my reaction when he told me that I loved him. I felt compelled to find him, to tell him how truly important he had been to me, to let him know that he had changed the direction of my life. This was before the Internet, so I had to work harder to find him than I would if I searched today.

I still had his old address; using a Haynes Cross-Index Directory, I got the names of all the people now living on that block. With the help of my family, I wrote to each, explaining that I was searching for an old friend and was asking for help. From telephone books and a database search, I got lists of people with his name (a very common one). I sent out more than 150 search letters all over his home state. The search became a driving force in my life, shaping all my days. It was something that I absolutely had to do, and I would not quit no matter how long it took.

I was very much heartened by the responses I received to my letters. It was amazing to me how many people took the time to reply, to explain that they were not the person I was seeking and to send their best wishes. Finally, through the help of a friend from Bob's former block, I got the name and address of his sister.

Five months after my search began, I received a letter from her, informing me sadly that Bob had died five years prior. He had taken his own life in a single-car accident. His sister told me that she and his other siblings would like to hear from me again and also talk to me if I wanted to. It was a kind, caring letter and it meant a great deal to me, despite the very real pain of knowing that I was too late to find Bob himself.

With some apprehension, since I didn't know if they were aware of his hospitalization, I wrote his siblings a long letter—33 single-spaced typed pages!—describing our relationship and why I had wanted to find him. I have spoken to Bob's sister twice since then, and she has been wonderfully warm and welcoming toward me. It has been so important to share details of Bob's life, knowing that she really loved him, and that she cares about this story. It has been affirming to hear about him from her, confirming that Bob really was the person I carried in my memories all these years.

In many ways his life was hard and disappointing, but I felt better knowing that he came from such a close and loving family. All four siblings wrote to me with their reactions to my letter. Then we all spoke together (her house has many telephone extensions!). This has clearly been an emotional experience for them; she tells me they all cried and spent a lot of time reminiscing about Bob, about the good times.

I cannot get over my sadness in knowing that I waited five years too long. I wish so much that I had told Bob what he meant to me while I had the chance. Yet the connection I have developed with his family assures me that my search was not in vain.

Truly exciting is Bob's siblings' decision to begin a search of their own—to find his grown children. Bob never saw them again after they were six and three years old; his ex-wife made visitations too difficult and told the children many venomous things about him, so he gave up. But his sister said that if I could find them after 25 years without even knowing their names, certainly they could track down Bob's grown children.

Bob enriched my life beyond measure. I pray that I may still have an opportunity to repay him, by restoring his children to his family and redeeming his reputation in their eyes through all of us who loved him.

CHAPTER 11

Still Thinking of You

Many people are still longing for their first loves. Why does young love create such haunting memories? Does the intensity of the lifelong feelings match the intensity of the original romance? Not always. In fact, a person's "first love" might have regarded him or her as "just a friend."

So what is first love? Is it dependent on the amount of time spent with that person many years ago? No, it is more enigmatic than that.

I first saw her at a small airport in Wisconsin in 1945. I had come home from the war and was working at the airport.

The moment I saw her I knew she was special. She was a little over five feet tall, with short dark hair. Her carriage was erect and she had the confident appearance of a young woman who was the product of private schools. And indeed, I found out that she was 17, almost 18, and the daughter of a wealthy family who lived near the country club.

She was at the airport to take flying lessons. I loved aviation and flying, and in those days it was very difficult to find a girl who had the same interests. I watched her take off and disappear, but I knew I would ask her out soon.

The very next day she was there for another lesson. It was July; the heat was oppressive on the ramp. The airplane's starter was not working, and her instructor in the back seat asked me to start the engine by hand. I agreed, and as I looked over the engine cowling into the coolest blue eyes I had ever seen, I tried to start the engine, but it refused to start (as it frequently did in hot weather).

As I repeatedly tried to start it, they were becoming very hot in the cockpit, which was surrounded by Plexiglas windows that did little but emphasize the sun's heat. Finally, she stopped my efforts by calling me to the side of the plane. I watched as she removed her blouse and handed it to me through the side window. She asked me to keep it until she returned from the flight. I was 21, and about to strangle at the sight of the lovely girl who was now clad only in a very full brassiere above her jeans. Her instructor, a woman pilot who was a complete prude, was flushed three shades of red and about to faint. To my delight, I knew in that instant that this girl was used to being her own woman! But I also immediately knew that the signal had been given, the gauntlet had been cast down. I was not about to ignore the signs that were so clear!

The engine started soon afterward and she took off on her training flight. An hour later I met the plane, as soon as it came to a stop, and gave her the blouse. I asked her for a date immediately, and she accepted. From that day on, for more than three years, we were very close and were together every summer day. In the winters, she went to a girl's prep school out of state, but we wrote hundreds of letters to each other and talked on the phone when we could. When summer returned each year, we resumed our relationship.

We were intimate on many occasions, but not in a final way. You have to understand that in the 1940's, in Wisconsin, young men and women did not reach majority until age 21, and I felt my responsibility to her acutely. The risk of pregnancy would have been dangerous to her and to her status in the community. The girl I was hopelessly in love with was no ordinary female. Her photo was often in the Society pages of the major newspaper in town, and an unwanted incident would have been too terrible to contemplate. Although I wanted to consummate our relationship, I needed to protect her more. Besides, I loved knowing that she was a virgin, even though I would desperately have loved to change that condition.

When it came time for her to enter a university, her mother sent her to England, too far for me to follow. And, I knew her mother wouldn't like that. I was not from a family of equal status; my parents were not wealthy like hers. She was going to continue her education, and I was going to work. One last night together was bittersweet, and I told her that I would always love her. It was a wrenching experience, and I knew that I was losing someone very important to me, but I was unable to stop what was happening.

I never saw her again. But I never stopped thinking about her. I am now in my seventh decade and still wish that I were with her. A few years after our separation, I married, as did she, and she still lives not far from the airport where we met. She has a husband and children, and I am divorced with grown children of my own.

I have talked to her by telephone a number of times over the half-century that separates us, not seeking a get-together, but merely speaking about aviation matters. But a few years ago, I wrote a short story about our flying experiences in which she was the heroine and which expressed thoroughly my love for her. She has a copy and therefore knows that my feelings for her have not changed over the years.

Still, even today, I feel a great need to protect her, and I would never do anything that would jeopardize her marriage, unless I knew that she desired such action on my part.

Although I am a writer, I don't have an ending for this story, and it may be one not to my liking when it happens. But I faithfully read the obituaries in my hometown paper, and you know what my hopes are in that regard. This much is certain: if the opportunity arises I will make this wonderful woman my wife, if she will have me, even if we have few years left to us.

If anyone told me as a young man that after fifty years I would feel this strongly about a lovely girl pilot I would meet in 1945, I would have laughed. But I am not laughing at all now, because I know that I have needed her through every one of those years we spent apart.

Usually I would never write to some stranger… but I do have a "first love" memory, and I have found your web site because I need to find a way to release the energy I spend wondering, thinking about whether my first love thinks about me the same way, and if I can ever love anyone else the same way.

The feelings of passion that I felt with my first love are incomparable to any other relationship I've ever had. I can literally take a vacation in my mind sometimes just thinking about when we dated. Thinking about it makes me feel dizzy and high!

But should I expect this type of feeling with the man who I will end up marrying? I know how passionate feelings can be. I love the guy who I am with now very much, although at times I become frustrated with him and I find myself comparing him to my "first love." Sometimes, I think that if my first love were to find me and say, "I'm sorry that I did not come for you sooner, I want to be with you, I have thought about you everyday, and I want to take you away and marry you" that I would follow, provided that we had the chance to know each other again and I still approved of him.

What if "first love" cannot be again? Then what? I choose to keep my memories of him close to my heart and leave them as memories. Presently, I have a beautiful loving relationship that has been built on trust, love, and laughter which is also incomparable. But I must close saying that my on and off thoughts of my first love keep me wondering if I should seek him out for peace of mind and soul or keep it a memory.

I read about your research. The premise is intriguing and has struck a chord with me. My "lost love" probably wouldn't qualify as anything real, because we were just turning eight when we were separated forever. But I can assure you we had most definitely established a bond that has lasted a lifetime in my memory.

I don't remember having any girlfriends in the first and second grade... only Eddy. I don't remember playing with girls at recess, just cowboys & Indians with Eddy and his friends. We lived in Placerville, California; it was May of 1942, and America had gone to war. During that school year of second grade, Eddy's mom brought him in one Saturday afternoon from their farm so we could attend a matinee at the movie theater. She sat well behind us and let us sit together in the second row from the front. It was a memorable occasion.

At school we sometimes played house at recess by making rooms of fallen pine needles and pretended to be a mother and father. We agreed we would marry when we grew up. I still can see his face... very blonde hair like my own, with deep blue eyes and full lips.

When my dad went off to Alaska to help build a base at Adak, I had to move to Sacramento to stay with an aunt, and they took me out of school several days before the end of the school year. Eddy and I sat on the bench under the big pine above the school yard and held hands and cried together as we said goodbye. I've never known how his life turned out but I've never, ever forgotten him. He was my first and truest love. We both knew we belonged together.

I haven't often mentioned Eddy to anyone, because they just look at me and laugh... or snort... or say something trite. So you've given me an opportunity to tell you another story about a love that was lost. Thank you.

I'm not sure why I am sending an email to a complete stranger about a lost love. I guess it may be the work you have done in this area. Here is my story:

I met this gal half my life ago, when I was a freshman at a college in Texas. It was second semester and I was at a tavern with some college buddies. I had met a gal at this tavern a few days before and she was there partying with us. I had no romantic interest in her, but we had played kissy-face a couple times. College freshman syndrome, I guess. On this particular night I saw Irene walk into the tavern. I felt my heart drop. I had never had this feeling before or since. I was so taken by this gal that when I was introduced to her, I failed to catch her name. So disgusted with myself, I couldn't think of asking my first and only true love what her name was AGAIN!! It was over a month before someone called her by name and I knew I would never forget it again.

We dated the rest of that school year and got together a lot in the summer following. I was a terrible student and she was brilliant. I was more concerned about partying while she was very studious. That didn't seem to interfere until I was kicked out of that college because of poor grades. I couldn't stand the thought of not being with her, so I moved to the college town (much to the chagrin of my parents) to be with her. I got a job and continued dating her. I have to admit I made some teenage mistakes, but letting her go was my biggest mistake in life.

I am very happily married now, with 2 children and one on the way. Not to Irene, though. I have no idea where she is. I will tell you one thing, Dr.—she has always been in my heart. I dream about her and wonder how she is, where she is, hope she is doing great. Sometimes she just jumps into my head for no reason. I have written around 100 poems that are inspired by thoughts of her. Some good, some bad. She remains in the forefront of my mind. Almost 20 years later I still think about her. Often! Is this normal?

I highly doubt that if she were to show up on my doorstep today that I would leave all I have to be with her. Why, then, all the memories and thoughts of her? This is very puzzling to me. My wife has no idea that I have these thoughts. It would hurt her to the bone if she were to know. Like I said, I'm not sure why I am telling you this or if you even care. I guess maybe to try and come to peace with it all? Is it possible for me to do that? Thanks for listening.

For hours I read and reread your *Dear Abby* contribution and peered out into the Pacific in the foreground. Dr. Kalish, for a lifetime I have had a lingering love for one who was destined to belong to someone else.

We met in high school, fell desperately in love, and became engaged to be married upon my graduation. But I was a recent Irish immigrant, and my fiancée's parents were worried about my ability to provide financial security for their daughter. My own parents joined this increasing hostility.

In time, Ana and I realized that she would not obtain parental permission to marry me. With broken hearts we pledged that we would hold hands and leap off a cliff to our demise into the Pacific Ocean. Separation was unthinkable.

Before we could carry out our sad ending, her parents found correspondence sent between us that warned them of our plan. Ana was moved quickly to an unknown destination—I would never see her again. A year later, I discovered Ana had been forced into an arranged marriage, and my young life seemed to have come to an end.

It was many years later that Kate came into my life. I made it quite clear that I still had love for someone else, that the love was still considerably more than just a memory. Kate took the chance—60 years ago.

Prosperity eventually came my way. I was the principal stockholder of a large company. Ironically, one of Ana's sons worked for that company; Henry knew his mother and I had once been engaged. In a thoughtless moment, Henry connected his mother into my private office phone. The phone rang and, unaware of the prank, I answered it and heard Ana's voice for the first time in more than 30 years. I suddenly felt faint. Her voice had changed very little since we had pledged to end our lives rather than face separation.

Nevertheless, the conversation began in a casual vein, with no reference to the mutual love we once knew. But not for long. Soon the voice on the phone broke into sobs as Ana poured out her heart; our love was the only love she had ever experienced. She had been married twice and both marriages had failed—her heart was left in the shadows of her first love.

I struggled to hold back the tears welling in my eyes. Yes, Ana knew about my happy life with Kate, but she considered this happiness something that could have, should have, belonged to her. Ana confessed that she had never forgotten our tender love of youth. She stopped crying and became subdued. There was a long moment of silence before she was able to ask the agonizing query: had I ever thought of her in those intervening years?

With poorly concealed emotion, I answered softly in the affirmative. Yet despite the lingering memories of young love, my marriage to Kate survived.

Ana died some years ago, still living with what might have been. In these sunset years of my life, it is still difficult to erase Ana and our love from my treasure chest of memories. No one should consider this narrative as evidence that lingering loves from the past do not return to their first loves. I could have been one.

My name is Sandy, and I have been thinking about a man I was engaged to more than 20 years ago. I met him by chance on a trip to visit my Mom in Surrey, England, and we fell in love at first glance. It was like our eyes met at the same second in this quaint local pub that I had to be persuaded to go to that evening.

Once I was there, I was enjoying myself and all of a sudden, I looked up and there he was—the most gorgeous guy I had ever seen in my life standing at the bar with a bunch of people, but he was accompanied by a female and, although they did not appear close, they were together. He looked at me at the same time, and I could feel the sparks. The fact that he was with someone kept me from starring foolishly at him. I was from Canada and had not much experience with pubs, bars or drinking places; being there that night was very out of character for me.

I tried hard to keep from concentrating on him and eventually the evening ended and I went back to my Mom's house… with this guy heavy on my mind. My mother was living in England at the time; she had been a war bride, and when she and my father divorced, she went back to England. So, missing her so very much back in Canada, I had arranged to go visit her at this time, in 1977. I had married young and had children and was getting over a divorce.

The next night I was dying to get back to this pub, as I had a feeling that this man would be there again. I talked my stepbrother into going there with me and, sure enough, the guy came in and was alone. After a short time he came over to me and asked where I was from, and that was the beginning of a passionate relationship. I had another few weeks in the UK and we spent every possible moment together. He had his job as head chef at a nearby hotel and I had my family to be with; it was like being a teen again, missing him every single second he was gone. I had never felt that way about anyone in my life. I had married the only guy I had ever known in school and we were more like friends than lovers. But Terry touched every single nerve in my body. We did not know how we would end up, so we just lived in the moment in the romantic settings of Merry Ol' England.

I cried when I had to leave him at the airport and return to Canada; we promised to be together no matter what happened in our lives. We wrote to each other every single day (no email back then), and called once every two weeks. There were times when he would go off the schedule and call me to surprise me, as he could not wait, and I would be so excited that I could hardly talk. It was definitely love.

I planned another trip to England and was ready to move into a little cottage on the grounds of the hotel where he was chef. The owner's wife did not like me and that was a problem, but he was insistent. Looking back, I realize that she liked him as more than just an employee. He lived in a room within the hotel.

I went with my children; he had never been married or had any children and was a couple of years younger than me. But that was never a problem with us. It was the geography that became a problem. He had his mom and friends in the UK, and I had my family and friends in Canada. But we had such a great time together—like baking a half hour before company was coming and having a flour fight in the kitchen and laughing so hard we were crying, trying to clean up in a hurry. He placed notes on my pillow when I woke up in the morning before he went to work very early. So many memories.

I stayed for the duration of my holiday time, then had to go back to Canada. He had decided to give up his job and move to Canada and we were to be married when he came. It was many months and still the longing and the letters, love songs, telephone calls… all that never died. His mother really liked me, but I was very sad that she was going to be alone, as Terry's father had died of cancer at a young age, leaving his Mom with just Terry. She depended on him for companionship. She was a very attractive woman, but she just stayed a recluse in her home, waiting for Terry's visits.

He came to Canada and it is was great, but it was too much all of a sudden and I started to get scared; suddenly one morning I woke up and told him I was not ready to get married. We had the marriage license, had booked the hall etc., but I just could not do it. I asked him to please go back to England as soon as he could and we would have to take it slower.

He was very upset, but I just needed to have him go back to the U.K. He did, and I didn't hear from him until a couple of years later; our love started again and then we were both too scared to go through it again. He sent me a photo and I did the same and then I got involved with my work and lost touch with him.

The past couple of weeks, things have been coming up that bring me back to him. I was on the Internet a few days ago and thought I would look up that pub where we met and where I had ended up working for a short time on my second trip to England. I had made lots of friends there. One was his best friend, Andy, who was the manager of the pub, and who gave me the job. So I sent an email to the pub, asking how things were with Andy, and told them that I had worked there back in 1978. I was not even sure who owned the pub. And I casually mentioned the name of the hotel where Terry was chef.

I received an email from the son of the owner. He said that the pub was doing very well, and it is nice to hear from former employees, especially those overseas. But he sadly told me that Andy had passed away the year before, after suffering with a long illness. I felt my heart sink. I was very close to Andy when I was in England, and I know I should have kept in touch, but when Terry and I split up, that sort of got lost too. The owner's son also told me that the hotel had burnt to the ground 5 years ago, and never been rebuilt. I wrote back and told him how sorry I was to hear about Andy, and then I asked if he knew whether Terry was still around. He did not know Terry, he said.

Years have gone by, but something very strong is pulling me to find him. I have thought of him through the years with a warmth, but never like this. Everything is stirring up memories. I have tried to find him using the Internet with no luck. He could be anywhere. If he is happily married, I would never try to disturb that; I just have this longing to talk to him and to tell him how scared I was back then to make a commitment. I used every imaginable excuse not to marry this man.

I wanted to share this with you, and I really need to get a grip here. I feel like I am now on a mission and need to tell him reasons why I acted as I did. I know there are times when things should just be left alone, but you could not imagine how completely connected we used to be. I have never had that since. Maybe I am just being silly and longing for that kind of love now in my life. I am certain that if God means us to find one another, for whatever reason, we will.

Can you understand, Dr. Kalish? There are tons more special times that I have inside my heart. Why on earth I did not go through with this marriage is a question I will ask myself till the end of time.

I found out about your research through your web site. I was looking around the Internet for information about lost loves and friends. I have a lost love, and although it's been more than 30 years since I saw her, I find myself missing her as much as ever. I am happily married with wonderful children, but I suspect there is also love for Robyn. I miss her every day.

I'm not quite sure I qualify for your research. Although I loved Robyn, I can't say for sure that she loved me. I do know that she had affection for me—she liked me a lot—and maybe it was love. Either way, she was *my* first love.

We met at work, at our first jobs after high school. I can still remember the first time I saw her. I was very shy, but it wasn't long before I decided to tell her how I felt about her. The end result was that, yeah, she liked me, but she didn't want to get serious. She was looking for someone a little more mature, like a father figure. Anyway, we became friends—very good friends.

I bought her a necklace for her birthday, and got my very first kiss. What was nice about that was that she sought me out ("Hey, where's my birthday kiss?") I can remember it exactly. I was so shy that I kissed her on the cheek. But after we talked a little, I asked her if I could kiss her again. She said yes, and I got it right.

Although my feelings for her sometimes made things a little messy, we got along very well. I miss her as a friend as much as anything. And she surprised me all that year with displays of affection. Most of our interactions took place at work, but there was also outside contact, and several all night telephone conversations—just gabbing the night away.

There was the time when she surprised me by coming back to work at night (sometimes we worked opposite shifts) to give me a ride home (I didn't have a car yet). And sometimes we rode around all night, just being with each other.

And there was the time when we saw each other for the first time in two weeks, after our vacations. Her boss told her to get back to work, but she said loudly, "It's been two weeks since I saw Mike, and I missed him." She said it "off the cuff" and was sincere—that sure got my attention!

But there were things that happened that seemed to indicate she didn't want to get serious, or was confused. One night after work, we went to a friend's house for a while. When we left, I walked her to her car, and on the spur of the moment I asked if I could kiss her goodnight. She said yes, and we kissed for about ten minutes! We each left in a very good mood. But the next day at work, she seemed to be avoiding me. I was very confused. It made me think back to that day several months before when she told me she needed a more mature guy. Was she falling for me and backing off?

The closest I came to telling her I was in love with her was one day when I said, "You know, you have me wrapped right around your little finger, and you know it." She said nothing at the time, but later she mentioned that my statement was something I should not have said. I didn't care.

We had a regular date also—very nice! When she was having personal problems, I wrote her a letter and told her that she could always call me when she needed someone to talk to. She did, and invited me over. The upshot was that we stayed out all night, driving, just talking about our lives. I loved being with her.

I like to think she still might have the necklace—I really hope so. But the end came that June when she quit her job. Separations are very hard for me, so I didn't go to work on her last day. Her leaving was much too hard to take. I saw her for the last time shortly thereafter when she stopped by work to talk to me. She surprised me by saying that she was sorry for all the hurts, for treating me badly (and there was probably a lot of that, though I choose not to remember). She said she wanted to go out with me seriously, if I wanted to. Why I didn't do so, I really can't remember. But I guess there were games with my heart, because it hurt; I decided to move on, without calling her.

That's the story of my old flame, Dr. Kalish. I could fill up pages with our other interactions—how she loved to pinch my butt, and put her hands over my eyes and say, "Guess who?!"

And that brings me to your book. Thank you, thank you, thank you! You and your book have become like friends. Because of your research, I found out that what I'm going through is not unique; that many people have a "special someone" in their hearts, someone they miss, and they wonder if they are remembered. Does Robyn remember me? Would she like to see me again? Would she want to hug me the way I damn sure want to hug her?

I can identify with some of the people in your book who needed antidepressants or other help to make it through a day without their lost loves. Although I use none of that, most of my days lately are up and down: I go from the hope of her remembering me, to the expectation that I'm forgotten. Although the missing her is especially strong right now, the truth is I've never forgotten about her. Every single September, when her birthday comes around, I send silent birthday wishes.

Dr. Kalish, you are in possession of many treasures; many people have opened their hearts to you and expressed things that are special, that have probably never been shared with anyone in the whole world. That is certainly true in my case. Robyn is very special to me, and I'm grateful to have had the chance to share my story. If you ever hear the song "Somewhere, Out There" by Linda Ronstadt and James Ingram, you will be hearing my prayer to God that this dream will come true.

I purchased and read your book this weekend. I read with relief. You have no doubt set yourself up to be barraged by people like me, in that we have no one to whom to sound our deepest, secret, and life altering thoughts. Brace yourself because here comes another story:

I have never contacted my lost love, but as you can guess, she has always been in my thoughts (28 years). My triumphs and setbacks in life have always been observed through her eyes as I perceived she would view them. While she has continually occupied a piece of my heart and my very soul, the thought of contacting her has always been a terrifying prospect. I was rejected, the dumpee. I don't know what a second rejection would leave of me. Simply, an unanswered letter would be all it might take to crush me, and my seemingly normal life might fly to pieces.

We were college sweethearts, and I was living in a dream world that I thought would surely never end. Her suggestions that we should marry were met with my assertions that that was a given, but "Gee, we sure are having a lot of fun now, there is no rush." I knew that we would be together forever; I had no way of knowing that what I was going to "be together" with was a haunting that would lurk in the innermost corridor of my very being. I'm sure now that an incident where we were discovered somewhat sexually compromised in her home (she lived at home until she married), coupled with my alarming disregard for my future, most likely brought parental concerns to bear that were beyond my ability to understand at the time. Though this was never discussed, I understand now. Anyway, I can only surmise these things because the relationship ended without explanation.

I have analyzed that relationship from every conceivable angle over the years. I have concluded that parental pressure probably played its part. If that were indeed the case, I would certainly never blame them, as being a father myself, I want the best for my own daughters as well. Who's to know, but maybe my lost love has had a life of gigantic proportions as measured in the things that truly count. I do hope and pray that that has been the case. I sure would like to know.

Except for an earlier span of time I have been able to keep track of my lost love. She has never lived more than a couple hundred miles from our hometown and from me, and searching phone books has enabled me to know where she is living and that she is still married to the husband who came from nowhere and whisked her away. There has been some comfort in this. Recently, my check on the Internet White Pages, which I check from time to time, showed her no longer at that location. I could not find her. Absolute panic of the heart! If she is well, I am confident that she can be found again. I pray she is well.

I tell myself, I only want to know that she is happy and, of course, for her to know that I turned out okay. But is that really the case? Would that be enough? I am miserable. I know that I cannot go back in time, nor should I want to. Everything that happened in the past has been preliminary to my children whom I love more than life. I think about her children and know that she must have been a loving mother; they are lucky.

My lost love's continual presence in my thoughts has cheated everyone who is close to me or who has dared to love me. In a just world, there should be no rivals in my heart. I should be capable of loving as I am loved. The guilt is crushing.

I have done better in life than I ever thought was possible. I have a wonderful marriage (my only marriage) to a beautiful sexy woman who has blessed me with wonderful bright, healthy and good-looking children. My wife loves me immensely, as I do her. I have enjoyed a challenging career that has enabled me to travel all over the world. My children are enrolled in private schools and I will financially be able to send them to the best colleges in this country. I live in a big and very impressive house and have reached financial independence. In my heart there is a hollowness.

Discovering your research and book was timely for me. I had already resolved that I must seek some kind of closure to this cursed thing. The risks are higher than anything I have ever faced. I am frightened to my core. I just want relief.

Nancy, even though we will never meet, I consider you a friend. Your work has helped me more than you will ever know.

Dear Bill, wherever you are:

Twenty-two years have gone by. In what abyss is that time hiding? I wish someone could tell me; I would hide there as well. Instead, I hide in your memory, burden myself with regret, and dream of a future that will never be mine.

Hundreds of letters I have written over the years. Some bitter, some written in times of need, humility, some sheltered in pride, but all written in love. No one tells you when you are young, "Make decisions you can live with for the rest of your life, because you will have to." No one warns you that you can never go back.

Twenty-two years ago I told you, "You will always be in my heart." That was a lie. You are all my heart consists of. You are the core of my inner being. Memories of our time together have damned my very existence. I have crossed every boundary I ever set for myself. Every relationship has been an attempt to reproduce what we felt, and every attempt was a failure.

In your arms I felt elevated to a state of grace, feeling your spirit I felt absolute, in your love I felt glory. You were my initiation to passion. Your memory makes me strive to be the person I want to be. With you I learned of pain, loss, pleasure, and sensibility. In your kiss I tasted conviction, in your eyes I saw perfection, wisdom, and escape. Just as we are meant to breathe, our love was meant to happen. Was our parting also meant to happen?

I have used our past as a barricade against change. I've walked the line between hope and regret, love and hate. I feel your breath in the dark, I see you when I close my eyes. I was too lost in love to know I had lost you. This is not the life I imagined, but it is mine. Many years ago our paths deviated from those we designed, but they are the lives in which we exist. The chaos is only that which I chose.

My intent in writing is of pure selfishness. I am not seeking pity or attempting to cultivate sentiment. All the stars have been wished on, every prayer prayed. I know you will never be mine again. God knows I'll never forget you, but this is my attempt to let you go.

I used to remember every detail of our time together, every conversation. I know that the first time you called my name, I loved you. The first time you whispered my name, I knew I would give you my life. Now I have bits and pieces of our short time together, fragments of memories. Hazy snapshots in my mind, like color that has faded to black and white. Your smile, the feel of your hands, the sound of your voice, the look in your eyes when we said good-bye; these are the things I have clung to. I promised to love you forever, probably the easiest and hardest promise I have ever kept.

My heart needs a reprieve. I have to know you have forgiven me for my immaturity, my lack of strength. Truly, I was not your equal; I was weak. Whether I have crossed your mind, caused you to smile, it doesn't matter. You have been loved regardless. The memory of you has seen me through so many difficult times, so thank you. In the time we had, you loved me enough to last a lifetime.

Thank you for the love you gave me, for the time you shared, and the impression you made in my life. You were and always will be the most beautiful, unforgettable man I know. I will cherish and adore you always.

You are my sweetest dream… .

I was the chosen one, A Genesis, like two spiritual entities that were meant to collide and make a profound impact on everything around them. Almost 20 years ago, when a phone call from Toronto to Vancouver was placed, I was changed forever.

I was mysteriously chosen to receive this call from a girl I never met. She was in our corporate head office and I was in a satellite branch office separated by more than half a country. She introduced herself on the phone and I managed to gather my composure enough to ask "why me?" as it is not everyday a boy of 23 gets a call from a girl, far from home, and introduces herself out of the blue. I have a difficult time remembering why she said she chose me, as we had never been in contact before. To this day I think this was a spiritual cupid connection that was meant to change destinies.

Very shortly after that call, I received a letter (you remember, the old fashion way of communication?). In that letter was a photo and a story of her background. To my total amazement, she was an incredibly beautiful girl, but why me? I must be dreaming… what did I do to deserve being chosen? This is what true fate stories are meant to be made of. I had always hoped it would happen that way.

Over the next several weeks, letters were exchanged, phone calls from Vancouver to Toronto were flip flopped during office hours, but they were kept short and since the office was wide open, the calls were no more than, "I was thinking of you."

We both just seemed to talk to each other about whatever seemed to tickle our fancy, feeling our way through an awkward long distance pseudo romance with what seemed like two peas in a pod. I always felt a sense of warmth and security. A cocoon of sorts. I just accepted her for who she was. I never felt challenged or threatened, just a feeling of inner peace and happiness. We were very innocent, and subjects of conversation were never in one particular direction or purpose. I never felt I had to impress her with anything. I was just me.

I left the company branch office and relocated to another firm shortly after a month or so of letters. I spoke to no one of my plans, including her. She found out when she called the office one morning and was told I had left. She wrote me and told me she was devastated that I had left without telling her. I explained that it was my fault, but I never expected that reaction. I was leaving to go to a competitor, and I did not want any problems from colleagues in the transfer.

The pace of our communication was now in a much more intense motion, with letters going back and forth two and three times a week, as we both had a passion to explore each others' thoughts and dreams. The letters were soon eclipsed by late night phone calls, as the letters were too slow to feed our frenzy of just wanting to be closer together.

A suggestion was raised that I make a trip to visit her in Toronto and stay at her family's home for four days. At first I was unsure of how to deal with being a stranger going to her family's home, since we had never met. But, I planned my trip, booked the flight, and flew to Toronto to meet her. I never mentioned this trip to my family.

My flight arrived early and I waited, listening to my Walkman in the emptiness of the airport, wondering how our first meeting would take place.

She arrived with her sister in tow, and a calm but subdued warm welcome was exchanged between us. We headed back to her parents' place, and I felt out of place, a traveler from afar in a unfamiliar set of circumstances, in the middle of an unconventional long distance relationship, staying in a family's home where only Spanish was spoken. My expectations of rejection by her parents remained a constant reminder to tiptoe through the minefield of etiquette and good grace.

The initial awkwardness was soon overcome with a warm welcome and friendly smiles from all of the family, so this could not be as bad as it seemed, I thought. With the language barrier with her father and mother came the opportunity for us to be alone and get comfortable with the idea of actually being together face to face alone, to figure out who we really were. It was nice to gain the trust of her sisters as well.

I remember vividly, she sat on one couch and I on another, and for a while it seemed perfectly natural… until I realized that we were 15 feet apart, just as it had been in the beginning of our relationship, a long distance affair separated by distance.

I suggested that, since I was technically there, we could sit together as a couple, because that was what we spoke of waiting to do for such along time. The true innocence of the moment, combined with the anticipation of that real first hug and kiss, seemed like an eternity before it happened. I have never since felt that kind of warm fuzzy tenderness for anyone and have never repeated that emotional bond again.

From that moment on we were "just us" together, we were a matching set. We did what seemed natural, just talk and gaze into each other's eyes on that couch, then disappear to the shores of the lake to lay out on the lawns and absorb each other's company for hours on end, just lost in being together.

I departed a number of days later, with tears and fond memories, I don't recall the return trip to Vancouver, but that spring of 1983 I left Vancouver and returned to my parents' home in Ottawa. I had no job and no money, as I had given everything up to move closer to her.

The phone calls migrated to weekend drives from Ottawa to Toronto, returning for Monday morning. We were hopelessly in love. To this point in time, we had never actually made love to each other, just hugs and kisses; it was not like we didn't want to, but we were content with holding onto each other's closeness and warmth.

We had set great plans. I had asked her father for his permission to wed his daughter, and this came as a huge shock to my parents, sparking their hasty trip to Toronto to see what I was up to. Her parents' household was abuzz with excitement from the news we were going to be married. My parents had big reservations about this relationship.

This is where the story takes a turn for the worse, as parental intervention and a young man's silly fears took over to erode the foundation of the love. The relationship was abruptly terminated with silly fears, motherly advice, lack of self-confidence, and lack of a job. I stopped the whole process as fast as we had started.

Six months afterwards, when I was employed again, I made a business trip back to Toronto to talk with her and give her an explanation that went over like the passing of a counterfeit bill. I had a chance to repair and mend, but I was so void of feelings, that was the last we ever spoke.

Her letters, the cards, and the pictures are all neatly stored with easy access, and once a year I sneak away and hide in shame; I cry as I read the words and see her face. The perfume from her letters has slowly faded, but if held very closely, the fragrance gently inhaled adds life to the letters and warm memories abound.

The old saying, "To have loved and lost is far better than to have never loved at all" must have been coined by a person who had no clue about true love. More appropriately stated, "To have loved and lost by not instinctively listening to your heart rather than to your silly fears is far worse."

I had failed to recognize that the chance for real love may only come along but once; if you fail, you rarely get a second chance to redeem yourself or to be chosen again. I had turned diamonds to dust; with the breath of an instant, I had breathed my last chance. I was doomed forever, banished from grace to the pointless forest, unable to return.

I have had a tortured soul for 20 years, trying to reconcile my mistake. I have a story to tell, and a real soft spot when it comes to reading stories from lost loves. From some of the stories I have read, I have had tears flowing and a tightening in my throat, as I now know that I am not as alone with these leftover emotions as I had once envisioned.

For over the years I have stood in deathly cold silence with the winter's winds stilling my smile. There are places of inspiration and solace wherefore I traveled; I have stood on the rocky shores of the ocean at evening's edge, gazing into an endless sky that never meets the water, my darkness, my thoughts, as deep, as far as I can see. I have stood atop a grand iron bridge with the river's silver waters roaring beneath my feet on a perfect moonlit night; the water's roar deafens my spirit, but calls my name. I have climbed a blue mountain with the snow at my waist, my beard frozen in ice with the summit in sight, not a word spoken; yet the pines whisper her name.

If all I ever get is a chance to say, "I'm sorry," I will have closure and move forward. I do not imagine that I cannot recapture what was lost. If, by the grace of the Stars, if all of the celestial circumstances are aligned positively for both of us, we will have a chance to communicate again.

Hi, Dr. Kalish. I am in the process of preparing to apply to law schools and have been spending all of my money on that endeavor. It's ridiculously expensive, especially if you are determined to go to one of the best schools! But when I happened to run across your site COMPLETELY by accident and saw the message boards, I KNEW I needed to spare some money on this book!

There is a lost love of mine that I have been thinking about constantly, daily, since he left, and I have a friend who is going through the same thing. We talk about our experiences and feelings, so I kind of had the feeling there were others like me out there. But finding your book has proved it—I immediately emailed my lost love after reading some of the chapters and sent him a link to your site!

My experience might be a bit different from the others since I am 23 and initially met my lost love on the Internet instead of at school, but the feelings are still the same. The distance was our primary problem, as well as a misunderstanding in our last conversation (never really letting each other know how we truly felt). And after reading your message boards and your book, I knew I didn't want to wait until I was 50 or 60 to find my lost love again or until one or both of us has made the mistake of marrying someone else (I doubt my lost love is married yet); I want to be together again as soon as possible and avoid having a story like many of the ones I read on your message boards and in your book.

Because of your book, I understand right NOW that none of our relationships with others has worked because we are right for each other, so I don't feel like wasting any more time. If the reconnection goes well, I would like to attend law school in my lost love's state and possibly settle down there, depending on how things go. I believe my lost love would be happy to hear from me and at least be friends, but if not, at least I will know where things stand—another thing I learned from your book—either way, I can't lose! So I really want to thank you for your work and this site!

I am a Choctaw Indian. When I was a boy, I used to float down the river in a rowboat lying on my back, listening to the hum of insects and birdcalls, and looking at eternity through the clouds. Once I was stirred from my reverie by silver laughter looping across the river and laying a smile on my face. Looking up over the edge of the boat, I saw an old shack partially hidden in a stand of trees by river's edge. Wild roses climbing the side of the shack were lit by golden shafts of sunlight streaming through the trees. Appearing in the door was a young girl in blue jeans rolled halfway up to her knees. She wore a faded yellow shirt, its ends tied in a knot at her waist. Long dark hair framed a dazzling smile. Cheerily she waved as I drifted by, sun struck by her beauty and innocence.

In all the years, I've never forgotten that day and that image. Try as I might, I could never find that place again. The adult in me says it's only a fantasy, but the boy in me is still looking for that girl with the silver laughter.

Social scientists, with our surveys and numbers and plausible explanations, cannot completely capture the essence of true love. And the power of first love—often our strongest romantic fantasy—is perhaps most elusive of all.

Praise for Dr. Kalish's first book,
Lost & Found Lovers

It's almost 3 a.m., and I have just finished reading Lost & Found Lovers *for the third time in two years. I am writing to thank you for such a wonderful book... and to encourage you to please, please write another book with more wonderful stories of Lost Loves for those of us who truly believe that everyone should get a second chance at first love.*

TRUST ME on this one: YOU have made an incredible difference in the lives of at least two people who walk this earth and are trying to "find themselves" so that they can make more of a contribution to the world. We will NEVER be able to thank you enough!!!!

Your book is on my night table so I can go to sleep reading excerpts nightly. Thank you for connecting me with others who have experienced this very powerful, everlasting feeling of true love. I am forever grateful for your study. I'm writing to let you know that your book changed my life. Write another book, ok?!

I love your book! Being in a situation newly revived, this was informative and helped me accept that the intensity is "normal" and that planning a future at 61 and 65 is not senility. For the first time, I am comfortable with what is happening.

Dr. Kalish, you have literally saved my life! I thought that I had gone truly CRAZY! I could not make it day to day without the knowledge and understanding I have gained from your research. Thank you from the bottom of my heart for writing this book. Absolutely no one understands this like you do!

Thank you for your wonderful book. I laughed, cried, felt anger, remorse, sadness, understanding, love—the entire gamut of emotions that one can feel. Your book has given us the strength to follow our hearts and to renew the love and happiness that has been missing in each of our lives. I hope you write a sequel. You have done a great work and I know that many have followed your lead and have found or have looked for their lost love. I thank God every day that I was fortunate to find mine.

Can't thank you enough for your research and book. You are an angel sent to those like me. Please write another book or a movie!

Everyone who finds themselves in the situation of "loving someone from the past" should read your book. Until I read it I thought I was alone in my broken-hearted existence, loving my ex-wife ten years later. It made me realize that dreams do come true and "real love" is just that..."real". I took a pink highlighter and highlighted the parts that read just like I had written them. When I got through half the book was pink. I realized, I am not alone. Thank God, I'm not crazy. Just in love. Thank you!

How to Order
Lost & Found Lovers

To learn about rekindled romance issues, it is recommended that you read Dr. Nancy Kalish's first book. *Lost & Found Lovers: Facts and Fantasies of Rekindled Romances* (William Morrow, 1997) contains results and explanations of lost love reconnections based on the author's landmark research project, as well as reunion love stories in the participants' own words.

Hardcover books are sold out! The unprecedented interest in Dr. Nancy Kalish's research has exhausted the supply of hardcover copies of *Lost & Found Lovers*. Hardcover books will not be reissued.

However, you can now purchase a paperback edition, or an ebook version, of the original 1997 *Lost & Found Lovers* at the author's web site, **Lostlovers.com**, by using the link below. All copies purchased through Dr. Nancy Kalish will be *signed,* and *inscribed* at your request, and will be sent to you immediately. There is a limited supply of these books available, so it's first come, first served.

Order A Signed Copy of *Lost & Found Lovers*

Unsigned copies of *Lost & Found Lovers* can be ordered at barnesandnoble.com, amazon.com, or through any bookstore:

Lost & Found Lovers: Facts and Fantasies of Rekindled Romances
by Nancy Kalish, Ph.D.
(Authors Guild, 2005). ISBN 0-595-34855-6

❀ ❀ ❀

Would you like to be part of the Lostlovers.com Message Board Community or have a private phone consultation with Dr. Kalish? Details can be found at **Lostlovers.com**.

❀ ❀ ❀

Made in the USA
Columbia, SC
20 April 2019